Arctic Explorations

Dr. Elisha Kent Kane

The Lakeside Classics

ARCTIC EXPLORATIONS

The Second Grinnell Expedition
In Search of
Sir John Franklin
1853, 54, 55

By
Elisha Kent Kane, M.D., U.S.N.

EDITED BY
CHAUNCEY LOOMIS
CONSTANCE MARTIN

The Lakeside Press

R.R. DONNELLEY & SONS COMPANY

CHICAGO

December, 1996

PUBLISHERS' PREFACE

"I HAVE AVAILED myself ... to connect together the passages of my journal that could have interest for the general reader," wrote Elisha Kent Kane, M.D., U.S.N., in the preface to his book, *Arctic Explorations.* The preface was dated July 4, 1856, an appropriately celebratory day for Kane. The year before, Kane and his crew emerged from two long winters of virtual imprisonment in the Arctic. They regained their freedom when they relinquished their quest to discover the whereabouts of a British explorer, Sir John Franklin, who had disappeared a few years earlier in the northern regions of Greenland.

Arctic Explorations is the ninety-fourth book in the Lakeside Classics, an annual series published by R.R. Donnelley & Sons Company since 1903. The Classics emphasize first-person narratives of American history, usually taken from books long out of print and not easily obtainable.

Kane's story struck a chord with his contemporary readers; some 250,000 copies of *Arctic Explorations* were sold before 1900, making it a major "bestseller" in its time. After the turn of the century, however, the book fell largely into obscurity.

In today's age of instant communications, when live broadcasts from breaking news halfway around the world appear on our televisions, when climbers near the top of Mount Everest call their homes through satellite transmissions, it's difficult to imagine how isolated the Kane party was. They were utterly separated from the rest of the world. There was no way to communicate with or to reach civilization, even though the party spent most of its two ice-locked years in Rensselaer Harbor, just 250 miles from Melville Bay, where both whalers and other expeditions would wait for good ice conditions before crossing Baffin Bay's northern waters.

Arctic exploration in the 1850s was not an adventure for the faint-hearted. Nor is this book. Kane graphically describes the ravages of scurvy, starvation, and frostbite; squalid living conditions; and deterioration of mind, spirit, and body as the crew survived at the very barest subsistence level. In the end, it is a story that celebrates endurance and sheer grit.

* * * *

As is our custom, we looked to experts in the field for help in editing and annotating the text, writing the Historical Introduction, and choosing illustrations. For the first time, a team worked on the Lakeside Classics: Chauncey C. Loomis, professor of English at Dartmouth College, Hanover, New Hampshire; and Constance Martin, research associate at the Arctic Institute of North America in Calgary, Alberta, Canada.

Loomis has traveled extensively in the Arctic and is the author of *Weird and Tragic Shores,* a biography of the nineteenth-century American Arctic explorer Charles Francis Hall, as well as numerous essays and reviews on Arctic literature and the visual arts.

Martin is an art historian and freelance curator. She curated the James Hamilton Exhibit at Calgary's Glenbow Museum and provided valuable assistance and direction in selecting and securing the four-color artwork starting on page 229. Her most recent book is *The Search for the Blue Goose: The Arctic Adventures of a Canadian Naturalist.*

Most of the illustrations in this book appeared in Kane's original edition published in 1856. We've supplemented these with several paintings from North American art collections. The book was significantly longer than can be accommodated in one volume of the Classics, so careful editing and judicious cutting pared the size of the book while retaining the narrative flow.

* * * *

Since 1903, one objective of the Lakeside Classics series has been to demonstrate high-quality bookmaking using advanced manufacturing methods. This edition is no different, although the digital processes used today are very different from bookmaking even a few years ago.

Editing and production were streamlined using computer-based technologies. The text was edited and pages designed using desktop publishing programs. Type was set and pages produced at our ComCom composition facility in Allentown, Pennsylvania. Maps, digitally drawn and proofed, were created by the cartographers at GeoSystems in Pennsylvania. (We maintain an ownership position in GeoSystems, a former subsidiary.)

Our Crawfordsville Book Manufacturing Division

scanned and proofed illustrations using digital technologies. Low resolution images were used by Com-Com for captioning, image placement, and final page proofing. Electronic page files were then transmitted to Crawfordsville for page imposition. Crawfordsville employed state-of-the-art computer-to-plate technologies to transform electronic pages into press-ready plates.

* * * *

Kane and his men survived a difficult physical and mental challenge, made more daunting by their enforced isolation. Many American corporations today also are facing new challenges. But our marketplace is not isolated. Instead, we face increased competition in every market and region worldwide.

To meet these challenges, we have set a course to align our business with the forces at work in our markets and create shareholder value. Critical to our value-creation effort is our adoption of an Economic Value Added (EVA) approach to capital budgeting, performance measurement, and compensation. EVA, a value-based rather than accounting-earnings-based gauge, ensures that we manage our business assets and invest our capital productively.

We strengthened our U.S. commercial printing capabilities in several ways over the past year. We are consolidating our gravure operations, for example, by closing two facilities in 1997 and transferring work from those plants to facilities where we could take best advantage of location and scale. Although this produced a one-time restructuring charge that affected our reported earnings, it is part of an overall strategy of becoming the industry's low-cost, high value-added service provider, positioning us to create long-term shareholder value.

We also realigned our book-printing assets by integrating our Scranton-based Haddon Craftsmen book bindery into Haddon's Bloomsburg, Pennsylvania, book-manufacturing operations. The move required an investment of about $20 million in plant expansions and new equipment, but will improve efficiency and reduce costs.

We repositioned Stream International, Inc., our software manufacturing, printing, kitting, and fulfillment business, moving away from traditional physical distribution vehicles to more electronic processes. The software business continues to evolve as developers and publishers move away from disk-based materials and printed documentation to electronic media, packaging, and delivery. Reflecting this shift, we closed Stream's Crawfordsville, Indiana, and Thorp Arch, England, manufacturing facilities to focus on Stream's strengths in technical support services and electronic software solutions.

As we address the scale and location of our global operations, we continue to selectively expand our presence in international markets in Central Europe, Latin America, and Asia. Also, earlier this year we added a directory module to our printing plant in

Krakow, Poland, to handle long-term directory printing agreements with PKT in Poland, and MediaTel in the Czech Republic. The two companies publish ninety directories with a combined circulation of six million.

We also streamlined operations and headquarters in Asia, Europe, and Latin America, focusing squarely on meeting customer needs.

Like many large companies, we continue to assess how each of our business units fits into our strategies and how to focus our business energy most effectively. In this process, we spun off two businesses through Initial Public Offerings (IPOs). We took Metromail Corporation, our demographic and behavioral list-management company, public in the early summer. In the fourth quarter, Donnelley Enterprise Solutions Incorporated was offered in an IPO. In both cases, we maintain a minority interest in these newly public companies.

Our first two strategies—strengthening our commercial printing capabilities in the United States and expanding selectively worldwide—focus on capabilities we know well. Our third strategy—using electronic media to enhance content management and distribution—is newer ground. Every day, new markets are being created by new digital processes and products. There are hundreds of ways we could participate in these exciting new markets. Our challenge is to discover which ways will create the *most* value. We are continuously exploring these possibilities and their impact on our businesses.

This year, we formed the Catalyst task force, consisting of some of the company's finest thinkers. The group's charter: To identify potential markets and technologies that will allow us to leverage our capabilities, to sort through the possibilities, and to make recommendations on how we can best take advantage of new media.

As our markets continue to evolve, we have become more nimble and more energetic. Our businesses remain sound. Strip away the unusual items affecting company earnings—notably the effects of restructuring and paper-price volatility—and you'll see that our print-related businesses have performed well in the most challenging markets we have seen in years.

The reason: our solid customer relationships. We continue to enjoy long-term relationships with most major telephone directory publishers. Strong activity in the capital markets globally has translated into excellent financial printing results.

Book publishers have challenged printers to print efficiently lower book quantities. We've responded by opening a new short-run, four-color book-manufacturing plant in Roanoke, Virginia; by improving cost controls; by offering manufacturing plans that emphasize faster turnarounds and smaller quantities; and through better distribution and fulfillment.

We continue to be the major printer of magazines, catalogs, and free-standing inserts, those colorful promotional inserts found in your Sunday paper. Stream International's restructuring better positions that company to meet the challenges of the global software business in the second half of the decade.

* * * *

In late October, John R. Walter, our chairman and chief executive officer since 1989, left R.R. Donnelley to join AT&T as president and chief operating officer. John M. Richman, a member of our board since 1988, has been elected chairman and CEO as the board searches for John Walter's successor.

We wish John the best in his new position, and thank him for his contributions to R.R. Donnelley's strength and development. Among those contributions, one stands out: the development of an exceptionally talented management team. Today the company is in the hands of capable and experienced executives focused on one goal: increasing shareholder value.

* * * *

R.R. Donnelley & Sons Company is the world leader in a significant industry. We are in a position to define the industry and its future. This is our challenge, and we invite you—our customers, our employees, and our friends—to join us on this exciting adventure.

Our best wishes to you and your families. Good health and good luck in the new year.

THE PUBLISHERS

December 1996

CONTENTS

xvi   *Contents*

ILLUSTRATIONS & MAPS

HISTORICAL INTRODUCTION

EXPLORATION OF the Arctic reached a climax in the last century. As expedition after expedition probed into the labyrinth of land, sea, and ice that stretches westward from Greenland through Canada's Arctic Archipelago to Alaska, the far north became a focus of international attention and excitement. Some explorers went north through Canada's tundra; others went by sea in ships specially equipped for arctic navigation, powered by sail early in the century and by steam later. Many endured terrible hardships and some never returned; all seemed figures from a saga. They were celebrated in their time, although most of their names are now forgotten except by arctic buffs and historians of exploration: Englishmen like the Rosses, Parry, Franklin, Back, Rae, McClintock, McClure—Americans like De Haven, Hartstene, Hayes, Hall, and Kane.[1]

In its earliest phase, following the end of the Napoleonic wars in 1815, nineteenth-century arctic

[1] It should be noted that during the seventeenth, eighteenth, and nineteenth centuries, the Hudson's Bay Company and the North West Company quietly pursued their own explorations of the Canadian north, but, because their interest was primarily trade in furs, they tended to stay south of its northern coastline and the Arctic Archipelago. They also avoided publicity, so most of the men who did the exploring remained virtually unknown. And in the maritime Arctic, of course, whalers came to know Baffin Bay, but they too did not penetrate into the Arctic Archipelago—and they too did their work quietly. It also should be noted that late in the nineteenth century and early in the twentieth century when the

exploration was mainly a continuation of the search for a northwest passage. That search had begun three centuries earlier when explorers, realizing that the New World was a huge landmass blocking any direct maritime trade route to the Orient, faced the fact that they might have to sail north around it if they wanted to avoid sailing thousands of miles south to the Straits of Magellan or Cape Horn. Merchants soon learned, at the cost of many ships and men, that even if there were a passage through the Arctic, it would be commercially useless. So, by the nineteenth century, motives for the search had changed.

Beginning in 1818, England in particular decided to use its victorious navy to pursue the search as a matter of scientific curiosity and national prestige. Second Secretary of the Navy John Barrow, who became a sort of midwife to English exploration in the first half of the century, wrote to the First Lord of the Admiralty that arctic exploration was "well deserving of a power like England" and that if England did not pursue the search for a passage she "would be laughed at by all the world."[2] In the seventeen years that followed, more ships were lost, more men died, but no passage was found. As the mid-century approached, the English

"race for the Pole" was at its peak such great Scandinavian explorers as Otto Sverdrup and Knud Rasmussen made extraordinary voyages in the high Arctic, traveling as the Inuit traveled without the sort of support systems that most previous expeditions had encumbered themselves with.

[2]Quoted in Richard Cyriax, *Sir John Franklin's Last Expedition* (London, 1939), p. 20.

decided to make their greatest effort. In the spring of 1845, two well-equipped ships, the *Erebus* and *Terror,* under the command of Sir John Franklin and with 129 carefully picked men aboard, sailed from England and disappeared into the Arctic Archipelago.

The next phase can be called "the search for Franklin." At worst the Admiralty had expected Franklin to be gone for two winters, and by 1848, alarm about him began to grow.

In the decade that followed, arctic exploration reached its peak of intensity as search expeditions went out one after another. They often found themselves locked in ice during brutal winters, suffering ordeals that hinted ominously about the fate of the Franklin Expedition. The Admiralty began to tire of the financial and human expense of the search, but Franklin's charismatic wife Lady Jane Franklin, playing on public opinion, not only goaded the Admiralty on, but also found private donors to create expeditions of their own.

Concern for the Franklin Expedition was international. Not only England, but European nations and the United States had a deep emotional investment in it and in the dramatic search following its disappearance. Arctic explorers had come to have almost allegorical significance: Larger than life, they appear to be courageous figures that moved through land and seascapes which were weird, beautiful, and ferocious. Somehow western mankind's faith in God's Providence and in itself—in its own technology, ingenuity, courage, stamina, and dominion in the world—seemed to be on the line.

The United States in particular became involved. Lady Jane wrote to her American friends to plead her cause. Wealthy and influential New York merchant Henry Grinnell, swayed by Lady Franklin, persuaded Congress to authorize an expedition if he supplied two ships, *Advance* and *Rescue*. Undoubtedly the members of Congress were willing to cooperate partly for nationalistic reasons, feeling impelled to show the American flag in the northern regions of the hemisphere that they considered to be their own. Under the command of Lieutenant Edwin De Haven, the First Grinnell Expedition sailed north in May of 1850. Sixteen months later, the expedition returned.

It had wintered over in the Arctic without losing a man; it had made several geographical discoveries; it had been present at tiny Beechey Island when British explorers found the first signs of the lost Franklin Expedition.

And it had given one of its members, Dr. Elisha Kent Kane, his first experience of the Arctic.

* * * *

Elisha Kent Kane was an improbable arctic explorer. He was born in 1820 to an affluent and influential Philadelphia family; his father was Attorney-General of Pennsylvania and Judge of a U.S. District Court. But privilege was no protection from ill health; as a boy he was stricken with rheumatic fever and endocarditis,

E. K. Kane.

an inflammation of the lining and the valves of the heart; the illnesses and their complications plagued him as long as he lived. He was slight and seemed frail, but in his short life he displayed a remarkable thirst for adventure and remarkable toughness in quenching that thirst.

Even before he joined the First Grinnell Expedition, he had led a life of adventure. After attending the University of Virginia, he went on to receive a medical degree from the University of Pennsylvania in 1842. All during this period he suffered ill health, but, as was later the case of Theodore Roosevelt, ill health may have been a spur to action; as Kane's roommate at medical school commented, "the uncertain state of his health had a good deal to do with his subsequent course of life, and the almost reckless exposure of himself to danger."[3] Soon after his graduation from medical school, he became a surgeon in the U.S. Navy, and was assigned to the frigate *Brandywine,* which in 1843 sailed in a fleet of four vessels on a special mission to China. It was a long cruise with many ports of call, and Kane, not only a medical doctor but also a naturalist and amateur artist, took full advantage of it. He hiked in the mountains behind Rio de Janeiro; he roamed the country around Bombay; he hunted elephants in Ceylon; he explored parts of the Philippines that few outsiders had ever seen and even had himself lowered by rope into a volcano near Manila; he went to see the

[3] Quoted in George W. Corner, *Doctor Kane of the Arctic Seas* (Philadelphia: Temple University Press, 1972), p. 28.

great Greek antiquities and climbed Mount Helicon; he took a boat up the Nile to see its ruins and suffered a wounded leg in a fight with Bedouins who attacked his party.

He returned home after this grueling two-year trip, but nine months later he was off again on a ship to West Africa, where he joined a caravan deep into the interior and suffered a debilitating bout of coast fever. Home again, then off again—this time to Mexico where he fought in a cavalry engagement in the Mexican War, wounded a Mexican officer in hand-to-hand combat, and was wounded by him at the same time. Although wounded, he saved the defeated Mexican officers from slaughter by the guerrilla troops with whom he was riding. One of the officers was a general; his son, the man who wounded and was wounded by Kane; when Kane became very sick soon after the battle, the general and his son, both paroled by the U.S. Army, took him to their estate and nursed him back to health. This chivalric behavior on the part of Kane and the Mexicans who were supposedly his enemies was described enthusiastically by Philadelphia's newspapers, and Kane was on his way towards the celebrity he later was to enjoy.

After returning from a relatively undemanding naval cruise to the Mediterranean and Rio de Janeiro, Kane, now age thirty, heard that the United States with the help of Henry Grinnell was organizing an expedition to go in search of the Franklin Expedition. Typically, he volunteered, and was enrolled as a surgeon.

Kane with the Magnetic Observatory

xxvii

The First Grinnell Expedition was not the ordeal that the Second Grinnell Expedition was to become, but nevertheless it was a test of Kane's mettle. Under command of Edwin J. De Haven, the *Advance* and *Rescue* sailed up the west coast of Greenland to the infamous "middle pack" in Baffin Bay—an ice pack that usually clogged much of the bay. Seeing what he thought was an opening in the pack, De Haven entered it, although previous expeditions had learned from whalers to avoid it by sailing north to the relative protection of Meville Bay then heading westward across the frequently open water in the northern parts of Baffin Bay. De Haven's ships were locked in ice for twenty-one days in mid-summer, an inauspicious beginning. Finally the ice broke up enough for them to reach Lancaster Sound, the entrance to the archipelago into which Franklin disappeared. In the months that followed, they encountered several English expeditions also looking for the Franklin Expedition and were present when three graves from Franklin's first winter were found on Beechey Island. After that, they sailed further west in Lancaster Sound, then north up into Wellington Channel, hoping that if they sailed far enough north they would find an open polar sea, and that Franklin survivors might be living on its shores.

The theory of an open polar sea was crucial in the planning of both the first and second of Kane's two voyages into the Arctic. The idea that beyond a rim of Arctic ice there might be a temperate and ice-free area was ancient: Greek cosmographers had speculated about the Hyperboreans, a people living beyond the source of the north wind (*Boreas*) in an ever-temperate paradise. In later centuries, scientists found less mythological reason to believe in the possibility, and in Kane's own time Matthew Fontaine Maury, an officer in the Naval Observatory, believed strongly in it on the basis of his study of ocean currents, ocean bottoms, and the phenomenon of the Russian "polynyas," areas of open water in the Russian Arctic. Maury played a very important role in creating the orders under which De Haven sailed, urging him to find some way to head directly north from Lancaster Sound. Wellington Channel appeared to offer the best due north route, but *Advance* and *Rescue* both became locked in ice while they were in it, and they drifted with that ice from mid-October to early June—all the way from Wellington Channel, through Lancaster Sound, out into Baffin Bay and then south to Davis Strait, where finally they were released from the ice and were able to sail for home. That drift suggests how powerful ice could be in determining the fate of an expedition.

When Kane returned from the Arctic in 1851, he set about giving lectures on the expedition and began to write a book about it—and he fell in love with a young woman, Margaret Fox. Margaret Fox and her sister were famous, or infamous, as "spirit rappers": they were spiritualists who had attracted national attention and considerable condemnation. Spiritualism was popular in the mid-nineteenth century, and many believed that the Fox sisters did indeed have contact with the spiritual world, but many others thought they were frauds. (They were indeed frauds: they had a remarkable ability to crack their double-jointed toes and thus make the sounds of rapping.) Kane apparently suspected they were frauds, but he still loved Margaret. His affair with her began on his return from the Arctic, went on over the protests of his parents while he was planning his next expedition, was suspended during it, and then was picked up again after it.

Romance or not, Kane also worked frantically to create his own expedition back to the Arctic. He felt that the first voyage had failed to fulfill one of its most important obligations—finding an open polar sea. His sense of that failure on the first was crucial in the creation of the Second Grinnell Expediton, Dr. Elisha Kent Kane commanding. Ostensibly Kane was searching for survivors of the Franklin Expedition, but his secondary—very possibly his primary—motive was to discover an open polar sea and perhaps even to reach the North Pole by sailing on it. The possibility of such a sea had been given additional credence when Commander Edward Inglefield returned from Baffin Bay while Kane was organizing his expedition and reported that he had seen open water to the north of Smith's Sound. Kane persuaded Lady Franklin that a plan to go directly north from Baffin Bay through Smith's Sound towards the hypothetical open polar sea rather than entering the Arctic Archipelago was worthwhile, arguing that the great bulk of Greenland might block the sort of southward drifting ice that the First Grinnell Expedition had found far to the west in Wellington Channel. He persuaded Henry Grinnell once again to give his blessing, some money, and his ship the *Advance* and the Navy to loan ten of its men. With Grinnell's help, he recruited more crew and laid in supplies.

On 31 May 1853 he sailed from New York on the *Advance* with a crew of seventeen men and officers, and headed towards one of the great ordeals by ice in the history of nineteenth-century exploration.

* * * *

Kane's account of that ordeal, *Arctic Explorations in the Years 1853, 54, 55,* was a true masterpiece of nineteenth-century book making. Printed in two elegant volumes, it was enriched by a multitude of superb illustrations, some given a full page, others bled into the text. By the seventeenth century, governments dispatching expeditions to faraway places had realized the importance of graphic records of discoveries—images not only of topography such as coastal views, but also of flora, fauna, native peoples, astronomical and meteorological events, and any other phenomena encountered by the expeditions. Draftsmen became important figures on the expedition rosters, and drawing became a part of a gentleman seaman's training. In the mid-eighteenth century England's Royal Society published a pamphlet giving instruction on how to describe and sketch discoveries, and by the end of the century manuals were available on such a specialized subject as the depiction of climactic conditions—how to draw cloud formations, or calm or rough seas.

Kane was well versed in these skills. He was a more than competent draftsman, and he brought back hundreds of sketches from his two arctic expeditions. He wanted them as a scientific record, but he also wanted to produce center-table books and knew that illustration would be of crucial importance in making his books popular. He and his publishers engaged James Hamilton, a fine artist of Turneresque sensibilities, to convert them into watercolors, then, with the assistance of other artists, into the engravings that embellished the books. Though enhanced by professional artists and engravers for the books, the illustrations were based on Kane's own drawings and descriptive prose, and essentially all were created under his supervision. Romantic as the illustrations were, they also remained essentially true to Kane's own sketched images of the strange world he had seen. Book, magazine, and newspaper graphics of this sort in the nineteenth century, as well as dioramas and exhibitions of paintings by such major artists as Frederick Church and William Bradford, had a profound effect on the nineteenth-century public, and the dramatic images of the Arctic they created linger on in our imaginations today.

Kane also was a literate and eloquent man. His verbal descriptions of the Arctic and his experiences in it are gripping, among the very best in an era when books about the Arctic appeared by the dozens. He narrates episodes with the skill of a master story teller. In Chapter xv—"After Seal," for example, he vividly describes how he and Hans, out hunting for seal on solid sea ice, suddenly realized that they were on thin ice. All Kane could do was drive the dogs faster, the ice cracking behind him, in hope that he could reach more solid ice before falling through. But fall through he did, and found himself floundering in frigid water with his dogs floundering around him. His description of his narrow and agonizing escape from this peril is hair-raising.

His reactions to the arctic environment itself were, like many other explorers', a mixture of delight at its beauty, horror at its ferocity. Text and illustration work together to create the sense of the otherworldly that struck so many explorers in the Arctic:

The moon is nearly full, and the dawning sunlight, mingling with hers, invests everything with an atmosphere of ashy gray. It clothes the gnarled hills that make the horizon of our bay, shadows out the terraces in dull definition, grows darker and colder as it sinks into the fiords, and broods sad and dreary upon the ridges and measureless plains of ice that make up the rest of our field of view. Rising above all this, and shading down into it in strange combination, is the intense moonlight, glittering on every crag and spire, tracing the outline of the background with contrasted brightness, and printing its fantastic profiles on the snow field. It is a landscape such as Milton or Dante might imagine—inorganic, desolate, mysterious. I have come down from deck

ARCTIC

EXPLORATIONS

IN THE YEARS 1853, '54, '55

BY

ELISHA KENT KANE, M.D., U.S.N.

VOL. I.

PHILADELPHIA

CHILDS AND PETERSON,

124 ARCH STREET.

1856.

Title page from Arctic Explorations, *published in 1856*

with the feelings of a man who has looked upon a world unfinished by the hand of its Creator (Ch. xxi—"Hanging On
and a Deserter").

* * * *

Today we see nature as protagonist, casting ourselves
and our technology as antagonists: we see ourselves as
endangering nature much more than nature en-
dangers us. But the very technology that we sometimes see as a threat to nature also protects us from it
and allows us the luxury of concerning ourselves with
its vulnerability and delicacy. Kane and his men had
little buffer between themselves and nature at its harsh-
est: often they were literally exposed to the elements,
and the elements in the Arctic were treacherous. In his
book, he makes real for a twentieth-century reader the
daily hardships and hazards faced by nineteenth-
century arctic explorers, many of these hardships and
hazards coming from natural phenomena: the long
winter darkness and bitter winter cold—of sudden
shifts in the ice, or sudden changes in weather (a thaw
could be as dangerous as a freeze)—of snow blindness and whiteouts—of water and fire (there were three
fires on board during the expedition)—above all, of
starvation and scurvy. Margins for error were very
slight, and minor changes in weather or in ice conditions could leave an area desolate one day that had
been alive with walrus, seal, and bear the day before.
Blaming it on his meager budget, early in the book
Kane admits that his supplies were too scanty when

they left New York, and during the long periods of deprivation that followed he often cried out in his journal for more supplies, such as walrus and seal meat, to feed his suffering crew.

The book is reasonably honest about his own sufferings and the sufferings of his men, less honest about the hostilities that burned on board the *Advance* during those two dreadful winters. Like many explorers, Kane self-censored his journals when he came to make them public. For example, Kane was very sick with rheumatic fever when they sailed from New York and he spent much of the cruise to Newfoundland and Greenland trying to recuperate in bed, although he made energetic appearances on deck to keep up a show. He makes no mention of that in the book. And a few days after their arrival in Greenland, he already had trouble with John Blake and William Godfrey. Those two toughs, who had been recruited by Henry Grinnell's son on the New York waterfront, cursed out First Officer Brooks. Kane had them tied up and incarcerated for several days in the booby hatch, a small space between decks. He makes no mention of that either, although he is more open in the book about his later troubles with these two men. One of the major crises in the expedition occurred during the second winter when almost half his men decided to leave the ship and head south on their own. In the book he seems sweet reason in his response to that desertion, in fact not even calling it that, but in an unpublished part of his journal, addressing his brother, he spits venom: "If I ever live to get home—home! and should meet Dr. Hayes or Mr. Bonsall, or Mr. Sontag, let them look to their skins. If I don't live to thrash them, which I'll try very hard to do (to live, I mean) why then, dear brother John, seek a solitary orchard and maul them for me. Don't honour them with a bullet and let the mauling be solitary . . . it would hurt your character to be [seen] wrestling with such . . . sneaks."[4]

We should not underestimate the psychological impact of duration and isolation on explorers of the past. Their expeditions usually lasted not days or months but years, and their isolation was often complete, with no communication possible between themselves and the worlds they had left behind. In the twenty-four-hour nights of winter, the men on the *Advance* must have felt deeply the great distances between themselves and their homes and suffered a sense of hopelessness, especially when they brooded on a second winter in the Arctic. Abrasions and hostilities were inevitable in the tightly packed quarters of the ship, and all anyone could do was to try to keep them under control. Kane apparently vented much of his anger in his journal and so was able to conceal it much of the time. When he allowed it to burst out there usually was reason for it, especially when he was dealing with Blake and Godfrey, who were out-and-out deserters, even mutineers.

But there also is evidence that Kane himself was at least partly responsible for problems of morale. In the

---

[4] Quoted in Corner, p. 179.

first autumn, Kane consulted with his officers about whether or not to head back south before the full brunt of winter struck them. All but one believed that they should head south, but Kane decided to ignore them and stay put in Rensselaer Harbor. That decision was fateful: the *Advance* was doomed by it, and so was the expedition. Looking back at it the men would all know how fateful it was, and would judge Kane accordingly. As commander, Kane had the right to make the decision, but by consulting with his officers in a pretense of democracy he complicated the situation. Clearly he was uneasy wielding the sort of power that naval commanders took for granted.

At least three of the men aboard disliked him intensely. The journal of sailing master John Wall Wilson, now in the U.S. National Archives, is filled with vituperation aimed at Kane, whom he called "the most self-conceited man I ever saw," and in another account Carl Petersen blames Kane's relative ignorance of the Arctic combined with his arrogance for much of what went wrong. William Godfrey actually published a book about the expedition after Kane's death, giving his side of the story and judging Kane a martinet.[5] With that much smoke there probably was fire, and Kane undoubtedly made mistakes and was erratic in his leadership. In his excellent survey of nineteenth-century arctic exploration, *The Arctic Grail,* Pierre

[5]Wilson is quoted in Pierre Berton, *The Arctic Grail* (New York: Viking, 1988), p. 254, and the other two are discussed at length by Berton in his section on Kane.

Berton gives more credence to these three men than to Kane and as a result characterizes Kane as a strutting braggart. But Berton does not take into account the fact that during the expedition Kane found all three wanting and let them know it. Their egos were stung, and we might expect them to get even in any way they could. Kane's account was probably partly self-serving, but so undoubtedly were theirs. And can we think badly of a man who, in order to let his sick men below decks see the return of the sun after the winter darkness, rigged up a system of mirrors?

As important as his relations with his own men were his relations with the Inuit.[6] It should be emphasized that except for Hans, who joined the expedition in Fiskenaes, the Inuit encountered by the expedition were northern and had little or no experience with outsiders. They were descendants of the Inuit whom John Ross encountered in 1818, calling them "Arctic Highlanders," and apparently no outsider had made contact with them since that time. Relations with them could have been disastrous, and their first meeting (Ch. IX—"Meeting with Esquimaux") was uneasy, but Kane apparently dealt with them well enough so that they became crucial in saving the expedition from many more casualties than it actually suffered—in fact, perhaps saving it from total destruction.

During the century white men's attitudes toward

---

[6]"Inuit" is the Eskimo name for themselves, and means simply "the people." "Eskimo" was an Indian name for them, meaning "eaters of raw flesh."

the Inuit varied. John Ross found them an interesting curiosity. Other arctic explorers pitied them and believed them fit subjects for conversion to Christianity. Still others thought them bestial. When the Hudson's Bay Company's John Rae returned from one of his remarkable overland sledge trips with a report that he had talked to Inuit who had seen men from the Franklin Expedition dying, and who told Rae that those men had been reduced to cannibalism, there was a cry of outrage from armchair travelers in England. Charles Dickens wrote in *Household Words* that Eskimos were "a gross handful of uncivilized people, with a domesticity of blood and blubber."[7] How could Rae believe such savages, the argument went, who more probably had murdered Franklin's men than seen them cannibalizing?

Most explorers were not so hasty in dismissing the Inuit as savages. Kane's attitude is not untypical, although probably better than most. Often in his book he displays a cultural, perhaps a racial, arrogance. He refers, for example, to the "egotistical self-conceit of savage life," (Ch. XVII—"Provisioning") blithely unaware of the obvious irony that by using the phrase he is showing the "egotistical self-conceit" of his own culture. At other times he is less arrogant but nevertheless he is condescending, using phrases like "these strange children of the snow" (Ch. XVII—"Provisioning") and indeed treating the Inuit as children. But

[7] "The Lost Arctic Voyagers," *Household Words,* 9 December 1854, p. 392.

often he shows genuine respect for their ingenuity, hardihood, and decency, and with Hans in particular he was able to establish a close relationship that at least partly cut across racial and cultural division. Our last image of Hans is of him sledging southward at high speed accompanied by a young woman. This is a desertion of sorts, but Kane forgives him with a laugh. The fact that Hans later joined several other expeditions attests to Kane's good relations with him.

The twentieth-century arctic explorer Vilhjalmur Stefansson passed a sweeping judgment on almost all nineteenth-century English and American arctic explorers. Many of them died, according to Stefansson, because they tried to carry their food and shelter with them rather than living off the land—they tried to insulate themselves against the environment rather than using the environment to support them. Above all, they did not hunt enough, and as a result they did not have enough fresh meat and fat to sustain them or to hold off the dreaded scurvy.[8] The Inuit, with one of the greatest hunting cultures on earth, set the example for them if only the explorers had used their eyes to see it. Most, largely because of their cultural arrogance— a refusal to "debase" themselves by living and eating as the Inuit lived and ate—they did not see it. When searchers finally found bodies of Franklin's men on King William Island, on the ground near them were silver plate and heavy gun cases that they had carried,

[8]Stefansson argues the point in much of his writing, but particularly in *The Friendly Arctic* (New York: Macmillan, 1927).

this while they were dying of exposure and starvation.

Kane, however, did see it. True, near the end of his narrative he asserts that one reason he finally determined to leave the *Advance* and head south over the ice was because "a third winter would force us, as the only means of escaping starvation, to resort to Esquimaux habits" (Ch. XXV—"Leaving the Brig"). That assertion, implying that if they did resort to Inuit habits they would be debasing themselves, rings only partly true. It directly contradicts more telling passages throughout the book in which Kane asserts, with no apparent sense of shame, that he and his men did indeed learn from the Inuit.

Although Kane did realize the virtual necessity of adapting to Inuit ways, however, he probably was of two minds about it—he undoubtedly had "civilized" reservations and restraints—and he did not act fully enough on his realization; as the second winter approached he attributed the sickness of his men to their civilized diet, and admits in the book that he did not do enough hunting when there had been game in the area (Ch. XIX—"Fire in the Brig!"). This was perhaps his greatest error. As Stefansson insisted, hunting had to be given priority over everything else if you expected to survive in the Arctic.

But even then you might not survive. Stefansson chooses not to emphasize the fact that the Inuit themselves, those master hunters, also could suffer famine and die of it in their unforgiving world. During the second winter Hans arrives at the *Advance* with the news that the Etah Inuit have run out of food, are debilitated by hunger, and are eating their dogs (Ch. XXI—"Hanging On and a Deserter").

Arctic Explorations in the Years 1853, 54, 55 is one of our great narratives of survival. Surely when all is said and done, survival is what it's about, the underlying subject of the entire book. The Second Grinnell Expedition failed in its stated purpose: it found no sign of the Franklin Expedition. It also made few geographical discoveries, and the main discovery it did make was actually a false one that did more harm than good: William Morton, when he achieved his farthest north, saw or thought he saw open water to the north and thereby encouraged continuing belief in the fiction of an open polar sea. (In fact, after returning with the Second Grinnell Expedition, Dr. Isaac Hayes organized an expedition to go after that chimera.) It failed to approach the North Pole, probably one of its unstated purposes. It can even be called a disaster. Three men died on it, many others had to endure amputations or had their health seriously damaged, and a good ship was lost to the ice.

It can be argued that Kane mishandled the expedition from beginning to end—by not having enough supplies at the outset—by not putting an experienced ice navigator in command of the ship and by relying too much on his own very limited arctic experience—by deciding not to head south as the first winter approached—by not emphasizing hunting more than he did—by not deserting his ship in the second autumn—by so alienating his men that his party split virtually in half.

Yet he and all but three of his men did survive the expedition, and, especially in the second winter, they survived in conditions appalling to modern readers. Some of them, unable to move any distance, were confined to the fetid sanctuary that they had created aboard the ship. Many were suffering scurvy, with its bleeding gums and festering sores, and all were suffering malnutrition and frostbite. For a period of time, their best source of food was rat meat rolled up into frozen tallow balls. The cold was bitter, and they were reduced to cannibalizing their very shelter, the ship itself, for fuel to warm themselves with.

But they survived. Some were able to work, hunt, and even to make demanding trips across the frozen waste back and forth between the ship and the Inuit settlement of Etah. And when the time came, those who had any strength left helped those who had none to escape from their prison. One of the many unforgettable images in the book is the image of Christian Ohlsen by main strength using a capstan bar to prevent one of the sledges from dropping through the ice when they were on their way to rescue. That final exertion of strength by a man who had lived through the deprivations Ohlsen had lived through cost him his life: he strained something inside of him terribly and in three days he was dead. But all the others on that last trek survived, including Elisha Kent Kane.

* * * *

Kane residence at Fern Rock, near Philadelphia

Courtesy Kane-Childs Album, Dreer Collection, Historical Society of Pennsylvania

Kane arrived home to fame. When he had not returned by the autumn of 1854, anxiety about him had mounted, and his family and friends had set about pleading for a search and rescue expedition. Kane's book on the First Grinnell Expedition had been published in his absence; he had become a public figure, so there was considerable popular support for such an expedition. Congress authorized one in February of 1855, and it set sail in May of 1855. Those events had been covered in detail by newspapers, which smelled another arctic tragedy in the making. But the return of the expedition with Kane and the other survivors on board was news too, even if not a tragedy, and the papers made much of it. The search for Franklin had produced many British heroes; now the Americans had their own hero.

While Kane had been gone, the Arctic Archipelago had been a hive of activity, with many British ships, sledges, and boats out looking for Franklin, some of them also hoping to complete a northwest passage themselves. But the Admiralty had given up and in the spring of 1854, over Lady Franklin's protestations, it had struck the names of Sir John Franklin and all his men from its rosters. Only a few weeks after this action by the Admiralty, John Rae had made his discoveries about the fate of Franklin, which he was able to report that autumn when he returned to civilization. The Inuit told John Rae that they had seen many white men dead or dying on King William Island and that there were signs of cannibalism; they also had sold him some relics, including a small silver plate with "Sir John Franklin K.C.H." engraved on it. Lady Franklin and a few others might resist admitting the worst and continue to press for more expeditions, but what had happened to Franklin and his men was now evident, and later discoveries would confirm this. Francis Leopold McClintock made the main discovery later in 1859 on an expedition suppported by Lady Franklin and a public subscription: he found a cairn on the west coast of King William Island with a brief report inside of it. Sir John had died in the spring of 1847 and many others had died later; the ships had been trapped in ice for nineteen months; the survivors, deserting the *Erebus* and *Terror,* were trying to reach the mainland when one of the officers scrawled the report. Obviously, in light of the evidence that Rae had offered a few years before, they all died on that trek— and what had happened to them could have happened to Kane had he been less adaptable to Inuit ways.

For a time at least Kane was well enough in health to enjoy the fruits of his fame. Newspapers continued to play up his return and he was lionized. At a dinner in New York's Century Association he was approached by the great English novelist William Makepeace Thackeray, who was in the United States on a lecture tour. After dinner Kane had been informally telling stories about his experiences—a man present that night said it was like listening to Marco Polo— when Thackeray got up from his chair and went over to him. Thackeray, a large man who loomed over

Kane, turned to their host and said: "Do you think the Doctor will permit me to stoop down and kiss his boots?"[9]

Kane apparently went to see Margaret Fox only days after his return. Newspapers soon picked up the story that they were engaged, and, since both were celebrities, gave it considerable play. The Kane family finally felt obliged to print a denial, stating that all Kane had done before his departure to the Arctic was give money to a fund that had been established by others to educate Margaret, and that when he returned from the Arctic he had gone to see what progress had been made in that education. We are almost entirely dependent on Margaret's book *The Love-Life of Dr. Kane* for what we know—or do not know—about what happened in the months that followed. According to her, Kane still loved her passionately but continued to be held in thrall by his family until finally, just before he departed on his last voyage, he made her his common-law wife in a private ceremony. Kane's most recent and best informed biographer, Dr. George W. Corner, speculates that when Kane returned from the Arctic he found his earlier passion for Maggie Fox had cooled, but he was too sensitive to hurt her by simply breaking off. By being gentle, he ended up implicating himself enough so that Margaret could, in a sense, lay claim to him. Corner emphasizes the fact that we have only Margaret's word for the story about the common-law marriage ceremony.

[9]Corner, p. 232.

Whatever was happening in his relations with Margaret Fox, Kane was also working strenuously on his book. Harper and Brothers had published the book on his first expedition while he was absent in the Arctic, and they had done excellent work on its typography, illustration, and binding, but Judge Kane, who had acted as agent for his son, believed that they had not been square in their financial dealings. Kane decided to change publishers for his second book, and contracted with Childs and Peterson of Philadelphia, a firm that was just establishing itself. George Childs, who took care of the business side of the firm while Peterson took care of the editorial side, was what we now would call a public relations man and urged Kane to write a popular book. Kane was willing to cooperate up to a point, although he complained to Childs that he was being forced to be "gaseous": "I attempt to be more popular and gaseous—this latter inflated quality in excess. Most certainly my efforts to make this book readable will destroy its permanency and injure me. It is a sacrifice."[10]

He insisted that he be allowed to include a considerable amount of scientific material, not only making the book more expensive to produce but also, in his opinion, more "permanent." He was wrong, of course; most of the scientific material, including various charts and tables in the appendices, became out of date. He was right, however, in insisting that he be allowed to

[10]Quoted in William Elder, *Biography of Elisha Kent Kane* (Philadelphia: Childs and Peterson, 1858), p. 216.

keep passages in his journal that evoked disagreeable aspects of his experiences—the violence, stench, bestiality, and suffering that he and the others endured. That quality of harsh realism in the book, offensive to some readers in the nineteenth century, makes it still potent today.

He worked steadily on writing the book and, in close cooperation with the artist James Hamilton, on its superb illustrations. The book was released in the autumn of 1856. Childs hoped that Congress would buy a large number to distribute to schools. (Congress had done that with another book some years before.) Kane thought it humiliating to lobby Congress for such a purpose, and to his relief nothing came of the scheme. As it turned out, the book sold so well that there was no need of a congressional subsidy anyway. Childs also hoped that Kane would tour the country giving lectures, but he actually gave only one talk on the expedition, and that to the very select but also very small American Philosophical Society. The plans for a lecture tour came to nothing because Kane had burned himself out working on the book; he was far too ill to face the demands of a lecture tour. He was more accurate than perhaps he knew when he wrote to Childs: "The book, poor as it is, has been my coffin."[11] He was, in fact, sick unto death. When he first arrived in New York, he had seemed in good health. The cruise from Greenland had allowed him to recover from the depredations the expedition had

[11]Elder, p. 218.

wreaked on him; he had gained weight and looked leathery and tough. But in the months that followed, he exhausted himself and soon paid the price for it. In consultation with doctors, he decided that he should go to a sanitarium in Switzerland.

The indefatigable Lady Franklin had been urging him to help her in an attempt to force the Admiralty to mount yet another search expedition. A ship from one of the British Navy's search expeditions had been abandoned to the ice of Barrow Strait in 1854 and had drifted entirely unattended along almost exactly the same route that the ships of the First Grinnell Expedition had floated when they had been trapped by the ice. An American whaler found her afloat in Baffin Bay, almost a year and a half after the time and almost a thousand miles from the place of her abandonment. The whaler manned her and brought her to New London. The Admiralty waived any claim to her, but Congress voted money to have her refurbished and then presented her to Queen Victoria. Lady Franklin began a campaign to persuade the Admiralty to dedicate the ship to continuing the search, and she also thought that Kane could be effective in pleading the cause. Kane intended to go to Europe to rest, but he agreed to go to England as well and do whatever he could do to help.

He first went to several American spas to gain at least some strength, and then sailed for England, accompanied only by the loyal William Morton, who had become his personal attendant. In London he was

Badge worn by committeemen at Kane obsequies,
Cincinnati, Ohio

Courtesy Kane-Childs Album, Dreer Collection, Historical Society of Pennsylvania

treated as a dignitary by the Admiralty and the Royal Geographical Society, and was so often visited by Lady Franklin that, as he wrote to his father, he felt she was using him unmercifully. While he was in London, however, he also went to see some of England's most eminent doctors, and they advised him to go to a warmer climate as soon as he could. Henry Grinnell's son Cornelius came from Paris immediately and made arrangements for himself, Kane, and Morton to take a ship to Saint Thomas, and from there to Cuba. On the ship to Cuba, Kane suffered a stroke, and in Havana he was carried off the ship on a stretcher.

Two of Kane's brothers and his mother went to Cuba to care for him, and in the weeks that followed he seemed to be on his way to at least partial recovery, but on 10 February he suffered another stroke, this one massive, and on 16 February 1857 he died at the age of thirty-six.

* * * *

Elisha Kent Kane's story does not end with his death. Following the news that he had died was a remarkable display of ritualized public sorrow that can be compared only to the national obsequies following the death of Lincoln some years later.

Four days after he died his casket was borne to the main plaza in Havana followed by Cuban and American officials and two military bands. From there it was taken to the waterfront, where it was placed on a special barge supplied by the Cuban government and tranferred to the steam packet *Catawba*. When the *Catawba* arrived in New Orleans two days later, it was met by the mayor of the city and a military guard and the casket was taken to City Hall, where it lay in state until it was carried in a large and solemn procession to a steamboat on the Mississipi. As the steamboat made its way up the Mississipi and Ohio rivers in the days that followed, in the small towns people gathered along the shore to pay their respects to the dead hero, and in the cities there were more formal ceremonies, with bells tolling, honor guards firing salvos, bands playing, and dignitaries giving speeches, the general tone of which is suggested by the following passage from one: "We could have wished that his enterprises had been crowned with fuller success—not, indeed for his fame's sake, for the glory of his name is secure—but to have made more complete his own happiness. But he heeds not these things now. He hath laid himself down with the brave to sleep. Death hath kissed him with lips colder than the north wind's breath. Life, with its behests and hopes, is over. He lives with the immortal dead."[12]

In Cincinnati the casket was transferred with considerable ceremony from boat to train, and the process was repeated. When the train stopped at smaller cities along the way, bells tolled and crowds gathered at the stations. At Baltimore when Kane's casket was trans-

[12]*Honors to Dr. Kane: Report of the Joint Committees Appointed to Receive the Remains and Conduct the Obsequies of the Late Elisha Kent Kane* (Philadelphia, 1857), p. 46.

ferred to another train for the last lap to Philadelphia, it was carried in procession on a gun carriage while the city's bells tolled for five hours.

And finally it reached home. At Philadelphia the casket was met by another large procession, and among those present were Isaac Hayes, Amos Bonsall, Henry Brooks, Henry Goodfellow, George Stephenson, William Godfrey, and Thomas Hickey. They joined William Morton, who had accompanied the body all the way from Havana, and laid the flag of the *Advance* over the casket, then walked beside it as it was carried to Independence Hall, where it lay in state for three days. Then, on 14 March 1857, with the Governor of Pennsylvania and its Chief Justice, two naval commodores, two famous doctors, and Henry Grinnell among the pallbearers, the casket was placed on an ornate funeral carriage that flew the flags of Great Britain, Spain, Denmark, and the United States, and in a procession of hundreds taken first to the church where there was a final public ceremony, and then to the Kane family vault.

CHAUNCEY LOOMIS

CONSTANCE MARTIN

April 1996

Arctic Explorations

GLOSSARY OF ARCTIC TERMS

BERG. Ice of recent formation, so called because forming most readily in bays and sheltered spots.

BERG. (See Iceberg.)

BESET. So enclosed by floating ice as to be completely unable to navigate.

BIGHT. An indentation.

BLASTING. Breaking the ice by gunpowder.

BLINK. (See Ice-blink.)

BORE. To force through loose or recent ice by sails or steam.

BRASH. Ice broken up into small fragments.

CALF. Detached masses from berg or glacier, rising suddenly to the surface.

CROW'S NEST. A lookout place attached to the top gallant masthead.

DOCK. An opening in the ice, artificial or natural, offering protection.

DRIFT-ICE. Detached ice in motion.

FIELD-ICE. An extensive surface of floating ice.

FIORD. An abrupt opening along the coastline, admitting the sea.

FIRE-HOLE. A well dug in the ice to be used as a safeguard in case of fire.

FLOE. A detached portion of a field.

GLACIER. A mass of ice derived from the atmosphere, sometimes abutting upon the sea.

HUMMOCKS. Ridges of broken ice formed by collision of the fields.

ICE-ANCHOR. A hook or grapnel adapted to take hold upon the ice.

ICE-BELT. A continued margin of ice, which in high northern latitudes adheres to the coast above the ordinary level of the sea.

ICEBERG. A large floating mass of ice, which is detached from a glacier.

ICE-BLINK. A peculiar appearance of the atmosphere over distant ice.

ICE-CHISEL. A long chisel for cutting holes in ice.

ICE-FACE. The abutting face of the ice-belt.

ICE-FOOT. The Danish name for the limited ice-belt of the more southern coast.

ICE-HOOK. A small ice-anchor.

ICE-RAFT. Ice, whether field, floe, or detached belt, transporting foreign matter.

ICE-TABLE. A flat surface of ice.

LAND-ICE. Floes or fields adhering to the coast or included between headlands.

LANE OR LEAD. A navigable opening in the ice.

NIP. The condition of a vessel pressed upon by the ice on both sides.

OLD ICE. Ice of more than a season's growth.

PACK. A large area of floating ices driven together more or less closely.

POLYNIA. A Russian term for an open water space.

RUE-RADDY. A shoulder belt to drag by.

TIDE-HOLE. A well sunk in the ice for the purpose of observing tides.

TRACKING. Towing along a margin of ice.

WATER-SKY. A peculiar appearance of the sky over open water.

YOUNG ICE. Ice formed before the setting in of winter; also, recent ice.

I

Preparations and Into the North Water

IN THE MONTH of December 1852, I had the honor of receiving special orders from the Secretary of the Navy, to "conduct an expedition to the Arctic seas in search of Sir John Franklin."

I had been engaged, under Lieutenant De Haven, in the First Grinnell Expedition, which sailed from the United States in 1850 on the same errand; and I had occupied myself for some months after our return in maturing the scheme of a renewed effort to rescue the missing party, or at least to resolve the mystery of its fate. Mr. Grinnell,[1] with a liberality altogether characteristic, had placed the *Advance*, in which I sailed before, at my disposal; and Mr. Peabody, of London, the generous representative of many American sympathies, had proffered aid largely toward her outfit. Then the Geographical Society of New York, also the Smithsonian Institution, the American Philosophical Society—I name them in the order in which they announced their contributions—and a number of scientific associations and friends of science besides, had come forward to help me; and by their aid I managed to secure a better outfit for purposes of observation

[1]For background on Henry Grinnell and the First and Second Grinnell Expeditions, see "Historical Introduction."

than would otherwise have been possible to a party so limited in numbers and absorbed in other objects.

Ten of our little party belonged to the United States Navy, and were attached to my command by orders from the Department; the others were shipped by me for the cruise, and at salaries entirely disproportionate to their services: all were volunteers. We did not sail under the rules that govern our national ships; but we had our own regulations, well considered and announced beforehand, and rigidly adhered to afterward through all the vicissitudes of the expedition. These included—first, absolute subordination to the officer in command or his delegate; second, abstinence from all intoxicating liquors, except when dispensed by special order; third, the habitual disuse of profane language. We had no other laws.

I had developed our plan of search in a paper read before the Geographical Society. It was based upon the probable extension of the land masses of Greenland to the Far North—a fact at that time not verified by travel, but sustained by the analogies of physical geography. Greenland, though looked upon as a congeries of islands connected by interior glaciers, was still to be regarded as a peninsula whose formation recognized the same general laws as other peninsulas having a southern trend.

From the alternating altitudes of its mountain ranges, continued without depression throughout a meridional line of nearly eleven hundred miles, I inferred that this chain must extend very far to the north, and that Greenland might not improbably approach nearer the Pole than any other known land.[2]

Believing, then, in such an extension of this peninsula, and feeling that the search for Sir John Franklin would be best promoted by a course that might lead directly to the open sea of which I had inferred the existence, and that the approximation of the meridians would make access to the west as easy from Northern Greenland as from Wellington Channel, and access to the east far more easy—feeling, too, that the highest protruding headland would be most likely to afford some traces of the lost party—I named, as the inducements in favor of my scheme:

1. Terra firma as the basis of our operations, obviating the capricious character of ice travel.
2. A due northern line, which, throwing aside the influences of terrestrial radiation, would lead soonest to the open sea, should such exist.
3. The benefit of the fan-like abutment of land, on the

[2]Kane's plan depended on two main theories. The first was that Greenland extended far to the north, and fanned out westward in its northern extremities. He believed that if this were so, then it would protect him from southward drifting ice of the sort that clogged Wellington Channel in the Arctic Archipelago or that had blocked Sir William Edward Parry when he tried to reach the North Pole via Spitzbergen in 1827. His second theory, discussed in the Historical Introduction, was that there was an "open polar sea" beyond the rim of ice that had endangered arctic explorers for centuries—that around the Pole itself would be more temperate open water rich in fish, birds, and mammals, and that Franklin's expedition might be surviving somewhere on the shores of that sea. The idea of an open polar sea had existed for centuries, and had supporters through the nineteenth century.

north face of Greenland, to check the ice in the course of its southern or equatorial drift, thus obviating the great drawback of Parry in his attempts to reach the Pole by the Spitzbergen Sea.

4. Animal life to sustain traveling parties.

5. The cooperation of the Esquimaux, settlements of these people having been found as high as Whale Sound and probably extending still farther along the coast.

We were to pass up Baffin's Bay at its most northern attainable point; and thence, pressing on toward the Pole as far as boats or sledges could carry us, examine the coastlines for vestiges of the lost party.

All hands counted, we were seventeen at the time of sailing. Another joined us a few days afterward. The party under my command, as it reached the coast of Greenland, consisted of:

Henry Brooks,	George Stephenson
FIRST OFFICER	William Morton
Isaac I. Hayes, M.D.,	George Whipple
SURGEON	Christian Ohlsen
John Wall Wilson	William Godfrey
August Sontag,	Henry Goodfellow
ASTRONOMER	John Blake
James McGary	Jefferson Baker
Amos Bonsall	Peter Schubert
George Riley	Thomas Hickey

Two of these, Brooks and Morton, had been my associates in the first expedition; gallant and trustworthy men, both of them, as ever shared the fortunes or claimed the gratitude of a commander.

The *Advance*[3] had been thoroughly tried in many encounters with the Arctic ice. She was carefully inspected, and needed very little to make her all a seaman could wish. She was a hermaphrodite brig of 144 tons, intended originally for carrying heavy castings from an iron foundry, but strengthened afterward with great skill and at large expense. She was a good sailer, and easily managed. We had five boats; one of them a metallic lifeboat, the gift of the maker, Mr. Francis.

Our equipment was simple. It consisted of little else than a quantity of rough boards to serve for housing over the vessel in winter; some tents made of India rubber and canvas, of the simplest description; and several carefully built sledges, some of them on a model furnished me by the kindness of the British Admiralty, others of my own devising.

Our store of provisions was chosen with little regard to luxury. We took with us some two thousand pounds of pemmican, a parcel of Borden's meat biscuit, some packages of an exsiccated potato, some pickled cabbage, and a liberal quantity of American dried fruits and vegetables; besides these, we had the salt beef and pork of the navy ration, hard biscuit, and flour. A very moderate supply of liquors, along with

---

[3] The *Advance* was the larger of the two vessels used on the First Grinnell Expedition, so Kane was familiar with her. An "hermaphrodite brig", it is two-masted, square-rigged forward and schooner-rigged aft.

the ordinary *et ceteras* of an Arctic cruiser, made up the diet list. I hoped to procure some fresh provisions before reaching the upper coast of Greenland; and I carried some barrels of malt, with a compact apparatus for brewing.

We had a moderate wardrobe of woolens; a full supply of knives, needles, and other articles for barter; a large, well-chosen library; and a valuable set of instruments for scientific observations.

We left New York on 30 May 1853 escorted by several noble steamers; and, passing slowly on to the Narrows amid salutes and cheers of farewell, cast our brig off from the steam tug and put to sea.

It took us eighteen days to reach St. John's, Newfoundland. The governor, Mr. Hamilton, a brother of the secretary of the Admiralty, received us with a hearty English welcome; and all the officials, indeed all the inhabitants, vied with each other in efforts to advance our views. I purchased here a stock of fresh beef, which, after removing the bones and tendons, we compressed into rolls by wrapping it closely with twine, according to the nautical process of *marling*, and hung it up in the rigging.

After two days we left this thriving and hospitable city; and, with a noble team of Newfoundland dogs on board, the gift of Governor Hamilton, headed our brig for the coast of Greenland.

We reached Baffin's Bay without incident. We took deep sea soundings as we approached its axis, and found a reliable depth of nineteen hundred fathoms:

Fiskenaes from the Governor's House, South Greenland

James Hamilton, from a sketch by Dr. Kane

an interesting result, as it shows that the ridge known to extend between Ireland and Newfoundland in the bed of the Atlantic is depressed as it passes farther to the north. A few days more found us off the coast of Greenland,[4] making our way toward Fiskenaes.

* * * *

We entered the harbor of Fiskenaes on 1 July amid the clamor of its entire population assembled on the rocks to greet us.

We found Mr. Lassen, the superintending official of the Danish Company, a hearty, single-minded man fond of his wife, his children, and his pipe. The visit of our brig was an incident to be marked in the simple annals of his colony; and, even before I had shown him my official letter from the Court of Denmark, he had most hospitably proffered everything for our accommodation. We became his guests, and interchanged presents with him before our departure; this last transaction enabled me to say, with confidence, that the inner fiords produce noble salmon trout, and that the reindeer tongue, a recognized delicacy in the old and new Arctic continents, is justly appreciated at Fiskenaes.

Feeling that our dogs would require fresh provisions, which could hardly be spared from our supplies on shipboard, I availed myself of Mr. Lassen's influence to obtain an Esquimaux hunter for our party. He

[4]Greenland was an integral part of the Kingdom of Denmark until it was granted home rule in 1979.

recommended to me one Hans Christian, a boy of nineteen, as an expert with the kayak and javelin; and after Hans had given me a touch of his quality by spearing a bird on the wing, I engaged him. He was fat, good natured, and, except under the excitements of the hunt, as stolid and unimpressible as one of our own Indians. He stipulated that, in addition to his very moderate wages, I should leave a couple of barrels of bread and fifty-two pounds of pork with his mother; and I became munificent in his eyes when I added the gift of a rifle and a new kayak. We found him very useful; our dogs required his services as a caterer, and our own table was more than once dependent on his energies.

No one can know so well as an Arctic voyager the value of foresight. My conscience has often called for the exercise of it, but my habits make it an effort. I can hardly claim to be provident, either by impulse or education. Yet, for some of the deficiencies of our outfit I ought not, perhaps, to hold myself responsible. Our stock of fresh meats was too small, and we had no preserved vegetables. But my personal means were limited, and I could not press more severely than a strict necessity exacted upon the unquestioning liberality of my friends.

While we were beating out of the fiord of Fiskenaes, I had an opportunity of visiting Lichtenfels, the ancient seat of the Greenland congregations, and one of the three Moravian settlements. I had read much of the history of its founders; and it was with feelings almost of devotion, that I drew near the scene their labors had consecrated.

We lingered along the coast for the next nine days, baffled by calms and light adverse winds; and it was only on 10 July that we reached the settlement of Sukkertoppen.

The Sukkertop, or Sugar-loaf, a noted landmark, is a wild isolated peak, rising some three thousand feet from the sea. The little colony which nestles at its base occupies a rocky gorge, so narrow and broken that a stairway connects the detached groups of huts, and the tide, as it rises, converts a part of the groundplot into a temporary island.

It was after twelve at night when we came into port; and the peculiar light of the Arctic summer at this hour—which reminds one of the effect of an eclipse, so unlike our orthodox twilight—bathed everything in gray but the northern background—an Alpine chain standing out against a blazing crimson sky.

Sukkertoppen is a principal depôt for reindeer skins; and the natives were at this season engaged in their summer hunt, collecting them. Four thousand had already been sent to Denmark, and more were on hand. I bought a stock of superior quality for fifty cents a piece. These furs are valuable for their lightness and warmth. I would have added to my stock of fish; but the cod had not yet reached this part of the coast, and would not for some weeks.

Bidding good-bye to the governor, whose hospitality we had shared liberally, we put to sea on Saturday, beating to the northward and westward in the teeth of a heavy gale.

The lower and middle coast of Greenland has been visited by so many voyagers, and its points of interest have been so often described, that I need not dwell upon them. From the time we left Sukkertoppen, we had the usual delays from fogs and adverse currents, and did not reach the neighborhood of Wilcox Point, which defines Melville Bay, until 27 July.

On the sixteenth we passed the promontory of Swartehuk, and were welcomed the next day at Proven by my old friend Christiansen, the superintendent, and found his family much as I left them three years before. Frederick, his son, had married a native woman, and added a summer tent, a half-breed boy, and a Danish rifle to his stock of valuables. My former patient, Anna, had united fortunes with a fat faced Esquimaux, and was the mother of a chubby little girl. Madame Christiansen, who counted all these and so many others as her happy progeny, was hearty and warm hearted as ever. She led the household in sewing up my skins into various serviceable garments; and I had the satisfaction, before I left, of completing my stock of furs for our sledge parties.

While our brig passed, half sailing, half drifting, up the coast, I left her under the charge of Mr. Brooks, and set out in the whaleboat to make my purchases of dogs among the natives. Gathering them as we went along from the different settlements, we reached Upernavik, the resting place of the First Grinnell Expedition in

1851 after its winter drift, and for a couple of days shared, as we were sure to do, the generous hospitality of Governor Flaischer.

Still coasting along, we passed in succession the Esquimaux settlement of Kingatok, the Kettle—a mountaintop so named from the resemblances of its profile—and finally Yotlik, the farthest point of colonization, beyond which, save the sparse headlands of the charts, the coast may be regarded as unknown. Then, inclining more directly toward the north, we ran close to the Baffin Islands—clogged with ice when I saw them three years before, now entirely clear— sighted the landmark known as Horse's Head, and, passing the Duck Islands, where the *Advance* was grounded in 1851, bore away from Wilcox Point.

We stood lazily along the coast, with alternations of perfect calm and offshore breezes, generally from the south or east; but on the morning of 27 July, as we neared the entrance of Melville Bay, one of those heavy ice-fogs, which I have described in my former narrative as characteristic of this region, settled around us. We could hardly see across the decks, and yet were sensible of the action of currents carrying us we knew not where. By the time the sun had scattered the mist, Wilcox Point was to the south of us; and our little brig, now fairly in the bay, stood a fair chance of drifting over towards Devil's Thumb, which then bore east of north. The bergs that infest this region, and which have earned for it among the whalers the title of the "Bergy Hole," showed themselves all around us.

It was a whole day's work, towing with both boats; but toward evening we had succeeded in crawling off-shore, and were doubly rewarded for our labor with a wind. I had observed with surprise, while we were floating near the coast, that the land ice was already broken and decayed; and I was aware, from what I had read, as well as what I had learned from whalers and observed myself of the peculiarities of this navigation, that the inshore track was in consequence beset with difficulty and delays. I made up my mind at once. I would stand to the westward until arrested by the pack, and endeavor to double Melville Bay by an outside passage.

On our road we were favored with a gorgeous spectacle, which hardly any excitement of peril could have made us overlook. The midnight sun came out over the northern crest of the great berg, our late "fast friend," kindling variously colored fires on every part of its surface, and making the ice around us one great resplendency of gemwork, blazing carbuncles, and rubies and molten gold.

* * * *

Our brig went crunching through all this jewelry; and, after a tortuous progress of five miles, arrested here and there by tongues that required the saw and ice-chisels, fitted herself neatly between two floes. Here she rested till toward morning, when the leads opened again, and I was able, from the crow's nest, to pick our way to a larger pool some distance ahead. In this we beat backward and forward, like China fish seeking an outlet from a glass jar, till the fog caught us again; and so the day ended.

The indentation known as Melville Bay is protected by its northern and northeastern coast from the great ice and current drifts that follow the axis of Baffin's Bay. The interior of the country that bounds upon it is the seat of extensive glaciers, which are constantly shedding off icebergs of the largest dimensions. The greater bulk of these is below the waterline, and the depth to which they sink when floating subjects them to the action of the deeper sea currents, while their broad surface above the water is, of course, acted on by the wind. It happens, therefore, that they are found not infrequently moving in different directions from the floes around them, and preventing them for a time from freezing into a united mass. Still, in the late winter, when the cold has thoroughly set in, Melville Bay becomes a continuous field of ice, from Cape York to the Devil's Thumb.

On the return of milder weather, the same causes renew their action; and that portion of the ice protected from the outside drift, and entangled among the icebergs that crowd the bay, remains permanent long after that which is outside is in motion. Step by step, as the year advances, its outer edge breaks off; yet its inner curve frequently remains unbroken through the entire summer. This is the "fast ice" of the whalers, so important to their progress in the earlier portions of the season; for, however it may be encroached upon by storms or currents, they can generally find room to track their vessels along its solid margin; or if the outside ice, yielding to offshore winds, happens to recede, the interval of water between the fast and the drift allows them not infrequently to use their sails.

It is, therefore, one of the whalers' canons of navigation, which they hold to most rigidly, to follow the shore. But it is obvious that this applies only to the early periods of the Arctic season, when the land ice of the inner bay is comparatively unbroken, as in May or June or part of July, varying of course with the circumstances. Indeed, the bay is seldom traversed except in these months, the northwest fisheries of Pond's Bay, and the rest, ceasing to be of value afterward. Later in the summer, the inner ice breaks up into large floes, moving with wind and tide, that embarrass the navigator, misleading him into the notion that he is attached to his "fast," when in reality he is accompanying the movements of an immense floating ice-field.

Now I felt sure, from the known openness of the season of 1852 and the probable mildness of the following winter, that we could scarcely hope to make use of the land ice for tracking, or to avail ourselves of leads along its margin by canvas. And this opinion was confirmed by the broken and rotten appearance of the floes during our coastwise drift at the Duck Islands. I therefore deserted the inside track of the whalers, and stood to the westward, until we made the first streams of the middle pack; and then, skirting the pack to the northward, headed in slowly for the middle portion of the bay above Sabine Islands. My object was to double, as it were, the loose and drifting ice that had stood in my way, and, reaching Cape York, as nearly as might be, trust for the remainder of my passage to warping and tracking by the heavy floes. We succeeded, not without some laborious boring and serious risks of entanglement among the broken ice-fields. But we managed, in every instance, to combat this last form of difficulty by attaching our vessel to large icebergs, which enabled us to hold our own, however swiftly the surface floes were pressing by us to the south. Four days of this scarcely varied yet exciting navigation brought us to the extended fields of the pack, and a fortunate northwester opened a passage for us through them. We are now in the North Water.

II

From Red Snow to the First Gale

M Y DIARY NOTES:
    "We passed the 'Crimson Cliffs' of Sir John Ross[1] in the forenoon of 5 August. The patches of red snow, from which they derive their name, could be seen clearly at the distance of ten miles from the coast. It had a fine deep rose hue, not at all like the brown stain I had noticed when I was here before. All the gorges and ravines in which the snows had lodged were deeply tinted with it. I had no difficulty now in justifying the somewhat poetical nomenclature Sir John Franklin applied to this locality;[2] for if the snowy surface were more diffused, as it is no doubt earlier in the season, crimson would be the prevailing color.

"Late at night we passed Conical Rock, the most insulated and conspicuous landmark of this coast; and, still later, Wolstenholme and Saunder's Islands, and

---

[1] Sir John Ross commanded the first British post-Napoleonic war expedition into the Arctic in 1818 and sailed past this area while exploring Baffin Bay.

[2] Kane is right that the Crimson Cliffs inspired poetic description, but wrong attributing the prose to Sir John Franklin. The only time Franklin would have seen the area was on his fateful trip of 1845 and no journal survives. Franklin's prior Arctic expeditions were overland.

Oomenak, the place of the *'North Star's'*[3] winter quarters—an admirable day's run; and so ends 5 August. We are standing along, with studding sails set, and open water before us, fast nearing our scene of labor. We have already got to work sewing up blanket bags and preparing sledges for our campaignings on the ice."

We reached Hakluyt Island in the course of the next day. The tall spire, probably of gneiss, rises six hundred feet above the water level and is a valuable landmark for very many miles around. We were destined to become familiar with it before leaving this region. Both it and Northumberland, to the southeast of it, afforded studies of color that would have rewarded an artist. The red snow was diversified with large surfaces of beautifully green mosses and alopecurus; and where the sandstone was bare, it threw in a rich shade of brown.

August 6, Saturday. "Cape Alexander and Cape Isabella, the headlands of Smith's Sound, are now in sight; and, in addition to these indications of our progress toward the field of search, a marked swell has set in after a short blow from the northward, just such as might be looked for from the action of the wind upon an open water-space beyond.

"Whatever it may have been when Captain Ingle-

---

[3]In 1849–50 the HMS *Northstar,* sent out from London to resupply one of the Franklin search expeditions, was forced by ice to winter over in Wolstenholme Sound. Four men died of scurvy during that winter.

field saw it a year ago, the aspect of this coast is now most uninviting.[4] As we look far off to the west, the snow comes down with heavy uniformity to the water's edge, and the patches of land seem as rare as the summer's snow on the hills about Sukkertoppen and Fiskenaes. On the right we have an array of cliffs, whose frowning grandeur might dignify the entrance to the proudest of southern seas. I should say they would average from four to five hundred yards in height, with some of their precipices eight hundred feet at a single steep. They have been until now the Arctic pillars of Hercules; and they look down on us as if they challenged our right to pass. Even the sailors are impressed, as we move under their dark shadow. One of the officers said to our lookout, that the gulls and eider that dot the water all around us were just as enlivening as the white sails of the Mediterranean. 'Yes, sir,' he rejoined, with sincere gravity; 'yes, sir, in proportion to their size.' "

AUGUST 7, SUNDAY. "We have left Cape Alexander to the south; and Littleton Island is before us, hiding Cape Hatherton, the latest of Captain Inglefields's positively determined headlands. We are fairly inside of Smith's Sound.

"On our left is a capacious bay; and deep in its northeastern recesses we can see a glacier issuing from a fiord."

---

[4]Captain Edward Inglefield, sponsored by Lady Franklin and public subscription, had cruised this coast in the *Isabel* the previous year.

We knew this bay familiarly afterward, as the residence of a body of Esquimaux with whom we had many associations; but we little dreamt then that it would bear the name of a gallant friend, who found there the first traces of our escape. A small cluster of rocks, hidden at times by the sea, gave evidence of the violent tidal action about them.

"As we neared the west end of Littleton Island, after breakfast this morning, I ascended to the crow's nest, and saw to my sorrow the ominous blink of ice ahead. The wind has been freshening for a couple of days from the northward, and if it continues it will bring down the floes on us.

"My mind has been made up from the first that we are to force our way to the north as far as the elements will let us; and I feel the importance therefore of securing a place of retreat, that in case of disaster we may not be altogether at large. Besides, we have now reached one of the points, at which, if anyone is to follow us, he might look for some trace to guide him."

I determined to leave a cairn on Littleton Island, and to deposit a boat with a supply of stores in some convenient place near it. One of our whaleboats had been crushed in Melville Bay, and Francis's metallic lifeboat was the only one I could spare. Its length did not exceed twenty feet, and our crew of twenty could hardly stow themselves in it with even a few days' rations; but it was air chambered and buoyant.

Selecting from our stock of provisions and field equipage such portions as we might by good luck be able to dispense with, and adding with reluctant liberality some blankets and a few yards of India rubber cloth, we set out in search of a spot for our first depot. It was essential that it should be upon the mainland; for the rapid tides might so wear away the ice as to make an island inaccessible to a foot party; and yet it was desirable that, while secure against the action of sea and ice, it should be approachable by boats. We found such a place after some pretty cold rowing. It was off the northeast cape of Littleton, and bore SSE from Cape Hatherton, which loomed in the distance above the fog. Here we buried our lifeboat with her little cargo. We placed along her gunwale the heaviest rocks we could handle, and, filling up the interstices with smaller stones and sods of andromeda and moss, poured sand and water among the layers. This, frozen at once into a solid mass, might be hard enough, we hoped, to resist the claws of the polar bear.

We found to our surprise that we were not the first human beings who had sought a shelter in this desolate spot. A few ruined walls here and there showed that it had once been the seat of a rude settlement; and in the little knoll we cleared away to cover in our storehouse of valuables, we found the mortal remains of their former inhabitants.

Nothing can be imagined more sad and homeless than these memorials of extinct life. Hardly a vestige of growth was traceable on the bare ice-rubbed rocks; and the huts resembled so much the broken fragments that surrounded them, that at first sight it was hard to distinguish one from the other. Walrus bones lay about in all directions, showing that this animal had furnished the staple of subsistence. There were some remains too of the fox and the narwhal; but I found no signs of the seal or reindeer.

These Esquimaux have no mother earth to receive their dead; but they seat them as in the attitude of repose, the knees drawn close to the body, and enclose them in a sack of skins. The implements of the living man are then grouped around him; they are covered with a rude dome of stones, and a cairn is piled above. This simple cenotaph will remain intact for generations to come. The Esquimaux never disturb a grave.

From one of the graves I took several perforated and rudely fashioned pieces of walrus ivory, evidently parts of sledge and lance gear. But wood must have been even more scarce with them than with the natives of Baffin's Bay north of the Melville Glacier. We found, for instance, a child's toy spear, which, though elaborately tipped with ivory, had its wooden handle pieced out of four separate bits, all carefully patched and bound with skin. No piece was more than six inches in length or half an inch in thickness.

We found other traces of Esquimaux, both on Littleton Island and in Shoal Water Cove, near it. They consisted of huts, graves, places of deposit for meat, and rocks arranged as foxtraps. These were evidently very ancient; but they were so well preserved, that it was impossible to say how long they had been abandoned, whether for fifty or a hundred years before.

Our stores deposited, it was our next office to erect a beacon and entrust to it our tidings. We chose for this purpose the Western Cape of Littleton Island, as more conspicuous than Cape Hatherton; built our cairn; wedged a staff into the crevices of the rocks; and, spreading the American flag, hailed its folds with three cheers as they expanded in the cold midnight breeze. These important duties performed—the more lightly for this little flicker of enthusiasm—we rejoined the brig early in the morning of the seventh, and forced on again toward the north, beating against wind and tide.

* * * *

August 8, Monday. "I had seen the ominous blink ahead of us from the Flagstaff Point of Littleton Island; and before two hours were over, we closed with ice to the westward. It was in the form of a pack, very heavy, and several seasons old; but we stood on, boring the loose stream-ice, until we had passed some forty miles beyond Cape Life-Boat Cove. Here it became impossible to force our way farther; a dense fog gathering around us, we were carried helplessly off to the east. We should have been forced upon the Greenland coast; but an eddy close inshore released us for a few moments from the direct pressure, and we were fortunate enough to get out a whale line to the rocks and warp into a protecting niche.

"In the evening I ventured out again with the change of tide, but it was only to renew a profitless conflict. The flood, after encountering the southward movement of the floes, drove them in upon the shore, and with such rapidity and force as to carry the smaller bergs along with them. We were too happy, when, after a manful struggle of some hours, we found ourselves once more out of their range.

"Our new position was rather nearer to the south than the one we had left. It was in a beautiful cove, landlocked from east to west, and accessible only from the north. Here we moored our vessel securely by hawsers to the rocks, and a whale line carried out to the narrow entrance. At McGary's suggestion, I called it 'Fog Inlet'; but we afterward remembered it more thankfully as Refuge Harbor."

August 9, Tuesday. "It may be noted among our little miseries that we have more than fifty dogs on board, the majority of whom might rather be characterized as 'ravening wolves.' To feed this family, upon whose strength our progress and success depend, is really a difficult matter. The absence of shore or land ice to the south in Baffin's Bay has prevented our rifles from contributing any material aid to our commissariat. Our two bears lasted the cormorants but eight days; and to feed them upon the meager allowance of two pounds of raw flesh every other day is an almost impossible necessity. Only yesterday they were ready to eat the caboose up, for I would not give them pemmican. Corn meal or beans, which Penny's dogs fed on, they disdain to touch; and salt junk would kill them.

"Accordingly, I started out this morning to hunt

walrus, with which the Sound is teeming. We saw at least fifty of these dusky monsters, and approached many groups within twenty paces. But our rifle balls reverberated from their hides like cork pellets from a popgun target, and we could not get within harpoon distance of one. Later in the day, however, Ohlsen, climbing a neighboring hill to scan the horizon and see if the ice had slackened, found the dead carcass of a narwhal or sea unicorn: a happy discovery, which has secured for us at least six hundred pounds of good fetid wholesome flesh. The length of the narwhal was fourteen feet, and his process, or 'horn,' from the tip to its bony encasement, four feet—hardly half the size of the noble specimen I presented to the Academy of Natural Sciences after my last cruise. We built a fire on the rocks and melted down his blubber to oil.

"While we were engaged getting our narwhal on board, the wind hauled round to the southwest, and the ice began to travel back rapidly to the north. This looks as if the resistance to the northward was not very permanent: there must be either great areas of relaxed ice or open water leads along the shore. But the choking up of the floes on our eastern side still prevents an attempt at progress. This ice is the heaviest I have seen; and its accumulation on the coast produces barricades, more like bergs than hummocks. One of these rose perpendicularly more than sixty feet. Except the 'ice-hills' of Admiral Wrangell on the coast of Arctic Asia, nothing of ice-upheaval has ever been described equal to this.

"Still, anxious beyond measure to get the vessel released, I forced a boat through the drift to a point about a mile north of us, from which I could overlook the sound. There was nothing to be seen but a melancholy extent of impacted drift, stretching northward as far as the eye could reach. I erected a small beacon cairn on the point; and, as I had neither paper, pencil, nor pennant, I burnt a 'K.' with powder on the rock, and scratching 'O.K.' with a pointed bullet on my cap lining, hoisted it as the representative of a flag."[5]

With the small hours of Wednesday morning came a breeze from the southwest, which was followed by such an apparent relaxation of the floes at the slackwater of flood tide that I resolved to attempt an escape from our little basin. We soon warped to a narrow cul-de-sac between the main pack on one side and the rocks on the other, and after a little trouble made ourselves fast to a berg.

There was a small indentation ahead, which I had noticed on my boat reconnaissance; and, as the breeze seemed to be freshening, I thought we might venture for it. But the floes were too strong: our eight-inch hawser parted like a whipcord. There was no time for hesitation. I crowded sail and bored into the drift, leaving Mr. Sontag and three men upon the ice: we did

[5]Kane reported: "It was our custom, in obedience to a general order, to build cairns and leave notices at every eligible point. One of these, rudely marked, much as I have described this one, was found by Captain Hartstene, and, strange to say, was the only direct memorial of my whereabouts communicated from some hundred of beacons."

not reclaim them till, after some hours of adventure, we brought up under the lee of a grounded berg.

I pass without notice our successive efforts to work the vessel to seaward through the floes. Each had its somewhat varied incidents, but all ended in failure to make progress. We found ourselves at the end of the day's struggles close to the same imperfectly defined headland that I have marked on the chart as Cape Cornelius Grinnell, yet separated from it by a barrier of ice, and with our anchors planted in a berg.

In one of the attempts that I made with my boat to detect some pathway or outlet for the brig, I came upon a long rocky ledge, with a sloping terrace on its southern face, strangely green with sedges and poppies. I had learned to refer these traces of vegetation to the fertilizing action of the refuse that gathers about the habitations of men. Yet I was startled, as I walked round its narrow and dreary limits, to find an Esquimaux hut, well preserved that a few hours' labor would have rendered it habitable. There were bones of the walrus, fox, and seal scattered round it in small quantities; a dead dog was found close by, with the flesh still on his bones; and, a little farther off, a bear skin garment that retained its fur. In fact, for a deserted homestead, the scene had so little of the air of desolation about it that it cheered my good fellows perceptibly.

AUGUST 12, FRIDAY. "After careful consideration, I have decided to try a further northing by following the coastline. At certain stages of the tides—generally from three-quarters flood to the commencement of the ebb—the ice evidently relaxes enough to give a partial opening close along the land. The strength of our vessel we have tested pretty thoroughly: if she will bear the frequent groundings that we must look for, I am persuaded we may seek these openings and warp along them from one lump of grounded ice to another. I am preparing the little brig for this novel navigation, clearing her decks, securing things below with extra lashings, and getting out spars to serve in case of necessity as shores to keep her on an even keel."

AUGUST 13, SATURDAY. "As long as we remain entangled in the wretched shallows of this bight, the long precipitous cape ahead may prevent the north wind from clearing us; and the nearness of the cliffs will probably give us squalls and flaws. Careful angular distances taken between the shore and the chain of bergs to seaward show that these latter do not budge with either wind or time. It looks as if we were to have a change of weather. Is it worth another attempt to warp out and see if we cannot double these bergs to seaward? I have no great time to spare: the young ice forms rapidly in quiet spots during the entire twenty-four hours."

AUGUST 14, SUNDAY. "The change of weather yesterday tempted us to forsake our shelter and try another tussle with the ice. We met it as soon as we ventured out; and the day closed with a northerly progress, by hard warping, of about three-quarters of a mile. The men were well tired; but the weather looked so threatening, that I had them up again at three o'clock this morning. My immediate aim is to attain a low rocky island that we see close into the shore, about a mile ahead of us.

"These low shallows are evidently caused by the rocks and foreign materials discharged from the great valley. It is impossible to pass inside of them, for the huger boulders run close to the shore. Yet there is no such thing as doubling them outside without leaving the holding ground of the coast and thrusting ourselves into the drifting chaos of the pack. If we can only reach the little islet ahead of us, make a lee of its rocky crests, and hold on there until the winds give us fairer prospects!"

MIDNIGHT. "We did reach it; and just in time. At 11:30 P.M. our first whale line was made fast to the rocks. Ten minutes later, the breeze freshened, and so directly in our teeth that we could not have gained our mooring ground. It is blowing a gale now, and the ice driving to the northward before it; but we can rely upon our hawsers. All behind us is now solid pack."

AUGUST 15, MONDAY. "We are still fast, and, from the grinding of the ice against the southern cape, the wind is doubtlessly blowing a strong gale from the southward. Once, early this morning, the wind shifted by a momentary flaw and came from the northward, throwing our brig with slack hawser upon the rocks. Though she bumped heavily, she started nothing till we got out a stern line to a grounded iceberg."

AUGUST 16, TUESDAY. "Fast still; the wind dying

out and the ice outside closing steadily. And here, for all I can see, we must hang on for the winter, unless Providence shall send a smart ice-shattering breeze to open a road for us to the northward.

"More bother with these wretched dogs! Worse than a street of Constantinople emptied upon our decks; the unruly, thieving, wild beast pack! Not a bear's paw, or an Esquimaux cranium, or basket of mosses, or any specimen whatever, can leave your hands for a moment without their making a rush at it, and, after a yelping scramble, swallowing it at a gulp. I have seen them attempt a whole feather bed; and here, this very morning, one of my Karsuk brutes has eaten up two entire birds' nests I had just before gathered from the rocks; feathers, filth, pebbles, and moss—a peckful at the least. One was a perfect specimen of the nest of the tridactyl, the other of the big burgomaster.

"When we reach a floe, or berg, or temporary harbor, they start out in a body, neither voice nor lash restraining them, and scamper off like a drove of hogs in an Illinois oak opening. Two of our largest left themselves behind at Fog Inlet, and we had to send off a boat party today to their rescue. It cost a pull through ice and water of about eight miles before they found the recreants, fat and saucy, beside the body of a dead narwhal. After more than an hour spent in attempts to catch them, one was tied and brought on board; but the other suicidal scamp had to be left to his fate."

III

Holding On

AUGUST 16, TUESDAY. "The formation of the young ice seems to be retarded by the clouds: its greatest nightly freezing has been three-quarters of an inch. But I have no doubt, if we had continued till now in our little Refuge Harbor, the winter would have closed around us, without a single resource or chance for escape. Where we are now, I cannot help thinking our embargo must be temporary. Ahead of us to the northeast is the projecting headland, which terminates the long shallow curve of Bedevilled Reach. This serves as a lee to the northerly drift, and forms a bight into which the south winds force the ice. The heavy floes and bergs that are aground outside of us have encroached upon the lighter ice of the reach, and choke its outlet to the sea. But a wind offshore would start this whole pack, and leave us free. Meanwhile, for our comfort, a strong breeze is setting in from the southward, and the probabilities are that it will freshen to a gale."

AUGUST 17, WEDNESDAY. "This morning I pushed out into the drift with the useful little specimen of naval architecture that I call 'Eric the Red,' but which the crew have named, less poetically, the 'Red Boat.' We succeeded in forcing her on to one of the largest bergs of the chain ahead, and I climbed it, in the hope of seeing something like a lead outside, which might be reached by boring. But there was nothing of the sort. The ice looked as if perhaps an offshore wind might spread it; but, save a few meager pools, which from our lofty eminence looked like the merest ink spots on a tablecloth, not a mark of water could be seen. I could see our eastern or Greenland coast extending on, headland after headland, no less than five of them in number, until they faded into the mysterious North. Everything else, Ice!

"Up to this time we have had but two reliable observations to determine our geographical position since entering Smith's Sound. These, however, were carefully made on shore by theodolite and artificial horizons; and, if our five chronometers, rated but two weeks ago at Upernavik, are to be depended upon, there can be no correspondence between my own and the Admiralty charts north of latitude 78°18´. Not only do I remove the general coastline some 2° in longitude to the eastward, but its trend is altered 60° of angular measurement. No landmarks of my predecessor, Captain Inglefield, are recognizable.

"In the afternoon came a gale from the southward. We had some rough rubbing from the floe pieces, with three heavy hawsers out to the rocks of our little icebreaker; but we held on. Toward midnight, our six-inch line, the smallest of the three, parted; but the other two held bravely. Feeling what good service this island has done us, what a Godsend it was to reach her, and how gallantly her broken rocks have protected us from the rolling masses of ice that grind by her, we have agreed to remember this anchorage as 'Godsend Ledge.'

"The walrus are numerous, approaching within twenty feet of us, shaking their grim wet fronts, and mowing with their tusks the sea ripples."

AUGUST 19, FRIDAY. "The sky looks sinister: a sort of scowl overhangs the blink under the great brow of clouds to the southward. The dovekies seem to distrust the weather, for they have forsaken the channel; but the walrus curved around us in crowds. I have heard that the close approach to land of these sphinx-faced monsters portends a storm. I was anxious to find a better shelter, and warped yesterday well down to the south end of the ledge; but I could not venture into the floes outside, without risking the loss of my dearly earned ground. It may prove a hard gale; but we must wait it out patiently."

AUGUST 20, SATURDAY, 3:30 P.M. "By Saturday morning it blew a perfect hurricane. We had seen it coming, and were ready with three good hawsers out ahead, and all things snug on board.

"Still it came on heavier and heavier, and the ice began to drive more wildly than I thought I had ever seen it. I had just turned in to warm and dry myself during a lull, and was stretching myself out in my bunk, when I heard the sharp twanging snap of a cord. Our six-inch hawser had parted, and we were swinging by the two others; the southward gale roaring like a lion.

"Half a minute more, and 'twang, twang!' came a second report. I knew it was the whale line by the shrillness of the ring. Our noble ten-inch manilla still held on. I was hurrying my last sock into its sealskin boot, when McGary came waddling down the companion ladders:—'Captain Kane, she won't hold much longer: it's blowing the devil himself, and I am afraid to surge.'

"The manilla cable was proving its excellence when I reached the deck; and the crew, as they gathered round me, were loud in its praises. We could hear its deep Aeolian chant, swelling through all the rattle of the running gear and moaning of the shrouds. It was the death song! The strands gave way, with the noise of a shotted gun; and, in the smoke that followed their recoil, we were dragged out by the wild ice, at its mercy.

"We steadied and did some petty warping, and got the brig a good bed in the rushing drift; but it all came to nothing. We then tried to beat back through the narrow ice-clogged waterway, that was driving, a quarter of a mile wide, between the shore and the pack. It cost us two hours of hard labor, I thought skillfully bestowed; but at the end of that time, we were at least four miles off, opposite the great valley in the center of Bedevilled Reach. Ahead of us, farther to the north, we could see the strait growing still narrower, and the heavy ice-tables grinding up, and clogging it between the shore cliffs on one side and the ledge on the other. There was but one thing left for us—to keep in some sort the command of the helm, by going freely where we must otherwise be driven. We allowed her to scud under a reefed foretopsail; all hands watching the enemy, as we closed, in silence.

"At seven in the morning, we were close upon the piling masses. We dropped our heaviest anchor with the desperate hope of winding the brig; but there was no withstanding the ice-torrent that followed us. We had only time to fasten a spar as a buoy to the chain and let her slip. So went our best bower!

"Down we went upon the gale again, helplessly scraping along a lee of ice seldom less than thirty feet thick; one floe, measured by a line as we tried to fasten to it, more than forty. I had seen such ice only once before, and never in such rapid motion. One upturned mass rose above our gunwale, smashing in our bulwarks, and depositing half a ton of ice in a lump upon our decks. Our stanch little brig bore herself through all this wild adventure as if she had a charmed life.

"But a new enemy came in sight ahead. Directly in our way, just beyond the line of floe-ice against which we were alternately sliding and thumping, was a group of bergs. We had no power to avoid them; and the only question was, whether we were to be dashed in pieces against them, or whether they might not offer us some providential nook of refuge from the storm. But, as we neared them, we perceived that they were at some distance from the floe-edge, and separated from it by an interval of open water. Our hopes rose, as the gale drove us toward this passage and into it; and we were ready to exult, when, from some unexplained cause—probably an eddy of the wind against the lofty ice-walls—we lost our headway. Almost at the same moment, we saw that the bergs were not at rest; that with a momentum of their own they were bearing down upon the other ice, and that it must be our fate to be crushed between the two.

"Just then, a broad sconce piece of low water-washed berg came driving up from the southward. The thought flashed upon me of one of our escapes in Melville Bay; and as the sconce moved rapidly close alongside us, McGary managed to plant an anchor on its slope and hold on to it by a whale line. It was an anxious moment. Our noble tow horse, whiter than the pale horse that seemed to be pursuing us, hauled us bravely on; the spray dashing over his windward flanks, and his forehead ploughing up the lesser ice as if in scorn. The bergs encroached upon us as we advanced: our channel narrowed to a width of perhaps forty feet: we braced the yards to clear the impending ice-walls.

"We passed clear; but it was a close shave—so close that our port quarterboat would have been crushed if we had not taken it in from the davits—and found ourselves under the lee of a berg, in a comparatively open lead. Never did men acknowledge with more gratitude their merciful deliverance from a wretched death.

"The day had already its full share of trials; but there were more to come. A flaw drove us from our shelter, and the gale soon carried us beyond the end of the lead. We were again in the ice, sometimes escaping its onset by warping, sometimes forced to rely on the strength and buoyancy of the brig to stand its pressure, sometimes scudding wildly through the half open drift. Our jib-boom was snapped off in the cap; we carried away our barricade stanchions, and were forced to leave our little Eric, with three brave fellows and their warps, out upon the floes behind us.

"A little pool of open water received us at last. It was just beyond a lofty cape that rose up like a wall, and under an iceberg that anchored itself between us and the gale. And here, close under the frowning shore of Greenland, ten miles nearer the Pole than our holding ground of the morning, the men have turned in to rest.

"I was afraid to join them; for the gale was unbroken, and the floes kept pressing heavily upon our berg—at one time so heavily as to sway it on its vertical axis toward the shore and make its pinnacle overhang our vessel. My poor fellows had but a precarious sleep before our little harbor was broken up. They hardly reached the deck, when we were driven astern, our rudder splintered, and the pintles torn from their boltings.

"Now began the nippings. The first shock took us on our port-quarter; the brig bearing it well, and after a moment of the old-fashioned suspense, rising by jerks handsomely. The next was from a veteran floe, tongues and honeycombed, but floating in a single table over twenty feet in thickness. Of course, no wood or iron could stand this; but the shoreward face of our iceberg happened to present an inclined plane, descending deep into the water; and up this the brig was driven, as if some great steam screw power was forcing her into a dry dock.

"At one time I expected to see her carried bodily up its face and tumbled over on her side. But one of those mysterious relaxations, which I have elsewhere called the pulses of the ice, lowered us quite gradually down again into the rubbish, and we were forced out of the line of pressure toward the shore. Here we succeeded in carrying out a warp, and making fast. We grounded as the tide fell; and would have heeled over to seaward, but for a mass of detached land-ice that grounded alongside of us, and, although it stove our bulwarks as we rolled over it, shored us up."

I could hardly get to my bunk, as I went down into our littered cabin on the Sunday morning after our hard-working vigil of thirty-six hours. Bags of clothing, food, tents, India rubber blankets, and the hundred little personal matters every man likes to save in time of trouble, were scattered around in places where the owners thought they might have them at hand. The pemmican had been on deck, the boats equipped, and everything of importance ready for a march, many hours before.

During the whole of the scenes I have been trying to describe, I could not help being struck by the composed and manly demeanor of my comrades. The turmoil of ice under a heavy sea often conveys the impression of danger when the reality is absent; but in

The nip off Cape Cornelius Grinnell, Force Bay

James Hamilton, from a sketch by Dr. Kane

this fearful passage, the parting of our hawsers, the loss of our anchors, the abrupt crushing of our stoven bulwarks, and the actual deposit of ice upon our decks, would have tried the nerves of the most experienced icemen. All—officers and men—worked alike. Upon each occasion of collision with the ice which formed our lee-coast, efforts were made to carry out lines; and some narrow escapes were incurred, by the zeal of the parties leading them into danger. Mr. Bonsall avoided being crushed by leaping to a floating fragment; and no less than four of our men at one time were carried down by the drift, and could only be recovered by a relief party after the gale had subsided.

As our brig, borne on the ice, began her ascent of the berg, the suspense was oppressive. Immense blocks piled against her, range upon range, pressing themselves under her keel and throwing her over upon her side, till, urged by the successive accumulations, she rose slowly and as if with convulsive efforts along the sloping wall. Still there was no relaxation of the impelling force. Shock after shock, jarring her to her very center, she continued to mount steadily on her precarious cradle. But for the groaning of her timbers and the heavy sough of the floes, we might have heard a pin drop. And then, as she settled down into her old position, quietly taking her place among the broken rubbish, there was a deep breathing silence, as though all were waiting for some signal before the clamor of congratulation and comment could burst forth.

IV

A Search for Wintering Ground

IT WAS NOT until the twenty-second that the storm abated, and our absent men were once more gathered back into their mess. During the interval of forced inaction, the little brig was fast to the ice-belt that lined the bottom of the cliffs, and all hands rested; but as soon as it was over, we took advantage of the flood tide to pass our tow lines to the ice-beach, and, harnessing ourselves in like mules on a canal, made a good three miles by tracking along the coast.

AUGUST 22, MONDAY. "Under this coast, at the base of a frowning precipice, we are now working toward a large bay which runs well in, facing at its opening to the north and west. I should save time if I could cross from headland to headland; but I am obliged to follow the tortuous land-belt, without whose aid we would go adrift in the pack again.

"The trend of our line of operations today is almost due east. We are already protected from the south, but fearfully exposed to a northerly gale. Of this there are fortunately no indications.

Our latitude, determined by the sun's lower culmination, if such a term can be applied to his midnight depression, gives 78°41′. We are farther north, therefore, than any of our predecessors, except Parry on his

49

Spitzbergen foot tramp.[1] There are those with whom,
no matter how great the obstacle, failure involves dis-
grace: we are safe at least from their censure."

AUGUST 26, FRIDAY. "My officers and crew are
stanch and firm men; but the depressing influences of
want of rest, the rapid advance of winter, and, above
all, our slow progress, make them sympathize but little with this continued effort to force a way to the
north. One of them, an excellent member of the party,
volunteered an expression of opinion this morning in
favor of returning to the south and giving up the attempt to winter."

It is unjust for a commander to measure his subor-
dinates in such exigencies by his own standards. The
interest which they feel in an undertaking is of a different nature from his own. With him there are always
personal motives, apart from official duty, to stimulate
effort. He receives, if successful, too large a share of the
credit, and he justly bears all the odium of failure.

An apprehension—I hope a charitable one—of this
fact leads me to consider the opinions of my officers
with much respect. I called them together at once, in
a formal council, and listened to their views in full.

[1]See note 2, Chapter 1. Kane was evidently unaware that
William Scoresby, the whaler and eminent natural scientist had attained 81° 30′ 42″ above Spitzbergen in 1806. His observations of
ice conditions in the Arctic over a period of seventeen years had
aided Britain's decision to search for new polar routes. See Constance Martin, "William Scoresby, Jr. (1789–1857) and the Open
Polar Sea: Myth and Reality," *Arctic*, v.41, No.1 (March 1988), pp.
39–47.

With but one exception, Mr. Henry Brooks, they were convinced that further progress to the north was impossible, and were in favor of returning southward to winter.

Not being able conscientiously to take the same view, I explained to them the importance of securing a position that might expedite our journeys in the future; and, after assuring them that such a position could only be attained by continuing our efforts, announced my intention of warping toward the northern headland of the bay. "Once there, I shall be able to determine from actual inspection the best point for setting out on the operations of the spring; and at the nearest possible shelter to that point I will put the brig into winter harbor." My comrades received this decision in a manner that was most gratifying, and entered zealously upon the hard and cheerless duty it involved.

The warping began again, each man, myself included, taking turn at the capstan. The ice seemed less heavy as we penetrated into the recess of the bay; our track lines and shoulder belts replaced the warps. Hot coffee was served; and, in the midst of cheering songs, our little brig moved off briskly.

Our success, however, was not complete. At the very period of high water she took the ground while close under the walls of the ice-foot. It would have been madness to attempt shoring her up. I could only fasten heavy tackle to the rocks that lined the base of the cliffs, and trust the noble craft's unassisted strength.

AUGUST 27, SATURDAY. "We failed, in spite of our efforts, to get the brig off with last night's tide; and, as our night tides are generally the highest, I have some apprehensions as to her liberation.

"We have landed everything we could get up on the rocks, put out all our boats and filled them with ponderables alongside, sunk our rudder astern, and lowered our remaining heavy anchor into one of our quarterboats. Heavy hawsers are out to a grounded lump of berg-ice, ready for instant heaving.

"Last night she heeled over again so abruptly that we were all tumbled out of our berths. At the same time, the cabin stove, with a full charge of glowing anthracite, was thrown down. The deck blazed smartly for a while; but, by sacrificing Mr. Sontag's heavy pilot cloth coat to the public good, I choked it down till water could be passed from above to extinguish it. It was fortunate we had water near at hand, for the powder was not far off.

"3 P.M. The ground-ice is forced in upon our stern, splintering our rudder, and drawing again the bolts of the pintle casings.

"5 P.M. She floats again, and our track lines are manned. The men work with a will, and the brig moves along bravely.

"10 P.M. Aground again; and the men, after a hot supper, have turned in to take a spell of sleep. The brig has a hard time of it with the rocks. She has been high and dry for each of the two last tides, and within three days has grounded no less than five times. I feel that this is hazardous navigation, but am convinced it is my duty to keep on. Except the loss of a portion of our false keel, we have sustained no real injury. The brig is still watertight; and her broken rudder and one shattered spar can be easily repaired.

AUGUST 28, SUNDAY. "By a complication of purchases, jumpers, and shores, we started the brig; and, Mr. Ohlsen having temporarily secured the rudder, I determined to enter the floe and trust to the calm of the morning for a chance of penetrating to the northern land-ice ahead.

"This land-ice is very old, and my hope is to get through the loose trash that surrounds it by springing, and then find a fast that may serve our tracking lines. I am already on my way, and, in spite of the ominous nods of my officers, have a fair prospect of reaching it.

"I took the boat this morning with Mr. McGary, and sounded along outside the land-floe. I am satisfied that the passage is practicable, and, by the aid of tide, wind, and springs, have advanced into the trash some two hundred yards.

"We have reached the floe, and find it as I hoped— the only drawback to tracking being the excessive tides, which expose us to grounding at low water."

We had now a breathing spell, and I could find time to look out again upon the future. The broken and distorted area around us gave little promise of successful sledge travel. But all this might change its aspect under the action of a single gale, and it was by no means certain that the ice-fields farther north would have the same rugged and dispiriting character. Besides, the ice-belt was still before us, broken sometimes and difficult to traverse, but practicable for a party on foot, apparently for miles ahead; and I felt sure that a resolute boat's crew might push and track their way for some distance along it. I resolved to make the trial, and to judge what ought to be our wintering ground from a personal inspection of the coast.

I had been quietly preparing for such an expedition for some time. Our best and lightest whaleboat had been fitted with a canvas cover that gave it all the comfort of a tent. We had a supply of pemmican packed in small cases, and a sledge taken to pieces was stowed away under the thwarts. In the morning of the twenty-ninth, Mr. Brooks, McGary, and myself walked fourteen miles along the marginal ice. It was heavy and complicated with drift, but there was nothing about it to make me change my purpose.

My boat crew consisted of seven, all of them volunteers and reliable: Brooks, Bonsall, McGary, Sontag, Riley, Blake, and Morton. We had buffalo robes for our sleeping gear, and a single extra day suit was put on board as common property. Each man carried his girdle full of woolen socks, so as to dry them by the warmth of his body, and a tin cup, with a sheath knife at the belt: a soup pot and lamp for the mess completed our outfit.

In less than three hours from my first order, the *Forlorn Hope* was ready for her work, covered with tin to prevent her being cut through by the bay-ice; and at half past three in the afternoon she was freighted, launched, and on her way.

I placed Mr. Ohlsen in command of the *Advance,* and Dr. Hayes in charge of her log: Mr. Ohlsen with orders to haul the brig to the southward and eastward into a safe berth, and there to await my return.

Many a warm shake of the hand from the crew we left showed me that our goodbye was not a mere formality. Three hearty cheers from all hands followed.

* * * *

In the first portions of our journey, we found a narrow but obstructed passage between the ice-belt and the outside pack. It was but a few yards in width, and the young ice upon it was nearly thick enough to bear our weight. By breaking it up we were able, with effort, to make about seven miles a day.

After such work, wet, cold, and hungry, the night's rest was very welcome. A couple of stanchions were rigged fore and aft, a sail tightly spread over the canvas cover of our boat, the cooking lamp lit, and the buffalo robes spread out. Dry socks replaced the wet; hot tea and pemmican followed; and very soon we forgot the discomforts of the day, the smokers musing over their pipes, and the sleepers snoring in dreamless forgetfulness.

We had been out something less than twenty-four hours when we came to the end of our boating. In front and on one side was the pack, and on the other a wall ten feet above our heads, the impracticable ice-belt. By waiting for high tide, and taking advantage of a chasm that a water-stream had worn in the ice, we managed to haul up our boat on its surface; but it was apparent that we must leave her there. She was stowed away snugly under the shelter of a large hummock; and we pushed forward in our sledge, laden with a few articles of absolute necessity.

Here, for the first time, we were made aware of a remarkable feature of our travel. We were on a table or shelf of ice, which clung to the base of the rocks overlooking the sea, but itself overhung by steep and lofty cliffs. Pure and beautiful as this icy highway was, huge angular blocks, some many tons in weight, were scattered over its surface; and long tongues of worn-down rock occasionally issued from the sides of the cliffs and extended across our course. The cliffs measured 1,010 feet to the crest of the plateau above them.

We pushed forward on this ice-table shelf as rapidly as the obstacles would permit, though embarrassed a good deal by the frequent watercourses, which created large gorges in our path, winding occasionally and generally steep sided. We had to pass our sledge carefully down such interruptions, and bear it upon our shoulders, wading, of course, through water of an extremely low temperature. Our night halts were upon knolls of snow under the rocks. At one of these, the tide overflowed our tent and forced us to save our buffalo sleeping gear by holding it up until the water subsided. This exercise, as it turned out, was more of a trial to our patience than to our health. The circulation was assisted perhaps by a perception of the ludicrous. Eight Yankee Caryatides, up to their knees in water, and an entablature sustaining such of their household goods as could not bear immersion!

After an absence of five days, we found by observation that we were but forty miles from the brig. Besides our small daily progress, we had lost much by the tortuous windings of the coast. The ice outside did not invite a change of plan in that direction; but I determined to leave the sledge and proceed over land on foot. With the exception of our instruments, we carried no weight but pemmican and one buffalo robe. The weather, not far below the freezing point, did not make a tent essential to the bivouac; and, with this light equipment, we could travel readily two miles to one with our entire outfit. On 4 September we made twenty-four miles with comparative ease and were refreshed by a comfortable sleep after the toils of the day.

The only drawback to this new method of advance was the inability to carry a sufficient quantity of food. Each man at starting had a fixed allowance of pemmican, which, with his other load, made an average weight of thirty-five pounds. It proved excessive: the Canadian voyagers will carry much more, and for an almost indefinite period; but we found—and we had good walkers in our party—that a very few pounds overweight broke us down.

Our progress on the fifth was arrested by another bay much larger than any we had seen since entering

Smith's Straits. It was a noble sheet of water, perfectly open, and thus in strange contrast to the ice outside. The cause of this then-inexplicable phenomenon was found in a roaring and tumultuous river, which, issuing from a fiord at the inner sweep of the bay, rolled with the violence of a snow torrent over a broken bed of rocks. This river, the largest probably yet known in North Greenland, was about three-quarters of a mile wide at its mouth and admitted the tides for about three miles. After that its bed rapidly ascended, and could be traced by the configuration of the hills as far as a large inner fiord. I called it Mary Minturn River, after the sister of Mrs. Henry Grinnell. Its course was afterward pursued to an interior glacier, from the base of which it issued numerous streams that united into a single trunk about forty miles above its mouth. By the banks of this stream we encamped, lulled by the unusual music of running waters.

Here, protected from the frost by the infiltration of the melted snows, and fostered by the reverberation of solar heat from the rocks, we met a flower growth, which, though drearily Arctic in its type, was rich in variety and coloring. Amid festuca and other tufted grasses twinkled the purple lychynis and the white star of the chickweed; and not without its pleasing associations I recognized a solitary hesperis, the Arctic representative of the wallflowers of home.

We forded our way across this river in the morning, carrying our pemmican as well as we could out of water, but submitting ourselves to a succession of plunge baths as often as we trusted our weight on the ice-capped stones above the surface. The average depth was not over our hips; but the crossing cost us so much labor that we were willing to halt half a day to rest.

Some seven miles farther on, a large cape projects into this bay and divides it into two indentations, each of them the seat of minor watercourses fed by the glaciers. From the numerous tracks found in the moss beds, they would seem to be the resort of deer. Our meridian observations by theodolite gave the latitude of but 78°52′: the magnetic dip was 84°49′.

It was plain that the coast of Greenland here faced toward the north. The axis of both these bays and the general direction of the watercourses pointed to the same conclusion. Our longitude was 78°41′ W.

Leaving four of my party to recruit at this station, I started the next morning, with three volunteers, to cross the ice to the northeastern headland, and thus save the almost impossible circuit by the shores of the bay.

This ice was new, and far from safe: its margin along the open water made by Minturn River required both care and tact in passing over it. We left the heavy theodolite behind us; and, indeed, carried nothing except a pocket sextant, my Fraunhöfer, a walking pole, and three-days' allowance of raw pemmican.

We reached the headland after sixteen miles of walk, and found the ice-foot in good condition, evidently better fitted for sledge travel than it was to the south.

This point I named Cape William Makepeace Thackeray. Our party knew it as Chimney Rock. It was the last station on the coast of Greenland, determined by intersecting bearings of theodolite, from known positions to the south. About eight miles beyond it is a large headland, the highest visible from the late position of our brig, shutting out all points farther north. It is indicated on my chart as Cape George Russell. We found the table-lands were twelve hundred feet high by actual measurement, and interior plateaus were seen of an estimated height of eighteen hundred.

I determined to seek some high headland beyond the cape and make it my final point of reconnaissance.

I shall never forget the sight, when, after a hard day's walk, I looked out from an altitude of eleven hundred feet upon an expanse extending beyond the eightieth parallel of latitude. Far off on my left was the western shore of the Sound, losing itself in distance toward the north. To my right, a rolling country led on to a low dusky wall-like ridge, which I afterward recognized as the Great Glacier of Humboldt; still beyond this, reaching northward from the north-northeast, was the land that now bears the name of Washington: its most projecting headland, Cape Andrew Jackson, bore 14° by sextant from the farthest hill, Cape John Barrow, on the opposite side. The great area between was a solid sea of ice. Close along its shore, almost looking down upon it from the crest of our lofty station, we could see the long lines of hummocks dividing the floes like the trenches of a beleaguered city. Farther out, a stream of icebergs, increasing in numbers as they receded, showed an almost impenetrable barrier. I could not doubt that among their recesses the ice was so crushed as to be impassable by the sledge.

Nevertheless, beyond these again, the ice seemed less obstructed. Distance is very deceptive upon the ice, subduing its salient features and reducing even lofty bergs to the appearance of a smooth and attractive plain. But, aided by my Fraunhöfer telescope, I could see that traversable areas were still attainable. Slowly, and almost with a sigh, I laid the glass down and made up my mind for a winter search.

I had seen no place combining so many of the requisites of a good winter harbor as the bay in which we left the *Advance*. Near its southwestern corner the wide streams and the watercourses on the shore promised the earliest chances of liberation in the coming summer. It was secure against the moving ice: lofty headlands walled it in beautifully to seaward, enclosing an anchorage with a moderate depth of water; yet it was open to the meridian sunlight, and guarded from winds, eddies, and drift. The space enclosed was only occupied by a few rocky islets and our brig. We soon came in sight of her on our return march, as she lay at anchor in its southern sweep, with her masts cutting sharply against the white glacier; and hurrying on through the gale, were taken on board without accident.

My comrades gathered anxiously near me, waiting

for the news. I told them in few words of the results of
our journey, and why I had determined upon remaining, and gave at once the order to warp in between the
islands. We found seven fathom soundings and a perfect shelter from the outside ice; and thus laid our little brig in the harbor, which we were fated never to
leave together, a long resting place to her indeed, for
the same ice is around her still.

Winter Harbor
"The same ice is around her still."

V

Approaching Winter

THE WINTER was now approaching rapidly. The thermometer had fallen by the tenth of September to fourteen degrees, and the young ice had cemented the floes so that we could walk and sledge round the brig. About sixty paces north of us, an iceberg had been caught, and was frozen in: it was our neighbor while we remained in Rensselaer Harbor. The rocky islets around us were fringed with hummocks; and, as the tide fell, their sides were coated with opaque crystals of bright white. The birds had gone. The sea swallows, which abounded when we first reached here, and even the young burgomasters that lingered after them, had all taken their departure for the south. Except the snowbirds, these are the last to migrate of all Arctic birds.

SEPTEMBER 10, SATURDAY. "We have plenty of responsible work before us. The long 'night in which no man can work' is close at hand: in another month we shall lose the sun. Astronomically, he should disappear on the twenty-fourth of October if our horizon were free; but it is obstructed by a mountain ridge, and, making all allowance for refraction, we cannot count on seeing him after the tenth.

"First and foremost, we have to unstow the hold

and deposit its contents in the storehouse on Butler Island. Brooks and a party are now briskly engaged in this double labor, running loaded boats along a canal that has to be recut every morning.

"Next comes the catering for winter diet. We have little or no game as yet in Smith's Sound; and, though the traces of deer that we have observed may be followed by the animals themselves, I cannot calculate upon them as a resource. I am entirely without the hermetically-sealed meats of our last voyage, and the use of salt meat in circumstances like ours is never safe.[1] A freshwater pond, which fortunately remains open at Medary, gives me a chance for some further experiments in freshening this portion of our stock. Steaks of salt junk, artistically cut, are strung on lines like dried apples, and soaked in festoons under the ice. The salmon-trout and salt codfish we bought at Fiskenaes are placed in barrels, perforated to permit a constant circulation of fresh water through them. Our pickled cabbage is similarly treated, after a little potash has been used to neutralize the acid. All these are submitted to twelve hours of alternate soaking and

---

[1]Kane's speculation is in error. Salted meats are not in themselves dangerous. Scurvy, the plague of all long-term expeditions, was caused by a lack of vitamin C or antiascorbic acid. As vitamin C was not isolated and crystallized until the 1930s, dietary supplements we have today did not exist. Until then, the prevention of scurvy on expeditions, far from fresh vegetables and fresh meats, was a process of trial and error. See Kenneth J. Carpenter's excellent in-depth study, *The History of Scurvy & Vitamin C* (Cambridge, 1986).

freezing, the crust of ice being removed from them before each immersion. This is the steward's province, and a most important one it is.

"Everyone is well employed; McGary arranging and Bonsall making the inventory of our stores; Ohlsen and Petersen building our deck-house; while I am devising the plan of an architectural interior, which is to combine, of course, the utmost of ventilation, room dryness, warmth, general accommodation, comfort—all the appliances of health.

"We have made a comfortable dog house on Butler Island; but though our Esquimaux *canaille* are within scent of our cheeses there, one of which they ate yesterday for lunch, they cannot be persuaded to sleep away from the vessel. They prefer the bare snow, where they can couch within the sound of our voices, to a warm kennel upon the rocks. Strange that this dog-distinguishing trait of affection for man should show itself in an animal so imperfectly reclaimed from a savage state that he can hardly be caught when wanted!"

September 11, Sunday. "Today came to us the first quiet Sunday of harbor life. We changed our log registration from sea time to the familiar home series that begins at midnight. It is not only that the season has given us once more a local habitation; but there is something in the return of varying day and night that makes it grateful to reinstate this domestic observance. The long staring day, which has clung to us for more than two months, to the exclusion of the stars, has begun to intermit its brightness.

"We had our accustomed morning and evening prayers; and the day went by, full of sober thought, and, I trust, wise resolve."

SEPTEMBER 12, MONDAY. "Still going on with Saturday's operations, amid the thousand discomforts of house cleaning and moving combined. I dodged them for an hour this morning, to fix with Mr. Sontag upon a site for our observatory; and the men are already at work hauling the stone for it over the ice on sledges. It is to occupy a rocky islet, about a hundred yards off, that I have named after a little spot that I long to see again, 'Fern Rock.'[2] This is to be for me the center of familiar localities. As the classic Mivins breakfasted lightly on a cigar and took it out in sleep, so I have dined on salt pork and made my dessert of home dreams."

SEPTEMBER 13, TUESDAY. "Besides preparing our winter quarters, I am engaged in the preliminary arrangements for my provision depots along the Greenland coast. Mr. Kennedy is, I believe, the only one of my predecessors who has used October and November for Arctic field work; but I deem it important to our movements during the winter and spring that the depots should be made before the darkness sets in. I propose arranging three of them at inter-

[2]"Fern Rock" was the name of a place much beloved by Kane's younger brother, Willie, who died while still a boy. The Kane family later built a house on the location and named it "Fern Rock." Another Kane house was named "Rensselaer"(a family name), and Kane named the harbor in which the *Advance* was forced to winter after that.

vals—pushing them as far forward as I can—to contain in all some twelve hundred pounds of provision of which eight hundred will be pemmican."

My plans of future search were directly dependent upon the success of these operations of the fall. With a chain of provision depots along the coast of Greenland, I could readily extend my travel by dogs. These noble animals formed the basis of my future plans: the only drawback to their efficiency as a means of travel was their inability to carry the heavy loads of provender essential for their support. A badly fed or heavily loaded dog is useless for a long journey; but with relays of provisions, I could start empty and fill up at our final station.

My dogs were both Esquimaux and Newfoundlanders. Of these last I had ten: they were to be carefully broken to travel by voice without the whip, and were expected to be very useful for heavy draught, as their tractability would allow the driver to regulate their pace. I was already training them in a light sledge to drive unlike the Esquimaux, two abreast, with a regular harness, a breast collar of flat leather, and a pair of traces. Six of them made a powerful traveling team; and four could carry me and my instruments for short journeys around the brig.

The sledge I used for them was built, with the care of cabinet work, of American hickory thoroughly seasoned. The curvature of the runners was determined experimentally: they were shod with annealed steel and fastened by copper rivets that could be renewed at pleasure. Except this, no metal entered into its construction. All its parts were held together by sealskin lashings, so that it yielded to inequalities of surface and to sudden shock. The three paramount considerations of lightness, strength, and diminished friction, were well combined. This beautiful and, as we later found, efficient and enduring sledge, was named the "Little Willie."

The Esquimaux dogs were reserved for the great tug of the actual journeys of search. They were now in the semisavage condition that marks their close approach to the wolf; and according to Mr. Petersen, under whose care they were placed, they were totally useless for journeys over such ice as was now before us. A hard experience had not then opened my eyes to the inestimable value of these dogs: I had yet to learn their power and speed; their patient, enduring fortitude; their sagacity in tracking these icy morasses, among which they had been born and bred.

I determined to hold back my more distant provision parties as long as the continued daylight would permit, making the Newfoundland dogs establish the depots within sixty miles of the brig. My previous journey had shown me that the ice-belt, clogged with the foreign matters dislodged from the cliffs, would not at this season of the year answer for operations with the sledge, and that the ice of the great pack outside was even more unfit on account of its want of continuity. It was now so consolidated by advancing cold as to have stopped its drift to the south; but the large floes or fields that formed it were imperfectly cemented together, and would break into hummocks under the action of winds or even of the tides. It was made still more impassable by the numerous bergs that kept on ploughing with irresistible momentum through the ice-tables and rearing up barricades that defied the passage of a sledge.

It was desirable, therefore, that our depot parties should not enter upon their work until they could avail themselves of the young ice. This now occupied a belt about one hundred yards in mean breadth close to the shore, and, but for the fluctuations of the tide, would already be a practicable road. For the present, however, a gale of wind or a spring tide might easily drive the outer floes upon it, and thus destroy its integrity.

The party appointed to establish this depot was furnished with a sledge, the admirable model of which I obtained through the British Admiralty. The only liberty that I ventured to take with this model—which had been previously tested by the adventurous journeys of McClintock in Lancaster Sound—was to lessen the height and somewhat increase the breadth of the runner; both of which, I think, were improvements, giving increased strength and preventing too deep a descent into the snow. I named her the "Faith." Her length was thirteen feet and breadth, four. She could readily carry fourteen hundred pounds of mixed stores.

This noble old sledge, which is now endeared to me by every pleasant association, bore the brunt of the

heaviest parties and came back, after the descent of the
coast, comparatively sound. The men were attached
to her in such a way as to make the line of draught or
traction as near as possible in the axis of the weight.
Each man had his own shoulder belt, or "rue-raddy,"
as we used to call it, and his own track line, which for
want of horse hair was made of Manilla rope: it traversed freely by a ring on a loop that extended from
runner to runner in front of the sledge. These track
ropes varied in length, so as to keep the members of
the party from interfering with each other by walking
abreast. The longest was three fathoms, eighteen feet,
in length; the shortest, directly fastened to the sledge
runner as a means of guiding or suddenly arresting and
turning the vehicle.

The cargo for this journey, without including the
provisions of the party, was almost exclusively pemmican. Some of this was put up in cylinders of tinned
iron with conical terminations, so as to resist the as-
saults of the white bear; but the larger quantity was in
strong wooden cases or kegs, well hooped with iron,
holding about seventy pounds each. Surmounting this
load was a light India rubber boat, made quite portable
by a frame of basket willow, which I hoped to launch
on reaching open water.

The personal equipment of the men was a buffalo
robe for the party to lie upon, and a bag of Mackinaw
blanket for each man to crawl into at night. India rubber cloth was to be the protection from the snow beneath. The tent was of canvas, made after the plan of our

English predecessors. We afterward learned to modify and reduce our traveling gear. Step by step, as long as our Arctic service continued, we went on reducing our sledging outfit until, at last, we came to the Esquimaux ultimatum of simplicity—raw meat and a fur bag.

While our arrangements for the winter were still in progress, I sent out Mr. Wilson and Dr. Hayes, accompanied by our Esquimaux, Hans, to learn something of the interior features of the country, and the promise it afforded of resources from the hunt. They returned on the sixteenth of September after a hard travel made with excellent judgment and abundant zeal. They penetrated into the interior about ninety miles when their progress was arrested by a glacier, four hundred feet high and extending to the north and west as far as the eye could reach. This magnificent body of interior ice formed on its summit a complete plateau—a *mer de glace*, abutting upon a broken plain of syenite. They found no large lakes. They saw a few reindeer at a distance, and numerous hares and rabbits but no ptarmigan.

SEPTEMBER 20, TUESDAY. "I was unwilling to delay my depot party any longer. They left the brig, McGary and Bonsall with five men, at half past one today. We gave them three cheers, and I accompanied them with my dogs as a farewell escort for some miles.

"Our crew proper is now reduced to three men; but all the officers, the doctor among the rest, are hard at work upon the observatory and its arrangements."

VI

Reaching the Midnight of the Year

SEPTEMBER 30, FRIDAY. "We have been terribly annoyed by rats. Some days ago we attempted to smoke them out with the vilest imaginable compound of vapors—brimstone, burnt leather, and arsenic—and spent a cold night in a deck bivouac to give the experiment fair play. But they survived the fumigation. We now determined to dose them with carbonic acid gas. Dr. Hayes burnt a quantity of charcoal; and we shut down the hatches, after pasting up every fissure that communicated aft and starting three stoves on the skin of the forepeak.

"As the gas was generated with extreme rapidity in the confined area below, great caution had to be exercised. Our French cook, good Pierre Schubert—who to a considerable share of bullheaded intrepidity unites a commendable portion of professional zeal—stole below without my knowledge or consent to season a soup. Morton fortunately saw him staggering in the dark; and, reaching him with great difficulty as he fell, both were hauled up in the end, Morton, his strength almost gone, the cook perfectly insensible.

"The next disaster was of a graver sort. I record it with emotions of mingled awe and thankfulness. We have narrowly escaped being burnt out of house and home. I had given orders that the fires, lit under my own eye, should be regularly inspected; but I learned that Pierre's misadventure had made the watch pretermit for a time opening the hatches. As I lowered a lantern, which was extinguished instantly, a suspicious odor, as of burning wood, reached me. I descended at once. Reaching the deck of the forecastle, my first glance toward the fires showed me that all was safe there; and, though the quantity of smoke still surprised me, I was disposed to attribute it to the recent kindling. But at this moment, while passing on my return near the door of the bulkhead, which leads to the carpenter's room, the gas began to affect me. My lantern went out as if quenched by water; and, as I ran by the bulkhead door, I saw the deck near it a mass of glowing fire for some three feet in diameter. I could not tell how much farther it extended; for I became quite insensible at the foot of the ladder and would have sunk had not Mr. Brooks seen my condition and hauled me out.

"When I came to, which happily was very soon, I confided my fearful secret to the four men around me, Brooks, Ohlsen, Blake, and Stephenson. It was of great importance to avoid confusion: we shut the doors of the galley, so as to confine the rest of the crew and officers aft; and then passed up water from the fire-hole alongside. It was done very noiselessly. Ohlsen and myself went down to the burning deck; Brooks handed us in the buckets, and in less than ten minutes we were in safety."

October 1, Saturday. "Upon inspecting the scene

Midnight in September

James Hamilton, from a sketch by Dr. Kane

of yesterday's operations, we found twenty-eight well-fed rats of all varieties of age. The cook, though unable to do duty, is better: I can hear him chanting through the blankets in his bunk, happy over his holiday, happy to be happy at everything. I had a larger dose of carbonic acid even than he, and am suffering considerably with palpitations and vertigo. If the sentimental asphyxia of Parisian charcoal resembles in its advent that of the Arctic zone, it must be, I think, a poor way of dying."

OCTOBER 3, MONDAY. "On shore to the southeast, above the first terrace, Mr. Petersen found unmistakable signs of a sledge passage. The tracks were deeply impressed, but certainly more than one season old. This adds to our hope that the natives, whose ancient traces we saw on the point south of Godsend Ledge, may return this winter."

OCTOBER 8, SATURDAY. "I have been practicing with my dog sledge and an Esquimaux team till my arms ache. To drive such an equipage a certain proficiency with the whip is indispensable, which, like all proficiency must be worked for. In fact, the weapon has an exercise of its own, quite peculiar and as hard to learn as single stick or broadsword.

"The whip is six yards long, and the handle but sixteen inches—a short lever, of course, to throw out such a length of seal hide. Learn to do it, however, with a masterly sweep, or else make up your mind to forego driving sledge; for the dogs are guided solely by the lash. You must be able not only to hit any particular dog out of a team of twelve, but to accompany this feat also with a resounding crack. After this, you find that to get your lash back involves another difficulty; for it is apt to entangle itself among the dogs and lines, or to fasten itself cunningly round bits of ice, so as to drag you head over heels into the snow.

"The secret by which this complicated set of requirements is fulfilled consists in properly describing an arc from the shoulder, with a stiff elbow, giving the jerk to the whip handle from the hand and wrist alone. The lash trails behind as you travel, and when thrown forward is allowed to extend itself without an effort to bring it back. You wait patiently after giving the projectile impulse until it unwinds its slow length, reaches the end of its tether, and cracks to tell you that it is at its journey's end. Such a crack on the ear or forefoot of an unfortunate dog is signalized by a howl quite unmistakable in its import.

"The mere labor of using this whip is such that the Esquimaux travel in couples, one sledge after the other. The hinder dogs follow mechanically, and thus require no whip; and the drivers change about so as to rest each other.

"I have amused myself, if not my dogs, for some days past with this formidable accessory of Arctic travel. I have not quite got the knack of it yet, though I might venture a trial of cracking against the postillion college of Lonjumeau."

OCTOBER 10, MONDAY. "Our depot party has been out twenty days, and it is time they were back: their provisions must have run very low, for I enjoined them to leave every pound at the depot they could spare. I am going out with supplies to look after them. I take four of our best Newfoundlanders, now well broken, in our lightest sledge; and Blake will accompany me with his skates. We have not hands enough to equip a sledge party, and the ice is too unsound for us to attempt to ride with a large team."

* * * *

I found little or no trouble in crossing the ice until we passed beyond the northeast headland, which I have named Cape William Wood. But on emerging into the channel, we found that the spring tides had broken up the great area around us, and that the passage of the sledge was interrupted by fissures, which were beginning to break in every direction through the young ice.

My first effort was of course to reach the land; but it was unfortunately low tide, and the ice-belt rose up before me like a wall. The pack was becoming more and more unsafe, and I was extremely anxious to gain an asylum on shore; for, though it was easy to find a temporary refuge by retreating to the old floes that studded the more recent ice, I knew that in doing so we should risk being carried down by the drift.

The dogs began to flag; but we had to press them: we were only two men; and, in the event of the animals failing to leap any of the rapidly multiplying fissures, we could hardly expect to extricate our laden sledge. Three times in less than three hours my shaft or dogs went in; and John and myself, who had been trotting alongside the sledge for sixteen miles, were nearly as tired as they were. This state of things could not last; and I therefore made for the old ice to seaward.

We were nearing it rapidly when the dogs failed in leaping a chasm that was somewhat wider than the others, and the whole concern came down in the water. I cut the lines instantly, and, with the aid of my companion, hauled the poor animals out. We owed the preservation of the sledge to their admirable docility and perseverance. The tin cooking apparatus and the air confined in the India rubber covering kept it afloat till we could succeed in fastening a couple of sealskin cords to the crosspieces at the front and back. By these John and myself were able to give it an uncertain support from the two edges of the opening, till the dogs, after many fruitless struggles, carried it forward at last upon the ice.

Although the thermometer was below zero, and in our wet state we ran a considerable risk of freezing, the urgency of our position left no room for thoughts of cold. We started at a run, men and dogs, for the solid ice; and by the time we had gained it we were steaming in the cold atmosphere like a couple of Nootka Sound vapor baths.[1]

We rested on the floe. We could not raise our tent,

[1]Probably refers to Hot Spring Cove, on the west coast of Vancouver Island, on Nootka Sound, British Columbia, a spectacular natural hot spring that has a series of three or four terraced hot-pools cascading down to the sea.

for it had frozen as hard as a shingle. But our buffalo robe bags gave us protection; and, though we were too wet inside to be absolutely comfortable, we managed to get something like sleep before it was light enough for us to move on again.

The journey was continued in the same way; but we found to our great gratification that the cracks closed with the change of the tide, and at high water we succeeded in gaining the ice-belt under the cliffs. This belt had changed very much since my journey in September. The tides and frosts together had coated it with ice as smooth as satin, and this glossy covering made it an excellent road. The cliffs discharged fewer fragments in our path, and the rocks of our last journey's experience were now fringed with icicles. I saw with great pleasure that this ice-belt would serve as a highway for our future operations.

The nights that followed were not so bad as one would suppose from the saturated condition of our equipment. Evaporation is not so inappreciable in this Arctic region as some theorists imagine. By alternately exposing the tent and furs to the air, and beating the ice out of them, we dried them enough to permit sleep. The dogs slept in the tent with us, giving it warmth as well as fragrance. What perfumes of nature are lost at home upon our ungrateful senses! How we relished the companionship!

We had averaged twenty miles a day since leaving the brig, and were within a short march of the cape I have named William Wood, when a broad chasm brought us to a halt. It was in vain that we worked out to seaward, or dived into the shoreward recesses of the bay: the ice everywhere presented the same impassable fissures. We had no alternative but to retrace our steps and seek among the bergs some place of security. We found a camp for the night on the old floe-ices to the westward, gaining them some time after the darkness had closed in.

On the morning of the fifteenth, about two hours before the late sunrise, as I was preparing to climb a berg from which I might have a sight of the road ahead, I perceived far off upon the white snow a dark object, which not only moved, but altered its shape very strangely—now expanding into a long black line, now waving, now gathering itself up into a compact mass. It was the returning sledge party. They had seen our black tent, and ferried across to seek it.

They were most welcome for their absence, in the fearfully open state of the ice, had filled me with apprehensions. We could not distinguish each other as we drew near in the twilight; and my first good news of them was when I heard that they were singing. On they came, and at last I was able to count their voices, one by one. Thank God, seven! Poor John Blake was so breathless with gratulation, that I could not get him to blow his signal horn. We gave them, instead, the good old Anglo Saxon greeting, "three cheers!" and in a few minutes were among them.

They had made a creditable journey, and were, on the whole, in good condition. They had no injuries worth talking about, although not a man had escaped some touches of the frost. Bonsall was minus a big toenail, and plus a scar upon the nose. McGary had attempted, as Tom Hickey told us, to *pluck* a fox, it being so frozen as to defy skinning by his knife; and his fingers had been tolerably frostbitten in the operation. "They're very horny, sir, are my fingers," said McGary, who was worn down to a mere shadow of his former rotundity; "very horny, and they water up like bladders." The rest suffered in their feet but as good fellows, postponed limping until reaching the ship.

Within the last three days they had marched fifty-four miles, or eighteen a day. Their sledge being empty, and the young ice north of Cape Bancroft smooth as a mirror, they had traveled, the day before we met them, nearly twenty-five miles. A very remarkable pace for men who had been twenty-eight days in the field.

My supplies of hot food, coffee, and marled beef soup, which I had brought with me, were very opportune. They had almost exhausted their bread; and, being unwilling to encroach on the depot stores, had gone without fuel in order to save alcohol. Leaving orders to place my own sledge stores in cache, I returned to the brig ahead of the party, with my dog sledge, carrying Mr. Bonsall with me.

* * * *

OCTOBER 28, FRIDAY. "The last remnant of walrus did not leave us until the second week of last month, when the temperature had sunk below zero. Till then they found open water enough to sport and even sleep in, between the fields of drift, as they opened with the tide; but they had worked numerous breathing holes besides, in the solid ice nearer shore. Many of these were inside the capes of Rensselaer Harbor. They had the same circular, cleanly finished margin as the seals' but they were in much thicker ice, and the radiating lines of fracture round them much more marked. The animal evidently used his own buoyancy as a means of starting the ice.

"Around these holes the ice was much discolored: numbers of broken clam shells were found near them, and, in one instance, some gravel, mingled with about half a peck of the coarse shingle of the beach. The use of the stones which the walrus swallows is still an interesting question. The ussuk or bearded seal has the same habit.[2]"

NOVEMBER 7, MONDAY. "The darkness is coming on with insidious steadiness, and its advances can only be perceived by comparing one day with its fellow of some time back. We still read the thermometer at noonday without a light, and the black masses of the hills are plain for about five hours with their glaring

[2]Both the walrus and the bearded seal feed on mussels, cockles and especially clams off the sea bottom. Often pebbles and stones are found in the mammals' stomachs. Until recently these were thought as a possible aid to digestion. Today scientists reject the theory for lack of evidence. Perry, Richard, *The World of the Walrus,* (Cassell. London, 1967), pp. 96–97. Also personal communication with Dr. Brendon Kelly, Insitute of Marine Science and Arctic Biology, University of Alaska. January 17, 1996.

patches of snow; but all the rest is darkness. Lanterns are always on the spar deck, and the lard lamps never extinguished below. The stars of the sixth magnitude shine out at noonday.

"Except upon the island of Spitzbergen, which has the advantages of an insular climate and tempered by ocean currents, no Christians have wintered in so high a latitude as this. They are Russian sailors who make the encounter there, men inured to hardships and cold. I cannot help thinking of the sad chronicles of the early Dutch, who perished year after year, without leaving a comrade to record their fate.

"Our darkness has ninety days to run before we shall get back again even to the contested twilight of today. Altogether, our winter will have been sunless for 140 days.

NOVEMBER 16, WEDNESDAY. "The great difficulty is to keep up a cheery tone among the men. Poor Hans has been sorely homesick. Three days ago he bundled up his clothes and his rifle to bid us all goodbye. It turns out that besides his mother there is another one of the softer sex at Fiskenaes that the boy's heart is dreaming of. He looked as wretched as any lover of a milder clime. I hope I have treated his nostalgia successfully, by giving him first a dose of salts, and, secondly, promotion. He has now all the dignity of henchman. He harnesses my dogs, builds my traps, and walks with me on my ice-tramps; and, except hunting, is excused from all other duty. He is really attached to me, and as happy as a fat man ought to be."

November 21, Monday. "We have schemes innumerable to cheat the monotonous solitude of our winter. We are getting up a fancy ball; and today the first of our Arctic newspaper, 'The Ice-Blink,' came out, with the motto, 'in tenebris servare fidem.' The articles are by authors of every nautical grade: some of the best from the forecastle."

November 27, Sunday. "I sent out a volunteer party some days ago with Mr. Bonsall to see whether the Esquimaux have returned to the huts we saw empty at the cape. The thermometer was in the neighborhood of forty degrees below zero, and the day was too dark to read at noon. I was hardly surprised when they returned after camping one night upon the snow. Their sledge broke down, and they were obliged to leave tents and everything else behind them. It must have been very cold, for a bottle of Monongahela whiskey of good stiff proof froze under Mr. Bonsall's head."

December 15, Thursday. "We have lost the last vestige of our midday twilight. We cannot see print, and hardly paper: the fingers cannot be counted a foot from the eyes. Noonday and midnight are alike, and, except a vague glimmer on the sky that seems to define the hill outlines to the south, we have nothing to tell us that this Arctic world of ours has a sun. In one week more we shall reach the midnight of the year."

VII

Daily Life

Mʏ ᴊᴏᴜʀɴᴀʟ for the first two months of 1854 is so devoid of interest that I spare the reader the task of following me through it. In the darkness and consequent inaction, it was almost in vain that we sought to create topics of thought, and by a forced excitement to ward off the encroachments of disease. Our observatory and the dogs gave us our only regular occupations.

Our magnetic observations went on; but the cold made it almost impossible to adhere to them with regularity. Our observatory was, in fact, an ice-house of the coldest imaginable description. The absence of snow prevented our backing the walls with that important nonconductor. Fires, buffalo robes, and an arras of investing sailcloth, were unavailing to bring up the mean temperature to the freezing-point at the level of the magnetometer;[1] and it was quite common to find the platform on which the observer stood full fifty degrees lower, or about twenty degrees below zero.

---

[1] A device to measure the magnetic field. The North Magnetic Pole was discovered by James Clark Ross on the west coast of Boothia Felix in 1831. Whether the pole was fixed or not remained a mystery until Amundsen returned to Boothia Felix in 1905 and found it had moved approximately thirty miles. See Berton, *The Arctic Grail*, pp. 114, 541.

Our astronomical observations were less protracted, but the apartment in which they were made was of the same temperature with the outer air. The cold was, of course, intense; and some of our instruments, the dip circle particularly, became difficult to manage because of the unequal contraction of the brass and steel.

On 17 January, our thermometers stood at forty-nine degrees below zero; and on the twentieth, the range of those at the observatory was at minus sixty-four degrees to minus sixty-seven degrees. The temperature on the floes was always higher than at the island, the difference being due, as I suppose, to the heat conducted from the seawater, which was at a temperature of twenty-nine degrees above zero; the suspended instruments being affected by radiation.

On 5 February, our thermometers began to show unexampled temperature. They ranged from sixty to seventy-five degrees below zero, and one very reliable instrument stood upon the taffrail of our brig at minus sixty-five degrees. The reduced mean of our best spirit standards gave minus sixty-seven degrees, or ninety-nine degrees below the freezing point of water.

The first traces of returning light were observed at noon on the twenty-first of January, when the southern horizon had for a short time a distinct orange tint. Though the sun had given us a band of illumination before, it was not distinguishable from the cold light of the planets. We had been nearing the sunshine for thirty-two days, and had just reached that degree of mitigated darkness which made the extreme midnight of Sir Edward Parry in latitude 74°47′. As late as the thirty-first, two very sensitive daguerreotype plates, treated with iodine and bromine, failed to indicate any solar influence when exposed to the southern horizon at noon—the camera being used indoors, to escape the effects of cold.

The influence of this long, intense darkness was most depressing. Even our dogs, although most of them were natives of the Arctic Circle, were unable to withstand it. Most of them died from an anomalous form of disease, to which, I am satisfied, the absence of light contributed as much as the extreme cold. I give a little extract from my journal of 20 January.

"This morning at five o'clock—for I am so afflicted with the insomnium of this eternal night, that I rise at any time between midnight and noon—I went up on deck. It was absolutely dark; the cold not permitting a swinging lamp. There was not a glimmer came to me through the ice-crusted windowpanes of the cabin. While I was feeling my way, half puzzled as to the best method of steering clear of whatever might be before me, two of my Newfoundland dogs put their cold noses against my hand, and instantly commenced the most exuberant antics of satisfaction. It then occurred to me how very dreary and forlorn must these poor animals be, at atmospheres of plus ten degrees indoors and minus fifty degrees without—living in darkness, howling at an accidental light as if it reminded them of the moon—and with nothing, either of instinct or of sensation, to tell them of the passing hours, or to explain the long-lost daylight. They shall see the lanterns more frequently."

I close my notice of these dreary months with a single extract more. It is of the date of 21 February.

"We have had the sun for some days: silvering the ice between the headlands of the bay; and today, toward noon, I started out to be the first of my party to welcome him back. It was the longest walk and toughest climb that I have had since our imprisonment; and scurvy and general debility have made me short of wind. But I managed to attain my object. I saw him once more upon a projecting crag nestled in the sunshine. It was like bathing in perfumed water."

The month of March brought back to us the perpetual day. The sunshine had reached our deck on the last day of February: we needed it to cheer us. We were not as pale as my experience in Lancaster Sound had foretold; but the scurvy spots that mottled our faces gave sore proof of the trials we had undergone. It was plain that we were all of us unfit for arduous travel on foot at the intense temperatures of the nominal spring; and the return of the sun, by increasing the evaporation from the floes, threatened us with a recurrence of still severer weather.

But I felt that our work was unfinished. The great object of the expedition challenged us to a more northward exploration. My dogs, that I had counted on so largely, the nine splendid Newfoundlanders and thirty-five Esquimaux of six months before, had perished; there were only six survivors of the whole pack, and one of these was unfit for draught. Still, they formed my principal reliance, and I busied myself from the very beginning of the month in training them to run together. The carpenter was set to work upon a small sledge, on an improved model adapted to the reduced force of our team; and, as we had exhausted our stock of small cord to lash its parts together, Mr. Brooks rigged up a miniature rope walk and was preparing a new supply from part of the material of our deep sea lines. The operations of shipboard, however, went on regularly; Hans and occasionally Petersen going out on the hunt, though rarely returning successful.

Meanwhile we talked encouragingly of spring hopes and summer prospects and managed sometimes to force an occasion for mirth out of the very discomforts of our unyielding winter life.

This may explain the tone of my diary.

MARCH 7, TUESDAY. "I have said very little in this business journal about our daily Arctic life. I have had no time to draw pictures.

"But we have some trials that might make up a day's adventures. Our Arctic observatory is cold beyond any of its class.

"The observer, if he were only at home, would be the 'observed of all observers.' He is clad in a pair of sealskin pants, a dog skin cap, a reindeer jumper, and walrus boots. He sits on a box that once held a transit instrument. A stove, glowing with at least a bucketful

of anthracite, represents pictorially a heating apparatus, and reduces the thermometer as near as maybe
to ten degrees below zero. The one hand holds a
chronometer, and is left bare to warm it: the other lux-
uriates in a fox skin mitten. The right hand and the left
take it 'watch and watch about.' As one burns with
cold, the chronometer shifts to the other, and the mitten takes its place.

"Perched on a pedestal comprised of frozen gravel
is a magnetometer; stretching out from it, a telescope:
and, bending down to this, an abject human eye. Every
six minutes, said eye takes cognizance of a finely divided arc, and notes the result in a cold memorandum
book. This process continues for twenty-four hours,
two sets of eyes taking it by turns; and, when twenty-
four hours are over, term day is over too.

"We have such frolics every week. I have just been
relieved from one, and after a few hours am to be called
out of bed in the night to watch and do it again. I have
been engaged in this way when the thermometer gave
twenty degrees above zero at the instrument, twenty
degrees below zero at two feet above the floor, and
minus forty-three degrees at the floor itself: on my
person, facing the little lobster-red fury of a stove,
ninety-four degrees; on my person, away from the
stove, ten degrees below zero. 'A grateful country' will
of course appreciate the value of these labors, and, as
it cons over hereafter the 480 results that go to make
up our record for each week, will never think of asking 'Cui bono all this?'

"Taking an ice-pole in one hand, and a dark lantern in the other, you steer through the blackness for a lump of greater blackness, the Fern Rock knob. Stumbling over some fifty yards, you come to a wall: your black knob has disappeared, and nothing but gray indefinable ice is before you. Turn to the right; plant your pole against that inclined plane of slippery smoothness, and jump to the hummock opposite: it is the same hummock you skinned your shins upon the last night you were here. Now wind along, half serpentine, half zigzag, and you cannot mistake that twenty-foot wall just beyond, creaking and groaning and even nodding its crest with a grave cold welcome: it is the 'seam of the second ice.' Tumble over it at the first gap, and you are upon the first ice: tumble over that, and you are at the ice-foot; and there is nothing else now between you and the rocks, and nothing after them between you and the observatory.

"But be a little careful as you come near this ice-foot. It is munching all the time at the first ice, and you have to pick your way over the masticated fragments. Don't trust yourself to the half balanced, half fixed, half floating ice lumps, unless you truly relish a bath like Marshall Suwarrow's[2]—it might be more pleasant if you were sure of getting out—but feel your way gingerly, with your pole held crosswise, not disdaining

[2]Marshall Suwarrow (also spelled Suvrov): In the 1790s, the Russian General Alexander Suvrov led a military campaign through the St. Gothard Pass to drive the French out of Switzerland. He was the first to traverse the Alps in winter and his campaign is considered one of the great feats of military history.

lowly attitudes, hands and knees, or even full length. That long wedge-like hole just before you, sending up its puffs of steam into the cold air, is the 'seam of the ice-foot': you have only to jump it and you are on the smooth level ice-foot itself. Scramble up the rocks now, get on your wooden shoes, and go to work observing an oscillating needle for some hours to come."

MARCH 9, THURSDAY. "How do we spend the day when it is not term day, or rather the twenty-four hours? for it is either all day here, or all night, or a twilight mixture of both. How do we spend the twenty-four hours?

"At six in the morning, McGary is called, with all hands who have slept in. The decks are cleaned, the ice-hole opened, the refreshing beef-nets examined, the ice-tables measured, and things aboard put to rights. At half past seven, all hands rise, wash on deck, open the doors for ventilation, and come below for breakfast. We are short of fuel and therefore cook in the cabin. Our breakfast is hard tack, pork, stewed apples frozen like molasses candy, tea and coffee, with a delicate portion of raw potato. After breakfast, the smokers take their pipe till nine: then all hands turn to, idlers to idle and workers to work; Ohlsen to his bench, Brooks to his 'preparations' in canvas, McGary to play tailor, Whipple to make shoes, Bonsall to tinker, Baker to skin birds—and the rest to the 'Office!' Take a look into the Arctic Bureau! One table, one salt pork lamp with rusty chlorinated flame, three stools, and as many waxen-faced men with their legs

drawn up under them, the deck at zero being too cold
for the feet. Each has his department: Kane is writing,
sketching, and projecting maps; Hayes copying logs
and meteorologicals; Sontag reducing his work at Fern
Rock. A fourth, as one of the working members of the
hive, has long been defunct: you will find him in bed,
or studying 'Littell's Living Age.' At twelve, a business round of inspection, and orders enough to fill up
the day with work. Next, the drill of the Esquimaux
dogs—my own peculiar recreation—a dog trot, specially refreshing to legs that creak with every kick, and
rheumatic shoulders that chronicle every descent of
the whip. And so we get on to dinner time; the occasion of another gathering, which misses the tea and
coffee of breakfast, but rejoices in pickled cabbage and
dried peaches instead.

"At dinner as at breakfast the raw potato comes in,
our hygienic luxury. Like doctor stuff generally, it is not
as appetizing as desirable. Grating it down nicely, leaving out the ugly red spots, and adding the utmost oil
as a lubricant, it is as much as I can do to persuade the
mess to shut their eyes and bolt it, like Mrs. Squeers's
molasses and brimstone and Dotheboys Hall.[3] Two
absolutely refuse to taste it. I tell of the Silesians using
its leaves as spinach, of the whalers in the South Seas
getting drunk on the molasses, which had preserved
the large potatoes of the Azores—I point to this gum,

---

[3]Dotheboys Hall is the dreadful school in the novel *Nicholas
Nickleby* by Charles Dickens. Mrs. Squeers is the wife of its brutal headmaster.

so fungoid and angry the day before yesterday, and so flat and amiable today—all by a potato poultice: my eloquence is wasted: they persevere in rejecting it.

"Sleep, exercise, amusement, and work at will, carry on the day till our six o'clock supper, a meal something like breakfast and something like dinner, only a little more scant: and the officers come in with the reports of the day.

"McGary is the next to come, with the cleaning up arrangement, inside, outside, and on decks; and Mr. Wilson follows with ice measurements. And last of all comes my own record of the day gone by; every line, as I look back upon it pages, giving evidence of a weakened body and harassed mind.

"We have cards sometimes, and chess sometimes— and a few magazines, Mr. Littell's thoughtful present, to cheer away the evening."

MARCH 11, SATURDAY. "All this seems tolerable for commonplace routine; but there is a lack of comfort which it does not tell of. Our fuel is limited to three bucketfuls of coal a day, and our mean temperature outside is forty degrees below zero; forty-six degrees below zero as I write. London Brown Stout, and somebody's Old Brown Sherry, freeze in the cabin lockers; and the carlines overhead are hung with tubs of chopped ice, to make water for our daily drink. Our lamps cannot be persuaded to burn salt lard; our oil is exhausted; and we work by muddy tapers of cork and cotton floated in saucers. We have not a pound of fresh meat, and only a barrel of potatoes left.

"Not a man now, except Pierre and Morton, is exempt from scurvy; and, as I look around upon the pale faces and haggard looks of my comrades, I feel that we are fighting the battle of life at disadvantage, and that an Arctic night and an Arctic day age a man more rapidly and harshly than a year anywhere else."

MARCH 13, MONDAY. "Since January, we have been working at the sledges and other preparations for travel. The death of my dogs, the rugged obstacles of the ice, and the intense cold have obliged me to reorganize our whole equipment. We have had to discard all our India rubber fancy work: canvas shoemaking, fur socking, sewing, carpentering are all going on; and the cabin, our only fire-warmed apartment, is the workshop, kitchen, parlor, and hall. Pemmican cases are thawing on the lockers; buffalo robes are drying around the stove; camp equipments occupy the corners; and our woebegone French cook, with an infinitude of useless saucepans, insists on monopolizing the stove."

MARCH 15, WEDNESDAY. "The mean temperature of the last five days has been,

March 10	$-46°.03$
March 11	$-45°.60$
March 12	$-46°.64$
March 13	$-46°.56$
March 14	$-46°.65$

giving an average of $-46°.30$, with a variation between the extremes of less than three-quarters of a degree.

"These records are remarkable. The coldest month of the Polar year has heretofore been February; but we are evidently about to experience for March a mean temperature not only the lowest of our own series, but lower than that of any other recorded observations.

"This anomalous temperature seems to disprove the idea of a diminished cold as we approach the Pole. It will extend the isotherm of the solstitial month higher than ever before projected.

"The mean temperature of Parry for March (in lat. 74°30′) was minus twenty-nine degrees; our own will be at least forty-one degrees below zero.

"At such temperatures, the ice or snow covering offers a great resistance to the sledge-runners. I have noticed this in training my dogs. The dry snow in its finely divided state resembles sand, and the runners creak as they pass over it. Baron Wrangell notes the same fact in Siberia at forty degrees below zero.

"The difficulties of draught, however, must not interfere with my parties. I am only waiting until the sun, now 13° high at noon, brings back a little warmth to the men in sleeping. The mean difference between bright clear sunshine and shade is now 5°. But on the tenth, at noon, the shade gave −42°2′, and the sun −28°; a difference of more than 14 degrees. This must make an impression before long."

MARCH 17, FRIDAY. "It is 9:00 P.M., and the thermometer outside at minus forty-six degrees. I am anxious to have this depot party off; but I must wait until there is a promise of milder weather. It must come

The pack off Sylvia Headland

James Hamilton, from a sketch by Dr. Kane

soon. The sun is almost at the equator. On deck, I can see to the northward all the bright glare of sunset, streaming out in long bands of orange through the vapors of the ice-foot, and the frost smoke exhaling in wreaths like those from the house chimneys a man sees in the valleys as he comes down a mountainside."

MARCH 18, SATURDAY. "Today our spring tides gave way to the massive ice that sustains our little vessel a rise and fall of seventeen feet. The crunching and grinding, the dashing of the water, the gurgling of the eddies, and the toppling over of the nicely poised ice-tables, were unlike the more brisk dynamics of hummock action, but conveyed a more striking expression of power and dimension.

"The thermometer at four o'clock in the morning was minus forty-nine degrees, too cold still, I fear, for our sledgemen to set out. But we packed the sledge and strapped on the boat, and determined to see how she would drag. Eight men attached themselves to the lines but were scarcely able to move her. This may be due in part to an increase of friction produced by the excessive cold, according the experience of the Siberian travelers; but I have no doubt it is principally caused by the very thin runners of our Esquimaux sledge cutting through the snow crust.

"The excessive refraction this evening, which entirely lifted up the northern coast as well as the icebergs, seems to give the promise of milder weather. In the hope that it may be so, I have fixed on tomorrow for the departure of the sledge, after very reluctantly dispensing with more than two hundred pounds of her cargo, besides the boat. The party think they can get along with it now."

MARCH 20, MONDAY. "I saw the depot party off yesterday. They gave the usual three cheers, with three for myself. I gave them the whole of my brother's great wedding cake and my last two bottles of port, and they pulled the sledge they were harnessed to famously. But I was not satisfied. I could see it was hard work; and, besides, they were without the boat or enough extra pemmican to make their deposit of importance. I followed them, therefore, and found that they encamped at 8:00 P.M. only five miles from the brig.

"When I overtook them, I said nothing to discourage them, and gave no new orders for the morning; but after laughing at good Ohlsen's rueful face, and listening to all Petersen's assurances that the cold and nothing but the cold retarded his Greenland sledge, and that no sledge of any other construction could have been moved at all through minus forty degree snow, I quietly bade them goodnight, leaving all hands under their buffaloes.

"Once returned to the brig, all my tired remainder-men were summoned: a large sled with broad runners, which I had built after the Admiralty model sent me by Sir Francis Beaufort, was taken down, scraped, polished, lashed, and fitted with track ropes and rue-raddies; the lines arranged to draw as near as possible in a line with the center of gravity. We made an entire cover of canvas, with snugly adjusted fastenings; and by one in the morning we had our discarded excess of pemmican and the boat once more in stowage.

"Off we went for the camp of the sleepers. It was very cold, but a thoroughly Arctic night; the snow just tinged with the crimson stratus above the sun, which, equinoctial as it was, glared beneath the northern horizon like a smelting furnace. We found the tent of the party by the bearings of the stranded bergs. Quietly and stealthily we hauled away their Esquimaux sledge, and placed her cargo upon the 'Faith.' Five men were then rue-raddied to the track lines; and with the whispered word, 'Now, boys, when Mr. Brooks gives his third snore, off with you!' off they went, and the 'Faith' after them, as free and nimble as a volunteer. The trial was a triumph. We awakened the sleepers with three cheers; and, giving them a second goodbye, returned to the brig, carrying the dishonored vehicle with us. And now, bating mishaps past anticipation, I shall have a depot for my long trip."

The rue-raddy

VIII

Rescue!

MARCH 27, MONDAY. "We have been for some days in all the flurry of preparation for our exploration trip: buffalo hides, leather, and tailoring utensils everywhere. Every particle of fur comes in play for mitts and muffs and wrappers. Poor Flora is turned into a pair of socks, and looks almost as pretty as when she was heading the team."

Everything looked promising, and we were only waiting for intelligence that our advance party had deposited its provisions in safety to begin our transit of the bay. Except a few sledge lashings and some trifling accoutrements to finish, all was ready.

We were at work cheerfully, sewing away at the skins of some moccasins by the blaze of our lamps, when, toward midnight, we heard the noise of steps above, and the next minute Sontag, Ohlsen, and Petersen came down into the cabin. Their manner startled me even more than their unexpected appearance on board. They were swollen and haggard, and hardly able to speak.

Their story was a fearful one. They had left their companions in the ice, risking their own lives to bring us the news: Brooks, Baker, Wilson, and Pierre were all lying frozen and disabled. Where? They could not tell: somewhere in among the hummocks to the north and east; it was drifting heavily round them when they parted. Irish Tom had stayed by to feed and care for the others; but the chances were sorely against them. It was in vain to question them further. They had evidently traveled a great distance, for they were sinking with fatigue and hunger, and could hardly be rallied enough to tell us the direction in which they had come.

My first impulse was to move on the instant with an unencumbered party: a rescue, to be effective or even hopeful, could not be too prompt. What pressed on my mind most was, where the sufferers were to be looked for among the drifts. Ohlsen seemed to have his faculties rather more at command than his associates, and I thought that he might assist us as a guide; but he was sinking with exhaustion, and if he went with us we must carry him.

There was not a moment to be lost. While some were still busy with the newcomers and getting ready a hasty meal, others were rigging out the "Little Willie" with a buffalo cover, a small tent, and a package of pemmican; and, as soon as we could hurry through our arrangements, Ohlsen was strapped on in a fur bag, his legs wrapped in dog skins and eiderdown, and we were off upon the ice. Our party consisted of nine men and myself. We carried only the clothes on our backs. The thermometer stood at minus forty-six degrees, seventy-eight degrees below the freezing point.

A well-known peculiar tower of ice, called by the men the "Pinnacly Berg," served as our first landmark;

other icebergs of colossal size, which stretched in long beaded lines across the bay, helped to guide us afterward; and it was not until we had traveled for sixteen hours that we began to lose our way.

We knew that our lost companions must be somewhere in the area before us, within a radius of forty miles. Mr. Ohlsen, who had been for fifty hours without rest, fell asleep as soon as we began to move, and awoke now with unequivocal signs of mental disturbance. It became evident that he had lost the bearing of the icebergs, which in form and color endlessly repeated themselves; and the uniformity of the vast field of snow utterly forbade the hope of local landmarks.

Pushing ahead of the party, and clambering over some rugged ice-piles, I came to a long level floe, which I thought might probably have attracted the eyes of weary men in circumstances like our own. I gave orders to abandon the sledge, and disperse in search of foot marks. We raised our tent, placed our pemmican in cache, except a small allowance for each man to carry on his person; and poor Ohlsen, now just able to keep his legs, was liberated from his bag. The thermometer had fallen by this time to $-49°.3$, and the wind was setting in sharply from the northwest. It was out of the question to halt: it required brisk exercise to keep us from freezing. I could not even melt ice for water; and, at these temperatures, any resort to snow for the purpose of allaying thirst was followed by bloody lips and tongue: it burnt like caustic.

It was indispensable then that we should move on,

looking out for traces as we went. Yet when the men were ordered to spread themselves, so as to multiply the chances, though they all obeyed heartily, some painful impress of solitary danger, or perhaps it may have been the varying configuration of the ice-field, kept them closing up continually into a single group. The strange manner in which some of us were affected I now attribute as much to shattered nerves as to the direct influence of the cold. Men like McGary and Bonsall, who had stood out our severest marches, were seized with trembling fits and short breath; and, in spite of all my efforts to keep up an example of sound bearing, I fainted twice on the snow.

We had been nearly eighteen hours out without water or food, when a new hope cheered us. I think it was Hans, our Esquimaux hunter, who thought he saw a broad sledge track. The drift had nearly effaced it, and we were some of us doubtful at first whether it was not one of those accidental rifts the gales make in the surface snow. But, as we traced it on to the deep snow among the hummocks, we were led to footsteps; and, following these with religious care, we at last came in sight of a small American flag fluttering from a hummock, and lower down a little Masonic banner hanging from a tent pole hardly above the drift. It was the camp of our disabled comrades: we reached it after an unbroken march of twenty-one hours.

The little tent was nearly covered. I was not among the first to come up; but, when I reached the tent curtain, the men were standing in silent file on each side of it. With more kindness and delicacy of feeling than is often supposed to belong to sailors, but which is almost characteristic, they intimated their wish that I should go in alone. As I crawled in, and, coming upon the darkness, heard before me the burst of welcome gladness that came forth from the four poor fellows stretched on their backs, and then for the first time the cheer outside, my weakness and gratitude together almost overcame me. "They had expected me: they were sure I would come!"

We were now fifteen souls; the thermometer seventy-five degrees below the freezing point; and our sole accommodation a tent barely able to contain eight persons: more than half our party were obliged to keep from freezing by walking outside while the others slept. We could not halt long. Each of us took a turn of two hours' sleep; and we prepared for our homeward march.

We took with us nothing but the tent, furs to protect the rescued party, and food for a journey of fifty hours. Everthing else was abandoned. Two large buffalo bags, each made of four skins, were doubled up to form a sort of sack, lined on each side by fur, and closed at the bottom but opened at the top. This was laid on the sledge; the tent, smoothly folded serving as a floor. The sick, with their limbs sewed up carefully in reindeer skins, were placed upon the bed of buffalo robes, in a half-reclining posture; other skins and blanket bags were thrown above them; and the whole litter was lashed together so as to allow but a single opening opposite the mouth for breathing capacity.

This necessary work cost us a great deal of time and effort; but it was essential to the lives of the sufferers. It took us no less than four hours to strip and refresh them, and then to embale them in the manner I have described. Few of us escaped without frostbitten fingers: the thermometer was at 55.6° below zero, and a slight wind added to the severity of the cold.

It was completed at last, however; all hands stood round; and, after repeating a short prayer, we set out on our retreat. It was fortunate indeed that we were not experienced in sledging over the ice. A great part of our track lay among a succession of hummocks; some of them extending in long lines, fifteen and twenty feet high, and so uniformly steep that we had to turn them by a considerable deviation from our direct course; others that we forced our way through, far above our heads in height, lying in parallel ridges, with the space between too narrow for the sledge to be lowered into it safely, and yet not wide enough for the runners to cross without the aid of ropes to stay them. These spaces too were generally choked with light snow, hiding the openings between the ice-fragments. They were fearful traps to disengage a limb from, for every man knew that a fracture or a sprain even would cost him his life. Besides all this, the sledge was top-heavy with its load: the maimed men could not bear to be lashed down tight enough to secure them against falling off. Notwithstanding our caution in rejecting every superfluous burden, the weight, including bags and tent, was a total of eleven hundred pounds.

And yet our march for the first six hours was very cheering. We made by vigorous pulls and lifts nearly a mile an hour, and reached the new floes before we were absolutely weary. Our sledge sustained the trial admirably. Ohlsen, restored by hope, walked steadily at the leading belt of the sledge lines; and I began to feel certain of reaching our halfway station of the day before, where we had left our tent. But we were still nine miles from it, when, almost without premonition, we all became aware of an alarming failure of our energies.

I was of course familiar with the benumbed and almost lethargic sensation of extreme cold; and once, when exposed for some hours in the midwinter of Baffin's Bay, I had experienced symptoms I compared to the diffused paralysis of the electro-galvanic shock. But I had treated the sleepy comfort of freezing as something like the embellishment of romance. I had evidence now to the contrary.

Bonsall and Morton, two of our stoutest men, came to me, begging permission to sleep: "They were not cold: the wind did not enter them now: a little sleep was all they wanted." Presently Hans was found nearly stiff under a drift; and Thomas, bolt upright, had his eyes closed, and could hardly articulate. At last, John Blake threw himself on the snow, and refused to rise. They did not complain of feeling cold; but it was in vain that I wrestled, boxed, ran, argued, jeered or reprimanded. An immediate halt could not be avoided.

We pitched our tent with much difficulty. Our hands were too powerless to strike a fire: we were obliged to do without water or food. Even the spirits (whisky) had frozen at the men's feet under all the coverings. We put Bonsall, Ohlsen, Thomas, and Hans, with the other sick men, well inside the tent, and crowded in as many others as we could. Then, leaving the party in charge of Mr. McGary, with orders to come on after four hours' rest, I pushed ahead with William Godfrey, who volunteered to be my companion. My aim was to reach the halfway tent, and thaw some ice and pemmican before the others arrived.

The floe was of level ice, and the walking excellent. I cannot tell how long it took us to make the nine miles; for we were in a strange sort of stupor, and had little apprehension of time. It was probably about four hours. We kept ourselves awake by imposing on each other a continued articulation of words; they must have been incoherent enough. I recall these hours as among the most wretched I have every gone through: we were neither of us in our right senses and retained a very confused recollection of what preceded our arrival at the tent. We both of us, however, remember a bear, who walked leisurely before us and tore up as he went a jumper that Mr. McGary had improvidently thrown off the day before. He tore it into shreds and rolled it into a ball, but never offered to interfere with our progress. I remember this and, with it, a confused sentiment that our tent and buffalo robes might probably share the same fate. Godfrey, with whom the memory of this day's work may atone for many faults of a later time, had a better eye than myself; and, looking some miles ahead, he could see that our tent was undergoing the same unceremonious treatment. I thought I saw it too, but we were so drunken with cold that we strode on steadily and, for aught I know, without quickening our pace.

Probably our approach saved the contents of the tent; for when we reached it the tent was uninjured, though the bear had overturned it, tossing the buffalo robes and pemmican into the snow; we missed only a couple of blanket bags. What we recollect, however, and perhaps all we recollect, is that we had great difficulty raising the tent. We crawled into our reindeer sleeping bags, without speaking, and for the next three hours slept on in a dreamy but intense slumber. When I awoke, my long beard was a mass of ice, frozen fast to the buffalo skin: Godfrey had to cut me out with his jackknife. Four days after our escape, I found my woolen comfortable with a goodly share of my beard still adhering to it.

We were able to melt water and get some soup cooked before the rest of our party arrived: it took them but five hours to walk the nine miles. They were doing well, and, considering the circumstances, in wonderful spirits. The day was most providentially windless, with a clear sun. All enjoyed the refreshment we had got ready. The crippled were repacked in their robes, and we sped quite briskly toward the hummock ridges that lay between us and the

Pinnacly Berg, clearly visible against the bright sky.

It required desperate efforts to work our way over it—literally desperate, for our strength failed us anew, and we began to lose our self control. We could not abstain any longer from eating snow: our mouths had swelled, and some of us became speechless. Happily the day was warmed by a clear sunshine, and the thermometer rose to minus four degrees in the shade: otherwise we must have frozen.

Our halts multiplied, and we fell half sleeping on the snow. I could not prevent it. Strange to say, it refreshed us. I ventured upon the experiment myself, making Riley wake me at the end of three minutes; and I felt so much benefited by it that I timed the men in the same way. They sat on the runners of the sledge, fell asleep instantly, and were forced to wakefulness when their three minutes were out.

By eight o'clock in the evening we emerged from the floes. The sight of the Pinnacly Berg revived us. Brandy, an invaluable resource in emergency, had already been served out in tablespoonful doses. We now took a longer rest, and a last but stouter dram, and reached the brig at 1:00 P.M., we believe without a halt.

I say we believe; and here perhaps is the most decided proof of our sufferings: we were quite delirious and had ceased to entertain a sane apprehension of the circumstances about us. We moved on like men in a dream. Our foot marks seen afterward showed that we had steered a beeline for the brig. It must have been by a sort of instinct, for it left no impress on the memory. Bonsall was sent staggering ahead, and reached the brig, God knows how, for he had fallen repeatedly at the track lines; but he delivered with punctilious accuracy the messages I had sent by him to Dr. Hayes. I thought myself the soundest of all; I went through all the formuli of sanity, and can recall the muttering delirium of my comrades when we got back into the cabin of our brig. Yet I have been told since of some speeches and some order too of mine, which I should have remembered for their absurdity if my mind had retained its balance.

Petersen and Whipple came out to meet us about two miles from the brig. They brought my dog team, with the restoratives I had sent for by Bonsall. I do not remember their coming. Dr. Hayes entered with judicious energy upon the treatment our condition called for, administering morphine freely, after the usual frictions. He reported that none of our brain symptoms as serious, referring them properly to the class of those indications of exhausted power that yield to generous diet and rest. Mr. Ohlsen suffered some time from strabismus[1] and blindness: two others underwent amputation of parts of the foot[2], without an unpleasant consequence; and two died in spite of all our efforts. This rescue party had been out for seventy-two hours. We had halted in all eight hours, half of our number sleeping at a time. We traveled between eighty and ninety miles, most of the way dragging a heavy sledge.

[1]Means squinting.
[2]Amputation was necessary if frozen limbs became gangrenous.

The mean temperature of the whole time, including the warmest hours of three days, was at minus 41°.2. We had no water except at our two halts, and were at no time able to intermit vigorous exercise without actually freezing.

APRIL 4, TUESDAY. "Four days have passed, and I am again at my record of failures, sound but aching still in every joint. The rescued men are not out of danger, but their gratitude is very touching. Pray God that they may live!"

Inside the Tent

IX

Meeting with Esquimaux

THE WEEK that followed has left me nothing to remember but anxieties and sorrow. Nearly all our party, as well the rescuers as rescued, were tossing in their sick bunks, some frozen, others undergoing amputations, several with dreadful premonitions of tetanus. I was myself among the first to be about: the necessities of the others claimed it of me.

Early in the morning of the seventh I was awakened by a sound from Baker's throat, one of those the most frightful and ominous that ever startle a physician's ear. The lockjaw[1] had seized him. His symptoms marched rapidly to their result; he died on 8 April. We placed him the next day in his coffin, and, forming a rude but heartful procession, bore him over the broken ice and up the steep side of the ice-foot to Butler Island; then, passing along the snow level to Fern Rock, and, climbing the slope of the observatory, we deposited his corpse upon the pedestals that had served to support our transit instrument and theodolite. We read the service for the burial of the dead, sprinkling over him snow for dust, and repeated the Lord's Prayer; and then, icing up again the opening in

[1]A *tetanic* infection. Scurvy causes skin sores and low immunity and, thus, susceptibility to infection of all kinds.

117

the walls we had made to admit the coffin, left him in his narrow house.

Jefferson Baker was a man of kind heart and true principles. I knew him when we were both younger. I passed two happy seasons at a little cottage adjoining his father's farm. He thought it a privilege to join this expedition, as in those green summer days when I had allowed him to take a gun with me on some shooting party. He relied on me with the affectionate confidence of boyhood, and I never gave him a harsh word or a hard thought.

We were out watching in the morning at Baker's deathbed, when one of our deck watch, who had been cutting ice for the melter, came hurrying down into the cabin with the report, "People hollaing ashore!" I went up, followed by as many as could mount the gangway; and there they were, on all sides of our rocky harbor, dotting the snow-covered shores and emerging from the blackness of the cliffs—wild and uncouth, but evidently human beings.

As we gathered on the deck, they rose upon the more elevated fragments of the land-ice, standing singly and conspicuously like the figures in a tableau of the opera, and distributing themselves around almost in a half circle. They were vociferating as if to attract our attention, or perhaps only to give vent to their surprise; but I could make nothing out of their cries, except "Hoah, ha ha!" and "Ka, kaah! ka, kaah!" repeated over and over again.

There was light enough for me to see that they bran-

dished no weapons, and were only tossing their heads
and arms about in violent gesticulations. A more un-
excited inspection showed us, too, that their numbers
were not as great nor their size as Patagonian as some
of us had been disposed to fancy at first. In a word, I
was satisfied that they were natives of the country; and
calling Petersen from his bunk to be my interpreter, I
proceeded, unarmed and waving my open hands, toward a stout figure who made himself conspicuous
and seemed to have a greater number near him than
the rest. He evidently understood the movement, for
he at once, like a brave fellow, leaped down upon the
floe and advanced to meet me fully halfway.

He was nearly a head taller than myself, extremely
powerful and well built, with swarthy complexion and
piercing black eyes. His dress was a hooded *capôte* or
jumper of mixed white and blue fox pelts, arranged
with something of fancy, and booted trousers of white
bear skin, which at the end of the foot were made to
terminate with the claws of the animal.

I soon came to an understanding with this gallant
diplomatist. Almost as soon as we commenced our
parley, his companions, probably receiving signals
from him, flocked in and surrounded us; but we had
no difficulty in making them know positively that they
must remain where they were, while Metek went with
me on board the ship. This gave me the advantage of
negotiating with an important hostage.

Although this was the first time he had ever seen a
white man, he went with me fearlessly; his companions

staying behind on the ice. Hickey took them out what he esteemed our greatest delicacies, slices of good wheat bread, and corned pork, with exorbitant lumps of white sugar; but they refused to touch them. They had evidently no apprehension of open violence from us. I found afterward that several among them were singly a match for the white bear and the walrus, and that they thought us a very pale-faced crew.

Being satisfied with my interview in the cabin, I sent out word that the rest might be admitted to the ship; and, although they, of course, could not know how their chief had been dealt with, some nine or ten of them followed with boisterous readiness upon the bidding. Others in the meantime, as if disposed to give us their company for the full time of a visit, brought up from behind the land-ice as many as fifty-six fine dogs with their sledges, and secured them within two hundred feet of the brig, driving their lances into the ice, and picketing the dogs to them by sealskin traces. The animals understood the operation perfectly, and lay down as soon as it commenced. The sledges were made up of small fragments of porous bone, admirably knit together by thongs of hide; the runners, which glistened like burnished steel, were of highly polished ivory, obtained from the tusks of the walrus.

The only arms they carried were knives, concealed in their boots; but their lances, which were lashed to the sledges, were quite a formidable weapon. The staff was of the horn of the narwhal, or else of the thighbones of the bear, two lashed together, or sometimes the mirabilis of the walrus, three or four of them united. This last was a favorite material also for the crossbars of their sledges. They had no wood. A single rusty hoop from a current drifted cask might have furnished all the knives of the party; but the flame-shaped tips of their lances were of unmistakable steel, and were riveted to the tapering bony point with no mean skill. I learned afterward that the metal was obtained in traffic from the more southern tribes.

When they were first allowed to come on board, they were very rude and difficult to manage. They spoke three or four at a time, to each other and to us, laughing heartily at our ignorance in not understanding them, and then talking away as before. They were incessantly in motion, going everywhere, trying doors and squeezing themselves through dark passages, round casks and boxes, and out into the light again, anxious to touch and handle everything they saw, and asking for, or else endeavoring to steal, everything they touched. It was the more difficult to restrain them, as I did not wish them to suppose that we were at all intimidated. But there were some signs of our disabled condition, which it was important they should not see: it was especially necessary to keep them out of the forecastle, where the dead body of poor Baker was lying: and, as it was in vain to reason or persuade, we had at last to employ the "gentle laying on of hands," which, I believe, the laws of all countries tolerate, to keep them in order.

They were lost in barbarous amaze at the new fuel—too hard for blubber, too soft for fire stone—but they were content to believe it might cook as well as seals' fat. They borrowed from us an iron pot and some melted water, and parboiled a couple of pieces of walrus meat; but the real *pièce de résistance*, some five pounds a head, they preferred to eat raw. Yet there was something of the gourmet in their mode of assorting their mouthfuls of beef and blubber. Slices of each, or rather strips, passed between the lips, either together or in strict alternation, and with a regularity of sequence that kept the molars well to their work.

They did not eat all at once, but each man when and as often as the impulse prompted. Each slept after eating, his raw chunk lying beside him on the buffalo skin; and, as he woke, the first act was to eat, and the next to sleep again. They did not lie down, but slumbered away in a sitting posture, with the head declined upon the breast, some of them snoring famously.

In the morning they were anxious to go; but I had given orders to detain them for a parting interview with myself. It resulted in a treaty, brief in its terms, that it might be certainly remembered, and mutually beneficial, that it might possibly be kept. I tried to make them understand what a powerful Prospero[2] they had had for a host, and how beneficent he would prove himself so long as they did his bidding. And, as an earnest of my favor, I bought all the walrus meat they

[2] The benign ruler of the island in Shakespeare's *The Tempest*.

had to spare, and four of their dogs, enriching them in return with needles and beads and a treasure of old cask staves.

In the fullness of their gratitude, they pledged themselves emphatically to return in a few days with more meat, and to allow me to use their dogs and sledges for my excursions to the north. I then gave them leave to go. They yoked in their dogs in less than two minutes, got on their sledges, cracked their two-fathom-and-a-half-long sealskin whips, and were off down the ice to the southwest at a rate of seven knots an hour.

They did not return: I had read enough of treaty makings not to expect them too confidently. But the next day came a party of five, on foot; two old men, one of middle age, and a couple of gawky boys. We had missed a number of articles soon after the first party left us, an axe, a saw, and some knives. We found afterward that our storehouse at Butler Island had been entered: we were too short handed to guard it by a special watch. Besides all this, reconnoitering stealthily beyond Sylvia Head, we discovered a train of sledges drawn up behind the hummocks.

There was cause for apprehension in all this; but I felt that I could not afford to break with the rogues. They had it in their power to molest us seriously in our sledge travel; they could make our hunts around the harbor dangerous; and my best chance of obtaining an abundant supply of fresh meat, our great desideratum, was by their agency. I treated the new party with marked kindness, and gave them many presents; but took care to make them aware that, until all the missing articles were restored, no member of the tribe would be admitted again as a guest on board the brig. They went off with many pantomimic protestations of innocence; but McGary, nevertheless, caught the incorrigible scamps stealing a coal barrel as they passed Butler Island, and expedited their journey homeward by firing among them a charge of small shot.

Still, one peculiar worthy—we thought it must have been the venerable of the party, whom I knew afterward as a stanch friend, old Shung-hu—managed to work round in a westerly direction, and to cut to pieces my India rubber boat, which had been left on the floe since Mr. Brooks's disaster, and to carry off every particle of the wood.

A few days after this, an agile, elfin youth drove up to our floe in open day. He was sprightly and good looking, and had quite a neat turnout of sledge and dogs. He told his name with frankness, "*Myouk*, I am,"—and where he lived. We asked him about the boat; but he denied all knowledge of it, and refused either to confess or repent. He was quite surprised when I ordered him to be confined to the hold. At first he refused to eat, and sat down in the deepest grief; but after a while he began to sing, and then to talk and cry, and then to sing again; and so he kept on rehearsing his limited *solfeggio* and crying and talking by turns, till a late hour of the night. When I turned in, he was still noisily disconsolate.

There was a simplicity and *bonhommie* about this

boy that interested me much; and I confess that when I made my appearance next morning—I could hardly conceal it from the gentleman on duty, whom I affected to censure—I was glad my bird had flown. Some time during the morning watch, he had succeeded in throwing off the hatch and escaping. We suspected that he had confederates ashore, for his dogs had escaped with as much address as himself. I was convinced, however, that I had the truth from him, where he lived and how many lived with him; my cross-examination on these points having been very complete and satisfactory.

It was a sad business for some time after these Esquimaux left us, to go on making and registering our observations at Fern Rock. Baker's corpse still lay in the vestibule, and it was not long before another was placed by the side of it. We had to pass the bodies as often as we went in or out; but the men, grown feeble and nervous, disliked going near them in the night-time. When the summer thaw came and we could gather stones enough, we built up a grave on a depression of the rocks, and raised a substantial cairn above it.

APRIL 19, WEDNESDAY. "I have been out on the floe again, breaking in my dogs. My reinforcement from the Esquimaux makes a noble team for me. For the last five days I have been striving with them, just as often and as long as my strength allowed me; and today I have my victory. The Society for Preventing Cruelty to Animals would have put me in custody, if they had been near enough; but, thanks to a merciless whip freely administered, I have been dashing along twelve miles in the last hour, and am back again; harness, sledge, and bones all unbroken. I am ready for another journey."

APRIL 22, SATURDAY. "Schubert has increasing symptoms of erysipelas[3] around his amputated stump; and everyone on board is depressed and silent except himself. He is singing in his bunk, as joyously as ever, 'Aux gens atrabilaires,' &c. Poor fellow! I am alarmed about him: it is a hard duty which compels me to take the field while my presence might cheer his last moments."

[3] A streptococcal infection that causes a rash. It is rare today.

X

To the Northern Coast

THE MONTH of April was about to close, and the short season available for Arctic search was upon us. The condition of things on board the brig was not such as I could have wished for; but there was nothing to exact my presence, and it seemed to me clear that the time had come for pressing on the work of the expedition. The arrangements for our renewed exploration had not been intermitted, and were soon complete. I leave to my journal its own story.

APRIL 25, TUESDAY. "A journey on the carpet; and the crew busy with the little details of their outfit: the officers the same.

"I have made a log line for sledge travel with a contrivance for fastening it to the ice and liberating it at pleasure. It will give me my dead reckoning quite as well as on the water. I have a team now of seven dogs, four that I bought of the Esquimaux, and three of my old stock. They go together quite respectably. Godfrey and myself will go with them on foot, following the first sledge on Thursday."

APRIL 26, WEDNESDAY. "McGary went yesterday with the leading sledge; and as Brooks is still on his back in consequence of the amputation, I leave Ohlsen in charge of the brig. He has my instructions in full:

among them I have dwelt largely upon the treatment of the natives.

"These Esquimaux must be watched carefully, at the same time that they are to be dealt with kindly, though with a strict enforcement of our police regulations and some caution as to the freedom with which they may come on board. No punishments must be permitted, either of them or in their presence, and no resort to firearms unless to repel a serious attack. I have given orders, however, that if the contingency does occur there shall be no firing overhead. The prestige of the gun with a savage is in his notion of its infallibility. You may spare bloodshed by killing a dog or even wounding him; but in no event should you throw away your ball. It is neither politic nor humane.

"Our stowage precautions are all arranged to meet the chance of the ice breaking up while I am away; and a boat is placed ashore with stores, as the brig may be forced from her moorings.

"The worst thought I have now in setting out is that, of the entire crew, I can leave but two behind in able condition, and the doctor and Bonsall are the only two officers who can help Ohlsen. This is our force, four able bodied and six disabled to keep the brig: the commander and seven men, scarcely better upon the average, out upon the ice. Eighteen souls, thank God! certainly not eighteen bodies!

"I am going this time to follow the ice-belt (Eisfod) to the Great Glacier of Humboldt, and there load up with pemmican from our cache of last October.

From this point I expect to stretch along the face of the glacier inclining to the west of north, and make an attempt to cross the ice to the American side. Once on smooth ice near this shore, I may pass to the west and enter the large indentation whose existence I can infer with nearly positive certainty. In this I may find an outlet, and determine the state of things beyond the ice-clogged area of this bay.

"I take with me pemmican, bread, and tea, a canvas tent, five feet by six, and two sleeping bags of reindeer skin. The sledge has been built on board by Mr. Ohlsen. It is very light, of hickory, and but nine feet long. Our kitchen is a soup kettle for melting snow and making tea, arranged so as to boil with either lard or spirits."

"For instruments I have a fine Gambey sextant, in addition to my ordinary pocket instrument, an artificial horizon, and a Barrow's dip circle. These occupy little room upon the sledge. Both my telescope and chronometer I carry on my person.

"McGary has taken the 'Faith.' He carries few stores, intending to replenish at the cache of Bonsall Point, and to lay in pemmican at McGary Island. Most of his cargo consists of bread, which we find it hard to dispense with in eating cooked food. It has a good effect in absorbing the fat of the pemmican, which is apt to disagree with the stomach."

Godfrey and I followed on the twenty-seventh. as I had intended. The journey was an arduous one to be undertaken, even if under the most favoring circumstances and by unbroken men. It would be the crowning expedition of the campaign, to attain the Ultima Thule of the Greenland shore, measure the waste that lay between it and the unknown west, and seek round the farthest circle of the ice for an outlet to the mysterious channels beyond. The scheme could not be carried out in its details. Yet it was prosecuted far enough in advance to indicate what must be our future fields of labor, and to determine many points of geographical interest. Our observations were in general confirmatory of those that had been made by Mr. Bonsall; and they accorded so well with our subsequent surveys as to trace for us the outline of the coast with great certainty.

The most picturesque portion of the North Greenland coast is to be found after leaving Cape George Russell and approaching Dallas Bay. The red sandstones contrast most favorably with the blank whiteness, associating the cold tints of the dreary Arctic landscape with the warm coloring of more southern lands. The seasons have acted on the different layers of the cliff so as to give them the appearance of jointed masonry, and the narrow line of greenstone at the top caps them with well-simulated battlements.

One of these interesting freaks of nature became known to us as the "Three Brother Turrets."

The sloping rubbish at the foot of the coast-wall led up, like an artificial causeway, to a gorge that was streaming at noonday with the southern sun; while everywhere else the rock stood out in the blackest

Tennyson's Monument

James Hamilton, from a sketch by Dr. Kane

shadow. Just at the edge of this bright opening rose the dreamy semblance of a castle, flanked with triple towers, completely isolated and defined. These were the "Three Brother Turrets."

I was still more struck with another of the same sort, in the immediate neighborhood of my halting-ground beyond Sunny Gorge, to the north of latitude 79°. A single cliff of greenstone, marked by the slaty limestone that once encased it, rears itself like the boldly chiseled rampart of an ancient city. At its northern extremity, on the brink of a deep ravine which has worn its way among the ruins, there stands a solitary column or minaret-tower, as sharply finished as if it had been cast for the Place Vendôme.[2] Yet the length of the shaft alone is 480 feet; and it rises on a plinth or pedestal itself 280 feet high.

I remember well the emotions of my party as it first broke upon our view. Cold and sick as I was, I brought back a sketch of it, though it scarcely suggests the dignity of this magnificent landmark. Those who are happily familiar with the writings of Tennyson, and have communed with his spirit in the solitudes of a wilderness, will apprehend the impulse that inscribed the scene with his name.

Still beyond this comes the archipelago that bears

[1] By comparing the magnificent natural landmark to the Place Vendôme and writing on his sketch "Alfred Tennyson," Kane was presenting a double compliment. Tennyson was the poet Kane most admired, *Ulysses* his favorite poem, and Tennyson's wife was the niece of Sir John Franklin. See Corner, *Doctor Kane of the Arctic Seas*, p.161.

the name of our brig, studded with the names of those on board of her who adhered to all the fortunes of the expedition; and at its eastern cape spreads out the Great Glacier of Humboldt.[2]

My recollections of this glacier are very distinct. The day was beautifully clear on which I first saw it; and I have a number of sketches made as we drove along in view of its magnificent face. They disappoint me, giving too much white surface and badly fading distances, the grandeur of the few bold and simple lines of nature being almost entirely lost.

I will not attempt to do better by florid description. Men only rhapsodize about Niagara and the ocean. My notes speak simply of the "long ever-shining line of cliff diminished to a well-pointed wedge in the perspective"; and again of "the face of glistening ice, sweeping in a long curve from the low interior, the facets in front intensely illuminated by the sun." But this line of cliff rose in solid glassy wall three hundred feet above the water level, with an unknown unfathomable depth below it; and its curved face, sixty miles in length, vanished into unknown space at not more than a single day's railroad travel from the Pole. The interior was an unsurveyed *mer de glace*, an ice ocean, to the eye of boundless dimensions.

It was in full sight—the mighty crystal bridge[2] that

[2]When Kane sees the Humboldt Glacier as a "crystal bridge" connecting Greenland to the continent of America, he is accepting an old theory, often demonstrated on maps from the sixteenth into the nineteenth century, that in the far North, Greenland bent around to connect with America.

connects the two continents of America and Greenland. I say continents; for Greenland, however insulated it may ultimately prove to be, is in mass strictly continental. Its least possible axis, measured from Cape Farewell to the line of this glacier, in the neighborhood of the eightieth parallel, gives a length of more than twelve hundred miles, not materially less than that of Australia from its northern to its southern cape.

Imagine, now, the center of such a continent, occupied through nearly its whole extent by a deep unbroken sea of ice, that gathers perennial increase from the water shed of vast snow covered mountains and all the precipitations of the atmosphere upon its own surface. Imagine this, moving onward like a great glacial river, seeking outlets at every fiord and valley, rolling icy cataracts into the Atlantic and Greenland seas; and, having at last reached the northern limit of the land that has borne it up, pouring out a mighty frozen torrent into unknown Arctic space.

It is thus, and only thus, that we must form a just conception of a phenomenon like this Great Glacier. I had looked in my own mind for such an appearance, should I be fortunate enough to reach the northern cost of Greenland. But now that it was before me, I could hardly realize it. I had recognized, in my quiet library at home, the beautiful analogies which Forbes and Studer have developed between the glacier and the river. But I could not comprehend at first this complete substitution of ice for water.

It was slowly that the conviction dawned on me, that I was looking upon the counterpart of the great river system of Arctic Asia and America. Yet here were no water feeders from the south. Every particle of moisture had its origin within the Polar Circle and had been converted into ice. There were no vast alluvions, no forest or any animal traces borne down by liquid torrents. Here was a plastic, moving, semisolid mass, obliterating life, swallowing rocks and islands, and ploughing its way with irresistible march through the crust of an investing sea.

Great Glacier

XI

Summer Arrives

"IT IS NOW the twentieth of May, and for the first time I am able, propped up by pillows and surrounded by sick messmates, to note the fact that we have failed again to force the passage to the north.

"Godfrey and myself overtook the advance party under McGary two days after leaving the brig. Our dogs were in fair traveling condition, and, except snow blindness, there seemed to be no drawback to our efficiency. In crossing Marshall Bay, we found the snow so accumulated in drifts that, with all our efforts to pick out a track, we became involved: we could not force our sledges through. We were forced to unload and carry forward the cargo on our backs, beating a path for the dogs to follow in. In this way we plodded on to the opposite headland, Cape William Wood, where the waters of Mary Minturn River, which had delayed the freezing of the ice, gave us a long reach of level travel. We then made a better rate; and our days' marches were such as to carry us by the fourth of May nearly to the glacier.

"This progress, however, was dearly earned. As early as the third of May, the winter's scurvy reappeared painfully among our party. As we struggled through the snow along the Greenland coast we sank up to our middle, and the dogs, floundering about, were so buried as to preclude any attempts at hauling. This excessive snow deposit seemed to be due to the precipitation of cold condensing wind suddenly wafted from the neighboring glacier; for at Rensselaer Harbor we had only four inches of general snow depth. It obliged us to unload our sledges again and carry their cargo, a labor that resulted in dropsical swellings with painful prostration. Here three of the party were taken with snow blindness, and George Stephenson had to be condemned as unfit for travel altogether on account of chest symptoms accompanying his scorbutic troubles. On the fourth, Thomas Hickey also gave in, although not quite disabled for labor at the track lines.

"Perhaps we would still have got on; but, to crown all, we found that the bears had effected an entrance into our pemmican casks, and destroyed our chances of reinforcing our provisions at the several caches. This great calamity was certainly inevitable; for it is simple justice to the officers under whose charge the provision depots were constructed to say that no means in their power could have prevented the result. The pemmican was covered with blocks of stone that it had required the labor of three men to adjust; but the extraordinary strength of the bear had enabled him to force aside the heaviest rocks, and his pawing had broken literally into chips the iron casks that held our pemmican. Our alcohol cask, which it had cost me a separate and special journey in the late fall to deposit, was so completely destroyed that we could not find a stave of it.

"Off Cape James Kent, about eight miles from 'Sunny Gorge,' while taking an observation for latitude, I was myself seized with a sudden pain and fainted. My limbs became rigid and certain obscure tetanoid symptoms of our late winter's enemy disclosed themselves. In this condition I was unable to make more than nine miles a day. I was strapped upon the sledge, and the march continued as usual; but my powers diminished so rapidly that I could not resist even the otherwise comfortable temperature of five degrees below zero. My left foot becoming frozen up to the metatarsal joint, caused a vexatious delay; and the same night it became evident that the immovability of my limbs was due to dropsical effusion.

"On the fifth, becoming delirious and fainting every time that I was taken from the tent to the sledge, I succumbed entirely.

"My comrades would kindly persuade me that, even had I continued sound, we could not have proceeded on our journey. The snows were very heavy and increasing as we went; some of the drifts perfectly impassable, and the level floes often four feet deep in yielding snow. The scurvy had already broken out among the men, with symptoms like my own; and Morton, our strongest man, was beginning to give way. It is the reverse of comfort to me that they shared my weakness. All that I should remember with pleasurable feeling is that to five brave men, Morton, Riley, Hickey,

Stephenson, and Hans, themselves scarcely able to travel, I owe my preservation. They carried me back by forced marches, after cacheing our stores and India rubber boat near Dallas Bay, in 79°5´ latitude, 66° longitude.

"I was taken into the brig on the fourteenth. Since then, fluctuating between life and death, I have by the blessing of God reached the present date, and can even feebly see the prospect of my recovery. Dr. Hayes regards my attack as one of scurvy, complicated by typhoid fever. George Stephenson is similarly affected. Our worst symptoms are dropsical effusion and night sweats."

MAY 22, MONDAY. "Let me, if I can, make up my record for the time I have been away or on my back.

"Poor Schubert is gone. Our gallant, merry-hearted companion left us some ten days ago, for, I trust, a more genial world. It is sad, in this dreary little homestead of ours, to miss his contented face and the joyous troll of his ballads.

"The health of the rest has, if anything, improved. Their complexions show the most cheery influence of sunlight, and I think several have a firmer and more elastic step. Stephenson and Thomas are the only two besides myself who are likely to suffer permanently from the effects of our breakdown. Bad scurvy both: symptoms still serious.

"Before setting out a month ago on a journey that should have extended into the middle of June, I had broken up the establishment of Butler Island and placed all the stores around the brig upon the heavy ice. My object in this was a double one. First, to remove from the Esquimaux the temptation and ability to pilfer. Second, to deposit our cargo where it could be restowed by very few men, if any unforeseen change in the ice made it necessary. Mr. Ohlsen, to whose charge the brig was committed, had orders to stow the hold slowly, remove the forward housing, and fit up the forecastle for the men to inhabit it again.

"All of these he carried out with judgment and energy. I find upon my return the brig so stowed and refitted that four days would prepare us for sea. The quarterdeck alone is now boarded in; and here all the officers and sick are sojourning. The wind makes this wooden shanty a somewhat airy retreat; but, for the health of our maimed scorbutic men, it is infinitely preferable to the less ventilated quarters below. Some of the crew, with one stove, are still in the forecastle; but the old cabin is deserted.

"I left Hans as hunter. I gave him a regular exemption from all other labor, and a promised present to his lady love on reaching Fiskenaes. He signalized his promotion by shooting two deer, *Tukkuk*, the first yet shot. We now have 145 pounds of fine venison, a gift of grace to our diseased crew. But, indeed, we are not likely to want for wholesome food, now that the night is gone, which made our need of it so pressing. On the first of May, those charming little migrants, the snow birds (*ultima coelicolum*), which only left us on the fourth of November, returned to our ice-crusted rocks, whence they seem to 'fill the sea and air with their sweet jargoning.' Seal literally abound too. I have learned to prefer this flesh to the reindeer's, at least that of the female seal, which has not the fetor of her mate's.

"By the twelfth, the sides of the *Advance* were free from snow, and her rigging clean and dry. The floe is rapidly undergoing its wonderful processes of decay; and the level ice measures but six feet in thickness. Today they report a burgomaster gull seen: one of the earliest but surest indications of returning open water. It is not strange, ice-leaguered exiles as we are, that we observe and exult in these things. They are the pledges of renewed life, the olive branch of this dreary waste: we feel the spring in all our pulses.

"The first thing I did after my return was to send McGary to Life-Boat Cove, to see that our boat and its buried provisions were secure. He made the journey by dog sledge in four days and has returned reporting that all is safe: an important help for us, should this heavy ice of our more northern prison refuse to release us.

"But the pleasantest feature of his journey was the disclosure of open water, extending up in a sort of tongue, with a trend of north by east to within two miles of Refuge Harbor, and there widening as it expanded to the south and west.

"Indeed, some circumstances he reports seem to point to the existence of a north water all the year round; and the frequent water skies, fogs, &c., that we have seen to the southwest during the winter, go to confirm the fact. The breaking up of the Smith Strait's ice commences much earlier than this; but as yet it has not extended farther than Littleton Island, where I should have wintered if my fall journey had not pointed to the policy of remaining here. The open water undoubtedly has been the cause of the retreat of the Esquimaux. Their sledge tracks have been seen all along the land foot; but, except a snow house at Esquimaux Point, we have met nothing which to the uninitiated traveler would indicate that they had rested upon this desert coast.

"As soon as I had recovered enough to be aware of my failure, I began to devise means for remedying it. But I found the resources of the party shattered. Pierre had died but a week before, and his death exerted an unfavorable influence. There were only three men able to do duty. Of the officers, Wilson, Brooks, Sontag, and Petersen were knocked up. There was no one except Sontag, Hayes, or myself who was qualified to conduct a survey; and, of us three, Dr. Hayes was the only one on his feet.

"The quarter to which our remaining observations were to be directed lay to the north and east of the Cape Sabine of Captain Inglefield. The interruption our progress along the coast of Greenland had met from the Great Glacier, and the destruction of our provision caches by the bears, left a blank for us of the entire northern coastline. It was necessary to ascertain whether the farthermost expansion of Smith's Strait did not find an outlet in still more remote channels;

and this became our duty the more plainly, since our theodolite had shown us that the northern coast trended off to the eastward, and not toward the west, as our predecessor had supposed. The angular difference of sixty degrees between its bearings on his charts and our own left me completely in the dark as to what might be the condition of this unknown area.

"I determined to trust almost entirely to the dogs for our travel in the future, and to send our parties of exploration, one after the other, as rapidly as the strength and refreshing of our team would permit.

"Dr. Hayes was selected specifically for that purpose; and I satisfied myself that, with a little assistance from my comrades, I could be carried round to the cots of the sick, and so avail myself of his services in the field.

"He was a perfectly fresh man, not having yet undertaken a journey. I gave him a team and my best driver, William Godfrey. He is to cross Smith's Straits above the inlet and make as near as may be a straight course for Cape Sabine. My opinion is that by keeping well south he will find the ice less clogged and easier sledging. Our experience proves, I think, that the transit of this broken area must be most impeded as we approach the glacier. The immense discharge of icebergs cannot fail to break it up seriously for travel.

"I gave him the small sledge built by Mr. Ohlsen. The snow was sufficiently thawed to make it almost unnecessary to use fire as a means of obtaining water: they could therefore dispense with tallow or alcohol, and could carry pemmican in far larger quantities.

Their sleeping bags were a very neat article of a light reindeer skin. The dogs were in excellent condition too, no longer footsore, but very well rested and completely broken, including the four from the Esquimaux, animals of great power and size. Two of these, the stylish leaders of the team, a span of thoroughly wolfish iron grays, have the most powerful and wild beast-like bound that I have seen in animals of their kind.

"I made up the orders of the party on the nineteenth, the first day that I was able to mature a plan; and with commendable zeal they left the brig on the twentieth."

MAY 23, TUESDAY. "They have had superb weather, thank heaven!—a profusion of the most genial sunshine, bringing out the seals in crowds to bask around their breathing holes. A ptarmigan was killed today, a male, with two brown feathers on the back of his neck to indicate the return of his summer plumage.

"The winter is gone! The Andromeda has been found on shore under the snow, with tops vegetating and green! I have a shoot of it in my hand."

MAY 25, THURSDAY. "Bands of soft mist hide the tops of the hills: the unbroken transparency of last month's atmosphere has disappeared, and the sky has all the ashen or pearly obscurity of the Arctic summer."

MAY 27, SATURDAY. "Everything showing that the summer changes have commenced. The ice is rapidly losing its integrity, and a melting snow has fallen for the last two days—one of those comforting home snows that we have not seen for so long."

MAY 28, SUNDAY. "Our day of rest and devotion. It was a fortnight ago last Friday since our poor friend Pierre died. For nearly two months he had been struggling against the enemy with a resolute will and mirthful spirit that seemed sure of victory. But he sunk in spite of them.

"The last offices were rendered to him with the same careful ceremonial that we observed at Baker's funeral. There were fewer to walk in the procession; but the body was encased in a decent pine coffin and carried to Observatory Island, where it was placed side-by-side with that of his messmate. Neither could yet be buried; but it is hardly necessary to say that the frost has embalmed their remains. Dr. Hayes read the chapter from Job, which has consigned so many to their last resting place, and a little snow was sprinkled upon the face of the coffin. Pierre was a volunteer not only of our general expedition, but of the party with which he met his death blow. He was a gallant man, a universal favorite on board, always singing some ballad or other, and so elastic in his merriment that even in his last sickness he cheered all that were about him."

XII

Progress of the Season

Mᴀʏ 30, Tᴜᴇꜱᴅᴀʏ. "We are gleaning fresh water from the rocks, and the icebergs are beginning to show commencing streamlets. The great floe is no longer a Sahara, if still a desert. The floes are wet, and their snows dissolve readily under the warmth of the foot, and the old floe begins to shed fresh water into its hollows. Puddles of salt water collect around the ice-foot. It is now hardly recognizable—rounded, sunken, broken up with water pools overflowing its base. Its diminished crusts are so percolated by the saline tides, that neither tables nor broken fragments unite any longer by freezing. It is lessening so rapidly that we do not fear it any longer as an enemy to the brig. The berg indeed vanished long before the sun thermometers indicated a noon temperature above thirty-two degrees.

"By means of the Esquimaux stratagem of a white screen pushed forward on a sledge until the concealed hunter comes within range, Hans has shot four seals. We have more fresh meat than we can eat. For the past three weeks we have been living on ptarmigan, rabbits, two reindeer, and seal.

"They are fast curing our scurvy. With all these resources how can my thoughts now turn despairingly to poor John Franklin and the fate of his crew?

"Can they have survived? No man can answer with certainty; but no man without presumption can answer in the negative.

"If, four months ago—surrounded by darkness and bowed down by disease—I had been asked the question, I would have turned toward the black hills and the frozen sea, and responded in sympathy with them, 'No.' But with the return of light a savage people come down upon us, destitute of any but the rudest appliances of the chase, who were fattening on the most wholesome diet of the region, only forty miles from our anchorage, while I was denouncing its scarcity.

"For Franklin, everything depends on locality: but, from what I can see of Arctic exploration thus far, it would be very hard to find a circle of fifty miles' diameter entirely destitute of animal resources. The most solid winter-ice is open here and there in pools and patches worn by currents and tides. Such were the open spaces that Parry found in Wellington Channel; such are the stream holes (stromhols) of the Greenland coast, the polynia of the Russians; and such we have ourselves found in the most rigorous cold of all.

"To these spots, the seal, walrus, and the early birds crowd in numbers. One which kept open, as we find from the Esquimaux, at Littleton Island, only forty miles from us, sustained three families last winter until the opening of the north water. Now, if we have been entirely supported for the past three weeks by the hunting of a single man—seal meat alone being plentiful enough to subsist us till we turn homeward—certainly a party of tolerably skillful hunters might lay up an abundant stock for the winter. As it is, we are making caches of meat under the snow, to prevent its spoiling on our hands, in the very spot which a few days ago I described as a Sahara. And, indeed, it was so for nine whole months, when this flood of animal life burst upon us like fountains of water and pastures and date trees in a southern desert.

"I have undergone one change in opinion. It is of the ability of Europeans or Americans to inure themselves to an ultra-Arctic climate. God forbid, indeed, that civilized man should be exposed for successive years to this blighting darkness! But around the Arctic Circle, even as high as 72°, where cold and cold only is to be encountered, men may be acclimatized, for there is light enough for outdoor labor.

"Of the 136[1] picked men of Sir John Franklin in 1846, Northern Orkney men, Greenland whalers, so many young and hardy constitutions, with so much intelligent experience to guide them, I cannot realize that some may not yet be alive; that some small squad or squads, aided or not aided by the Esquimaux of the expedition, may not have found a hunting ground, and laid up from summer to summer enough of fuel and food and sealskins to brave three or even four more winters in succession."

June 1, Thursday. "At ten o'clock this morning the wailing of dogs outside announced the return of Dr.

[1] There actually were only 129 men on the Franklin expedition.

Hayes and William Godfrey. And a lamentable state of affairs it was. Both of them were completely snow blind, and the doctor had to be led to my bedside to make his report."

This journey connected the northern coast with the survey of my predecessor; but it disclosed no channel or any form of exit from this bay.

It convinced me, however, that such a channel must exist; for this great curve could be no cul-de-sac. Even were my observations since my first fall journey of September 1853 not decisive on this head, the general movement of the icebergs, the character of the tides, and the equally sure analogies of physical geography would point unmistakably to such a conclusion.

To verify it, I at once commenced the organization of a double party. This, which is called in my Report the Northeast Party, was to be assisted by dogs, but was to be subsisted as far as the Great Glacier by provisions carried by a foot party in advance.

* * * *

For the continuation of my plans I again refer to my journal.

JUNE 2, FRIDAY. "There is still this hundred miles wanting to the northwest to complete our entire circuit of this frozen water. This is to be the field for our next party. I am at some loss how to organize it; for myself, I am down with scurvy. Dr. Hayes is just from the field, worn out and snow blind. His health roll makes a sorry parade. It runs thus:

Officers

Mr. Brooks	Unhealed stump.
Mr. Wilson	do.
Mr. Sontag	Down with scurvy.
Mr. Bonsall	Scurvy knee, but mending.
Mr. Petersen	General scurvy.
Mr. Goodfellow	Scurvy.
Mr. Ohlsen	Well.
Mr. McGary	Well.

Crew

William Morton	Nearly recovered.
Thomas Hickey	Well.
George Whipple	Scurvy.
John Blake	Scurvy.
Hans Christian	Well.
George Riley	Sound.
George Stephenson	Scurvy from last journey.
William Godfrey	Snow blind.

JUNE 3, SATURDAY. "McGary, Bonsall, Hickey, and Riley were detailed for the first section of the new parties: they will be accompanied by Morton, who has orders to keep himself as fresh as possible, so as to enter on his own line of search to the greatest possible advantage. I keep Hans a while to recruit the dogs and do the hunting and locomotion for the rest of us; but I shall soon let him follow, unless things grow so much worse on board as to make it impossible.

"They start light, with a large thirteen-foot sledge, arranged with broad runners on account of the snow, and are to pursue my own last track, feeding at the caches which I deposited, and aiming directly for the glacier barrier on the Greenland side. Here, sustained as I hope by the remnants of the great cache of last fall, they will survey and attempt to scale the ice, to look into the interior of the great *mer de glace.*

"My notion is that the drift to the southward both of berg and floe, not being reinforced from the glacier, may leave an interval of smooth frozen ice; but if this route should fail, there ought still to be a chance by sheering to the southward and westward and looking out for openings among the hummocks.

"I am intensely anxious that this party should succeed: it is my last throw. They have all my views, and I believe they will carry them out unless overruled by a higher Power.

"Their orders are, to carry the sledge forward as far as the base of the Great Glacier and fill up their provisions from the cache of my own party of last May. Hans will then join them with the dogs; and while McGary and three men attempt to scale and survey the glacier, Morton and Hans will push to the north across the bay with the dog sledge and advance along the more distant coast. Both divisions are provided with clampers to steady them and their sledges on the irregular ice-surfaces; but I am not without apprehensions that, with all their efforts, the glacier cannot be surmounted.

"In this event, the main reliance must be on Mr. Morton: He takes a sextant, an artificial horizon, and a pocket chronometer; he also has intelligence, courage, and the spirit of endurance in full measure."

JUNE 5, MONDAY. "The last party are off: they left yesterday at 2:00 P.M. I can do nothing more but await the ice-changes that are to determine for us our liberation or continued imprisonment.

"The sun is shining bravely, and the temperature feels like a home summer."

JUNE 9, FRIDAY. "Today I was able to walk out upon the floe for the first time. I was very much struck by the condition of the floe-ice. Hitherto I have been dependent upon the accounts of my messmates, and believed that the work of thaw was going on with extreme rapidity. They are mistaken: we have a late season. The ice-foot has not materially changed either in breadth or level, and its base has been hardly affected at all, except by the overflow of the tides. The floe, though undergoing the ordinary molecular changes which accompany elevation of temperature, shows less surface change than the Lancaster Sound ices in early May. All this, but especially the condition of the ice-foot, warns me to prepare for the contingency of not escaping. It is a momentous warning. We have no coal for a second winter here; our stock of fresh provisions is utterly exhausted; and our sick need change, as essential to their recovery."

* * * *

JUNE 10, SATURDAY. "Hans was ordered yesterday to hunt in the direction of the Esquimaux huts in the hope of determining the position of the open water. He did not return last night; but Dr. Hayes and Mr. Ohlsen, who were sent after him this morning with the dog sledge, found the hardy savage fast asleep not five miles from the brig. Alongside of him was a large usuk or bearded seal, (*P. barbata*,) shot, as usual, in the head. He had dragged it for seven hours over the ice-foot.

"Mr. Ohlsen and Dr. Hayes are off on an overland tramp. I sent them to inspect the open water to the southward. The immovable state of the ice-foot gives me anxiety: last year, a large bay above us was closed all summer, and the land-ice, as we find it here, is as perennial as the glacier."

JUNE 20, TUESDAY. "This morning, to my great surprise, Petersen brought me quite a handful of scurvy grass (*C. fenestrata*). In my fall list of the stinted flora here, it had quite escaped my notice. I felt grateful to him for his kindness, and, without the affectation of offering it to anyone else, ate it at once."

JUNE 21, WEDNESDAY. "A snow, moist and flaky, melting upon our decks and cleaning up the dingy surface of the great ice-plain with a new garment. We are at the summer solstice, the day of greatest solar light! Would that the traditionally verified but meteorologically disproved equinoctial storm could break upon us, to destroy the tenacious floes!"

JUNE 22, THURSDAY. "The ice changes slowly, but the progress of vegetation is excessively rapid. The growth on the rocky group near our brig is surprising."

June 23, Friday. "The eiders have come back: a pair were seen in the morning, soon followed by four ducks and drakes. The poor things seemed to be seeking breeding grounds, but the ice must have scared them. They were flying southward."

June 25, Sunday. "Walked on shore and watched the changes: andromeda in flower, poppy and ranunculus the same: saw two snipe and some tern.

"Mr. Ohlsen returned from a walk with Mr. Petersen. They saw reindeer and brought back a noble specimen of the king duck. It was a solitary male, resplendent with the orange, black, and green of his head and neck.

"Stephenson is better; and I think that a marked improvement, although a slow one, shows itself in all of us. I work the men lightly, and allow plenty of basking in the sun. In the afternoon we walk on shore, to eat such succulent plants as we can find amid the snow. The pyrola I have not found, nor the cochlearia, save in one spot, and then dwarfed. But we have the lychnis, the young sorrel, the andromeda, the draba, and the willow bark; this last an excellent tonic, and, in common with all the Arctic vegetable astringents, I think, powerfully antiscorbutic."

XIII

No Retreat

Mr. Morton left the brig with the relief party of McGary on the fourth of June. He took his place at the track-lines like the others; but he was ordered to avoid all extra labor, so as to husband his strength for the final passage of the ice.

On the fifteenth he reached the base of the Great Glacier, and on the sixteenth was joined by Hans with the dogs. A single day was given to feed and refresh the animals, and on the eighteenth the two companies parted. Morton's account I have not felt myself at liberty to alter.

Mr. Morton, after traveling due north over a solid area choked with bergs and frozen fields, was startled by the growing weakness of the ice: its surface became rotten and the snow wet and pulpy. His dogs, seized with terror, refused to advance. Then for the first time the fact broke upon him, that a long dark band seen to the north beyond a protruding cape—Cape Andrew Jackson—was water. With danger and difficulty he retraced his steps and, reaching sound ice, made good his landing on a new coast.

The journeys which I had made myself, and those of my different parties, had shown that an unbroken surface of ice covered the entire sea to the east, west, and south. From the southernmost ice, seen by Dr. Hayes only a few weeks before, to the region of this mysterious water, was, as the crow flies, 106 miles. But for the unusual sight of birds and the unmistakable giving way of the ice beneath them, they would not have believed in the evidence of eyesight. Neither Hans nor Morton was prepared for it.

Landing on the cape, and continuing their exploration, new phenomena broke upon them. They were on the shores of a channel, so open that a frigate, or a fleet of frigates, might have sailed up it. The ice, already broken and decayed, formed a sort of horseshoe-shaped beach, against which the waves broke in surf. As they traveled north, this channel expanded into an iceless area; "for four or five small pieces"—lumps—were all that could be seen over the entire surface of its white-capped waters. Viewed from the cliffs and taking thirty-six miles as the mean radius open to reliable survey, this sea had a justly-estimated extent of more than four thousand square miles.

Animal life, which had so long been a stranger to us to the south, now burst upon them. At Rensselaer Harbor, except the Netsik seal or a rarely encountered Harelda, we had no life available for the hunt. But here the Brent goose (*Anas bernicla*), the eider, and the king duck were so crowded together that our Esquimaux killed two at a shot with a single rifle ball.

The Brent goose had not been seen since entering Smith's Straits. It is well known to the Polar traveler as a migratory bird of the American continent. Like the others of the same family, it feeds upon vegetable matter, generally on marine plants with their adherent molluscous life. It is rarely or never seen in the interior and, from its habits may be regarded as singularly indicative of open water. The flocks of this bird, easily distinguished by their wedge-shaped line of flight, now crossed the water obliquely and disappeared over the land to the north and east. I had shot these birds on the coast of Wellington Channel in latitude 74°50', nearly six degrees to the south; they were flying in the same direction.

The rocks on shore were crowded with sea-swallows (*Sterna Artica*), birds whose habits require open water, and they were already breeding.

It may interest others besides the naturalist that all of these birds occupied the southern limits of the channel for the first few miles after reaching open water; but as the party continued their progress to the north, they disappeared and marine birds took their place. The gulls were now represented by no less than four species. The kittiwakes (*Larus tridactylis*)—reminding Morton of "old times in Baffin's Bay"—were again stealing fish from the water, probably the small whiting (*Merlangus Polaris*) and their grim cousins, the burgomasters, enjoying the dinner thus provided at so little cost to themselves. It was a picture of life all round.

It is another remarkable fact that, as they continued their journey, the land-ice and snow, which had served as a sort of pathway for their dogs, crumbled and melted, and at last ceased altogether; so that, during the final stages of their progress, the sledge was rendered useless, and Morton found himself at last toiling over rocks and along the beach of a sea, which like the familiar waters of the south, dashed in waves at his feet.

Here for the first time he noticed the Arctic Petrel (*Procellaria glacialis*), a fact which shows the accuracy of his observation, though he was then unaware of its importance. This bird had not been met with since we left the North Water of the English whalers, more than two hundred miles south of the position on which he stood. Its food is essentially marine, the acalephae, &c. &c.; and it is seldom seen in numbers, except in the highways of open water frequented by the whale and the larger representatives of ocean life. They were in numbers, flitting and hovering over the crests of the waves, like their relatives of kinder climates, the Cape of Good Hope Pigeons, Mother Carey's Chickens, and the petrels everywhere else.

As Morton, leaving Hans and his dogs, passed between Sir John Franklin Island and the narrow beach-line, the coast became more wall-like, and dark masses of porphyritic rock abutted into the sea. With growing difficulty, he managed to climb from rock to rock, in hopes of doubling the promontory and sighting the coasts beyond, but the water kept encroaching more and more on his track.

It must have been an imposing sight as he stood at this termination of his journey, looking out upon the great waste of waters before him. Not a "speck of ice," to use his own words, could be seen. There, from a height of 480 feet, which commanded a horizon of almost forty miles, his ears were gladdened with the novel music of crashing waves; and a surf, breaking in among the rocks at his feet, stayed his farther progress.

Beyond this cape all is surmise. The high ridges to the northwest dwindled off into low blue knobs, which blended finally with the air. Morton called the cape, which baffled his labors, after his commander; but I have given it the more enduring name of Cape Constitution.

The homeward journey, as it was devoted to the completion of his survey and developed no new facts I need not give. But I am reluctant to close my notice of this discovery of an open sea without adding that the details of Mr. Morton's narrative harmonized with the observations of all our party. I do not propose to discuss here the causes or conditions of this phenomenon. How far it may extend—whether it exists simply as a feature of the immediate region or as part of a great and unexplored area communicating with a Polar Basin—and what may be the argument in favor of one or the other hypothesis, or the explanation which reconciles it with established laws—may be questions for men skilled in scientific deductions. Mine has been the more humble duty of recording what we saw. Coming as it did, a mysterious fluidity in the midst of vast plains of solid ice, it was calculated to arouse emotions of the highest order; and I do not believe there was a man among us who did not long for the means of embarking upon its bright and lonely waters. But those who follow our story will feel that a controlling need made the desire a fruitless one.

An open sea near the Pole, or even an open Polar basin, has been the topic of theory for a long time, and has been shadowed forth to some extent by actual or supposed discoveries. As far back as the days of Barentz, in 1596, without referring to the earlier and more uncertain chronicles, water was seen to the eastward of the northernmost cape of Novaia Zemlia[1]; and, until its limited extent was defined by direct observation, it was assumed to be the sea itself. The Dutch fishermen above and around Spitzbergen pushed their adventurous cruises through the ice into open spaces that varied in size and form with the season and the winds; and Dr. Scoresby, a venerated authority, alludes to such vacancies in the floe as pointing in argument to a freedom of movement from the north, inducing open water in the area or neighborhood of the Pole. Baron Wrangell, when forty miles from the coast of Arctic Asia, saw, as he thought, a "vast, illimitable ocean," forgetting for the moment how narrow are the limits of human vision on a sphere. So, still more recently, Captain Penny proclaimed a sea in Wellington Sound, on the very spot where Sir Edward Belcher has since left his frozen ships; and my predecessor Captain Inglefield, from the mast-head of his little vessel, announced an "open Polar Basin," but fifteen miles off from the ice that arrested our progress the next year.

[1] Novaya Zemlya

All these discoveries were no doubt chronicled with perfect integrity; and it may seem to others, as since I have left the field it sometimes does to myself, that my own, though on a larger scale may one day pass within the same category. Unlike the others, however, that which I have ventured to call an open sea has been traveled for many miles along its coast, and was viewed from an elevation of 580 feet, still without a limit, moved by a heavy swell, free of ice, and dashing in surf against a rock-bound shore.

It is impossible in reviewing the facts which connect themselves with this discovery—the melted snow upon the rocks, the crowds of marine birds, the limited but still advancing vegetable life, the rise of the thermometer in the water—not to be struck with their bearing on the question of a milder climate near the Pole. To refer them all to the modification of temperature induced by the proximity of open water is only to change the form of the question; for it leaves the inquiry unsatisfied—what is the cause of the open water?

This, however, is not the place to enter upon such a discussion. There is no doubt on my mind that at a time within historical and even recent limits, the climate of this region was milder than it is now. I might base this opinion on the fact, abundantly developed by our expedition, of a secular elevation of the coastline. But, independently of the ancient beaches and terraces and other geological marks which show that the shore has risen, the stone huts of the natives are found scattered along the line of the bay in spots now so fenced in by ice as to preclude all possibility of the hunt and, of course, of habitation by men who rely on it for subsistence.

Tradition points to these as once favorite hunting grounds near open water. At Rensselaer Harbor, called by the natives *Aunatok*, or the Thawing-place, we met with huts in quite tolerable preservation, with the stone pedestals that used to sustain the carcasses of the captured seals and walrus still standing. Sunny Gorge, and a large indentation in Dallas Bay that bears the Esquimaux name of the Inhabited Place, showed us the remains of a village surrounded by the bones of seals, walrus, and whales—all now cased in ice. In impressive connection with the same facts, showing not only the former extension of the Esquimaux race to the higher north, but the climatic changes that may perhaps be still in progress there, is the sledge-runner that Mr. Morton saw on the shores of Morris Bay in latitude 81°. It was made of the bone of a whale, and worked out with skillful labor.

In this recapitulation of facts, I am not entering upon the question of a warmer climate impressed upon this region in virtue of a physical law that extends the isotherms toward the Pole. Still less am I disposed to express an opinion as to the influence ocean-currents may exert on the temperature of these far-northern regions: there is at least one man, an officer in the same service with myself, and whose scientific investigations do it honor, with whom I am content to leave that discussion. But I would respectfully suggest to those whose opportunities facilitate the inquiry, whether it may not be that the Gulf Stream traced already to the coast of Novaia Zemlia, is deflected by that peninsula into the space around the Pole. It would require a change in the mean summer temperature of only a few degrees to develop the periodical recurrence of open water. The conditions that define the line of perpetual snow and the limits of the glacier formation may have certainly a proximate application to the problem of such water-spaces near the Pole.[2]

For more than two months we had been imprisoned in ice and throughout all that period, except during the enforced holiday of the midwinter darkness or while repairing from actual disaster, had been constantly in the field. The summer was wearing on, but still the ice did not break up as it should. As far as we could see, it remained inflexibly solid between us and the North Water of Baffin's Bay. The questions and speculations of those around me began to show that they too had anxious thoughts for the coming year.

JULY 8, SATURDAY. "I know by experience how soon the ice breaks up after it once begins to go, and I hardly think that it can continue advancing so slowly much longer. Indeed, I look for it to open, if it opens at all, about the beginning of September at farthest, somewhere near the date of Sir James Ross's liberation at Leopold. But then I have to remember that I am much farther to the north than my predecessors, and that by

[2]For discussion of Open Polar Sea, see "Historical Introduction."

the twenty-eighth of last August I had already, after twenty days of unremitting labor, forced the brig nearly forty miles through the pack, and that the pack began to close on us only six days later, and that on the seventh of September we were fairly frozen in. Yet last summer was a most favorable one for ice melting. Putting all this together, it looks as if the winter must catch us before we can get halfway through the pack, even though we should begin warping to the south at the earliest moment that we can hope for water.

"It is not a pleasant conclusion of the argument; for there never was, and I trust never will be, a party worse armed for the encounter of a second Arctic winter. We have neither health, fuel, nor provisions. Dr. Hayes, and indeed all I have consulted about it indirectly, despond at the thought; and when I look round upon our diseased and disabled men, and think of the fearful work of the last long night, I am tempted to feel as they do.

"The alternative of abandoning the vessel at this early stage of our absence, even if it were possible, would, I feel, be dishonoring; but resolving the question as one of practicability alone, I would not undertake it. In the first place, how are we to get along with our sick and newly amputated men? It is a dreary distance, at the best, to Upernavik or Beechey Island[3], our only seats of refuge, and a precarious traverse if

[3]Beechey Island was a small island in the Arctic Archipelago where an early search and rescue expedition found the first signs of the Franklin Expedition, including the graves of three sailors who had died in the winter of 1846. It later became a base for the many search and rescue expeditions.

we were all fit for moving; but we are hardly one-half in efficiency of what we count in number. Besides, how can I desert the brig while there is still a chance of saving her? There is no use of noting pros and cons: my mind is made up; I will not do it.

"But I must examine this ice-field for myself. I have been maturing through the last fortnight a scheme of relief, based upon a communication with the English squadron to the south, and tomorrow I set out to reconnoiter. Hans will go with me. We will fit out our poor travel-worn dogs with canvas shoes and cross the floes to the true water edge, or at least be satisfied that it is impossible. 'He sees best who uses his own eyes.' After that I have my course resolved on."

JULY 11, TUESDAY. "We got back last night: a journey of sixty miles—comfortless enough, with only three hours' sleep on the ice. For thirty-five miles south the straits are absolutely tight. Off Refuge Inlet and Esquimaux Point we found driving leads; but between these points and the brig, not a crack. I pushed the dogs over the drift-ice, and, after a fair number of mischances, found the North Water. It was flowing and free; but since McGary saw it last May, it has not advanced more than four miles. It would be absurd at this season of the year to attempt escaping in open boats with this ice between us and water. All that can be done is to reinforce our energies as we may and look the worst in the face.

"In view of these contingencies, I determined to attempt in person to communicate with Beechey Island, or at least make the effort. If I can reach Sir Edward Belcher's squadron, I am sure of all that I want. I will take a light whaleboat and pick my companions for a journey to the south and west. I may find perhaps the stores of the *North Star* at the Wostenholm Islands, or by great good luck come across some passing vessel of the squadron, and make known our whereabouts and wants; or, failing these, we will try and coast it along to Wellington Channel.

"A depot of provisions and a seaworthy craft large enough to carry us—if I had these, everything would be right. Even Sir John Ross's launch, the Little Mary, which he left at Union Bay, would serve our purpose. If I had her, I could make a southern passage after the fall tides. The great enemy of that season is the young shore-ice, which would cut through our frail boats like a saw. Or, if we can only renew our stock of provisions for the winter, we may await the chances of next year.

"I know it is hazardous venture, but it is a necessary one, and under the circumstances an incumbent duty. I should have been glad, for some reasons, if the command of such an attempt could have been delegated to a subordinate; but I feel that I have no right to devolve this risk upon another, and I am, besides, the only one possessed of the necessary local knowledge of Lancaster Sound and its ice-movements.

"As a prelude to this solemn undertaking, I met my officers in the evening and showed them my ice-charts; explaining what I found needed little explanation, the prospect immediately before us. I then discussed the probable changes, and, giving them my personal opinion that the brig might after all be liberated at a late date, I announced my project. I will not say how gratified I was with the manner in which they received it. It struck me that there was a sense of personal relief experienced everywhere. I told them that I did not choose to call a council or connect any of them with the responsibilities of the measure, for it involved only the personal safety of those who chose to share the risk. Full instructions were then left for their guidance during my absence.

"It was the pleasantest interview I ever had with my associates. I believe every man on board would have volunteered, but I confined myself to five active men: James McGary, William Morton, George Riley, Hans Christian, and Thomas Hickey make up my party."

Our equipment had been getting ready for some time, though without its object being understood or announced. The boat was our old *Forlorn Hope,* mended up and revised for her new destinies. She was 23 feet long, had a 6¼ foot beam, and was 2¼ feet deep. Her build was the characteristic one of the American whaleboats, too flat-bottomed for ordinary use, but much improved by a false keel, which Ohlsen had given her throughout her entire length. After all, she was a mere cockle shell.

Her great fault was her knife-like bow, which cut into the short seas most cruelly. To remedy this in some degree, and to make up for her want of height, I devised a sort of half deck of canvas and gum elastic cloth, extending back beyond the foremast and continued along the gunwale—a sort of weather cloth that might possibly add to her safety and would certainly make her more comfortable in heavy weather.

I left her rig altogether to McGary. She carried what anyone but a New London whaler would call an inordinate spread of canvas, a light cotton foresail of twelve feet lift, a stouter mainsail of fourteen feet lift with a spreet eighteen feet long and a snug little jib. Her masts were, of course, selected very carefully, for we could not carry extra sticks: and we trusted to the good old-fashioned steering oar rather than a rudder.

Morton, who was in my confidence from the first, had all our stores ready. We had no game, and no meat but pork, of which we took some 150 pounds. I wanted pemmican, and sent the men out in search of the cases left on the floe by the frozen depot party during the rescue of last March; but they could not find a trace of them, or indeed of anything else we abandoned at that time: a proof, if we wanted one, of how blurred all our faculties must have been by suffering, for we marked them as we thought with marvelous care.

We lifted our boat over the side in the afternoon and floated her to the crack at the Observatory Island; mounted her there on our large sledge, "The Faith," by arrangement of cradles of Mr. Ohlsen's devising, we stowed in everything but the provisions, and carried her on to the bluff of Sylvia Headland; and the next morning a party consisting of all but the sick was detailed to transport her to open water, while McGary, Hans, and myself followed with our St. John's sledge carrying our stores.

The surface of the ice was very irregular and covered with water pools. Our sledge broke down with repeated strainings, and we had a fatiguing walk of thirty-six miles to get another. We passed the first night wet and supperless on the rocks; a bad beginning, for the next day found us stiff and out of sorts.

The ice continued troublesome, the land-ices swaying hither and thither with the tide. The second day's progress, little as it was, cost us very hard labor. But another night of repose on the rocks refreshed us; so that, the day after, we were able to make about seven miles along the ice-belt. Two days more, and we had carried the boat across twenty miles of heavy ice-floe, and launched her in open water. It was not far from the hut on Esquimaux Point.

The straits were much clogged with drift, but I followed the coast southward without difficulty. We traveled at night, resting when the sun was hottest. I had every reason to be pleased with the performance of the whaleboat, and the men kept up their spirits well. We landed at the point where we left our lifeboat a year ago, and to our great joy found it untouched: the cove and inlet were still fast in ice.

We now neared the Littleton Island of Captain Inglefield, where a piece of good fortune awaited us. We saw a number of ducks, both eiders and hareldas; and it occurred to me that by tracking their flight we should reach their breeding grounds. There was no trouble in doing so, for they flew in a beeline to a group of rocky islets, above which the whole horizon was studded with birds. A rugged little ledge, which I named Eider Island, was so thickly colonized that we could hardly walk without treading on a nest. We killed with guns and stones over two hundred birds in a few hours.

It was near the close of the breeding season. The nests were still occupied by the mother birds, but many of the young had burst the shell, and were nestling under the wing, or taking their first lessons in the water pools. Some, more advanced, were already in the ice-sheltered channels, greedily waiting for the shell fish and sea urchins, which the old bird busied herself in procuring for them.

Nearby was a low and isolated rock ledge, which we called Hans Island. The glaucous gulls, those cormorants of the Arctic seas, had made it their peculiar homestead. Their progeny, already full fledged and voracious, crowded the guano-whitened rocks; and the mothers, with long necks and gaping yellow bills, swooped above the peaceful shallows of the eiders, carrying off the young birds, seemingly just as their wants required. A more domineering and insatiable rapacity I have never witnessed. The gull would gobble up and swallow a young eider in less time than it takes me to describe the act. For a moment you would see the paddling feet of the poor little wretch protruding from the mouth; then came a distension of the neck as it descended into the stomach; a few moments more, and the hungry young gulls were feeding on the ejected morsels.

The mother duck, although distracted, battles, and battles well; but she cannot always reassemble her brood; and in her efforts to defend one, uncovering the others, I have seen her left as destitute as Niobe. Hans tells me that in such cases she adopts a new progeny; and, as he is well versed in the habits of the bird, I see no reason to doubt his assertion.

I could sentimentalize on these bereavements of the ducks and their companions in diet: it would be only the every day sermonizing of the world. But while the gulls were fattening their young on the eiders, the eiders were fattening theirs on the lesser life of the sea, and we were as busily engaged upon both in true predatory sympathy. The squab gull of Hans Island has a well-earned reputation in South Greenland for its delicious juices, and the eggs of Eider Island can well afford to suffer from the occasional visits of gulls and other bipeds; for a locust swarm of foragers might fatten without stint on their surplus abundance.

We camped at this nursery of wild fowl, and laid in four large India rubber bags full, cleaned and rudely boned. Our boat was hauled up and refitted; and, the trial having shown us that she was too heavily laden for safety, I made a general reduction of our stores and cached the surplus under the rocks.

On Wednesday, the nineteenth, we left Flagstaff Point, where we fixed our beacon last year; and stood

W10°S under full canvas. My aim was to take the channel obliquely at Littleton Island; and, making the drift-ice or the land to the southwest in the neighborhood of Cape Combermere, push on for Kent Island and leave a cairn there.

Toward night the wind freshened from the northward, and we passed beyond the protection of the straits into the open seaway. My journal gives no picture of our new life. The oldest sailor, who treads the deck of his ship with the familiar confidence of a man at home, has a distrust of open boat navigation that a landsman hardly shares. The feeling grew upon us as we lost the land. McGary was an old Behring's Straits whaler, and there is no better boatman in the world than he; but I know that he shared my doubts, as the boat buried herself again and again in the trough of a short chopping sea, which taxed all his dexterity in steering to meet.

Baffin passed around this gulf in 1616 with two small vessels; but they were giants beside ours. I thought of them as we crossed his track steering for Cape Combermere, then about sixty miles distant, with every prospect of a heavy gale.

We were in the center of this large area of open water when the gale broke upon us from the north. We were near foundering. Our false bow of India rubber cloth was beaten in, and our frail weather boarding soon followed it. With the utmost exertion we could hardly keep our boat from broaching to: a broken oar or an accidental twitch would have been fatal to us at any time. But McGary handled that whaler's marvel, the long steering oar, with admirable skill. None of us could pretend to take his place. For twenty-two unbroken hours he stuck to his post without relaxing his attention or his efforts.

I was not prepared for such a storm. I do not think I have seen a worse sea raised by the northers of the Gulf of Mexico. At last the wind hauled to the eastward, and we were glad to drive before it for the inshore floes. We had passed several bergs; but the sea dashed against their sides so furiously as to negate all hope of protection at their base: the pack or floe, so much feared before, was now looked to for a refuge.

I remember well our anxiety as we entered the loose streams of drift after four hours' scudding, and our relief when we felt their influence upon the sea. We fastened to an old floe not quite fifty yards in diameter and, with the surf breaking over our heads, rode out the storm under a warp and grapnel.

* * * *

The obstacle we had now to encounter was the pack that stretched between us and the south.

When the storm abated, we commenced boring into it—slow work at the best of times; but my companions encountered it with a persevering activity quite as admirable as their fortitude in danger. It had its own hazards too; and more than once it looked as if we were permanently beset. I myself knew that we might rely on the southerly wind to liberate us from such an imprisonment; but I saw that the men thought otherwise, as the ice-fields closed around us and the horizon showed an unchanging circle of ice.

We were still laboring on, hardly past the middle of the bay, when the floes began to relax. On Sunday, the twenty-third of July, the whole aspect around us changed. The sun came out cheeringly, the leads opened more and more, and, as we pulled through them to the south, each ice-tongue that we doubled brought us nearer to the Greenland shore. A slackening of the ice to the east enabled us after a while to lay our course for Hakluyt Island. We spread our canvas again, and reached the inshore fields by one in the afternoon. We made our camp, dried our buffalo skins, and sunned and slept away our fatigue.

I was confident that I should find the "Eastern Water" if I could only reach Cape Parry, and that this would give me a free track to Cary Islands. I therefore looked anxiously for a fissure in the pack, and pressed our little craft into the first one that seemed at all practicable.

For the next three days we worked painfully through the half-open leads, making in all some fifteen miles to the south. We had very seldom room enough to row; but, as we tracked along, it was not difficult to escape nippings by hauling up the boat on the ice. Still she received some hard knocks, and a twist or two that did not help her seaworthiness; she began to leak, and this, with the rain that fell heavily, forced us to bale her out every other hour. Of course, we could not sleep, and one of our little party fell sick with the unmitigated fatigue.

On the thirty-first, at the distance of ten miles from Cape Parry, we came to a dead halt. A solid mass lay directly across our path, extending onward to our farthest horizon. There were bergs in sight to the westward, and by walking for some four miles over the moving floe in that direction, McGary and myself succeeded in reaching one. We climbed it to the height of 120 feet, and, looking out from it, we saw that all within a radius of thirty miles was a motionless, unbroken, and impenetrable sea.

I had not counted on this. Captain Inglefield found open water two years before at this very point. I myself met no ice here only seven days later in 1853. Yet it was plain, that from Cape Combermere on the west side and an unnamed bay immediately to the north of it across to Hakluyt Island, there extended a continuous barrier of ice. We had scarcely penetrated beyond its margin.

We had, in fact, reached the dividing pack of the two great open waters of Baffin's Bay. The experience of the whalers and of the expedition ships that have traversed this region have made all of us familiar with that great expanse of open sea to the north of Cape Dudley Digges, which has received the name of the North Water. Combining the observations of Baffin, Ross, and Inglefield, we know that this sometimes extends as far north as Littleton Island, embracing an area of ninety thousand square miles. The voyagers I have named could not, of course, be aware of the fact that this water is divided, at least occasionally, into two distinct bodies; the one comprehended between Lancaster and Jones's Sounds, the other extending from the point we had now reached to the upper pack of Smith's Straits. But it was evident to all that the barrier that now arrested us was made up of the ices that Jones's Sound on the west and Murchison's on the east had discharged and driven together.

It was obvious that a further attempt to penetrate to the south must be hopeless till the ice-barrier before us should undergo a change. I had observed, when passing Northumberland Island, that some of its glacier slopes were margined with verdure, an almost unfailing indication of animal life; and, as my men were much wasted by diarrhea and our supplies of food had become scanty, I resolved to work my way to the island and recruit therefore another effort.

Tracking and sometimes rowing through a heavy rain, we traversed the leads for two days, working eastward; and on the morning of the third gained the open water near the shore. Here a breeze came to our aid, and in a couple of hours more we passed with now unwonted facility to the southern face of the island. We met several flocks of auks as we approached it, and found on landing that it was one enormous homestead of the auks, dovekies, and gulls.

We encamped on the thirty-first, on a low beach at the foot of a moraine that came down between precipitous cliffs of surpassing wildness. It had evidently been selected by the Esquimaux for a winter settlement: five well-built huts of stone attested to this. Three of them were still tolerably perfect, and bore marks of recent habitation. The droppings of the birds had fertilized the soil, and it abounded in grasses, sorrel, and cochlearia to the water's edge. The foxes were about in great numbers, attracted, of course, by the abundance of birds. They were all of them of the lead-colored variety, without a white one among them. The young ones, as yet lean and seemingly unskilled in hospitable courtesies, barked at us as we walked about.

Gulls

XIV

Losing Hope

I T WAS with mingled feelings that we neared the brig. Our little party had grown fat and strong upon the auks and eiders and scurvy grass; and surmises were rife among us as to the condition of our comrades and the prospects of our ice-bound little ship.

The tide leads, which one year ago had afforded a precarious passage to the vessel, now barely admitted our whaleboat; and, as we forced her through the broken ice, she showed such signs of hard usage that I had her hauled up upon the land belt and housed under the cliffs at Six-Mile Ravine. We crossed the rocks on foot, aided by our jumping poles, and startled our shipmates by our sudden appearance.

In the midst of the greeting that always met our returning parties, and that gave to our little vessel the endearing associations of a homestead, our thoughts turned to the feeble chances of our liberation, and the failure of our recent effort to secure a retreat.

The brig had been imprisoned by closely cementing ice for eleven months, during which period she had not budged an inch from her icy cradle. My journal will show the efforts and the hopes which engrossed our few remaining days of uncertainty and suspense:

AUGUST 8, TUESDAY. "This morning two saw lines were passed from the open water pools at the sides of our sternpost, and the ice was bored for blasting. In the course of our operations the brig surged and righted, rising 2½ feet. We are now trying to warp her a few yards toward Butler Island, where we again go to work with our powder canisters."

AUGUST 11, FRIDAY. "Returned yesterday from an inspection of the ice toward the Esquimaux settlements.

"As I traveled back along the coast, I observed the wonderful changes brought about by the disruption of the pack. It was my hope to have extricated the brig, if she was ever to be liberated, before the drift had choked the land leads; but now they are closely jammed with stupendous ice-fragments, records of inconceivable pressures. The bergs, released from their winter cement, have driven down in crowds, grounding on the shallows, and extending in reefs or chains out to seaward, where they have caught and retained the floating ices. The prospect was really desolation itself. One floe measured nine feet in mean elevation above the water level; thus implying a tabular thickness by direct congelation of sixty-three feet. It had so closed in with the shore, too, as to rear up a barricade of crushed ice, which it was futile to attempt to pass. All prospect of forcing a passage ceased north of Six-Mile Ravine.

"On reaching the brig, I found that the blasting had succeeded: one canister cracked and uplifted two hundred square yards of ice with but five pounds of powder. A prospect showed itself of getting inside the island at high water; and I determined to attempt it at the highest spring tide, which takes place on the twelfth."

AUGUST 12, SATURDAY. "The brig bore the strain of her new position very well. The tide fell fifteen feet, leaving her high and dry; but, as the water rose, everything was replaced, and the deck was put in order for warping again. Everyone in the little vessel turned to; and after much excitement, at the very top of the tide, she passed 'by the skin of her teeth.' She was then warped into a bight of the floe near Fox Trap Point, and there she now lies.

"We congratulated ourselves upon effecting this crossing. Had we failed, we should have had to remain fast probably for the high tides a fortnight hence. The young ice is already making, and our hopes rest mainly upon the gales of late August and September."

AUGUST 13, SUNDAY. "Still fast to the old floe near Fox Trap Point, waiting a heavy wind as our only means of liberation. The land trash is cemented by young ice, which is already an inch-and-a-half thick. The thermometer has been as low as twenty-nine degrees; but the fog and mist that prevail today are in our favor. The perfect clearness of the past five days hastened the growth of young ice, and it has been forming without intermission."

AUGUST 15, TUESDAY. "Today I made another ice inspection to the northeast. The floe on which I have trudged, often the bay floe of our former mooring, is nearly the same as when we had left it. I recognized the holes and cracks through the fog by a sort of instinct. McGary and myself had little difficulty in reaching the Fiord Water by our jumping poles.

"I have my eye on this water; for it may connect with the Northeast Headland and hereafter give us passage.

"The season travels on: the young ice grows thicker, and my messmates' faces grow longer every day. I have again to play buffoon to keep up the spirits of the party.

"A raven! The snowbirds begin to fly to the south in groups, coming at night to our brig to hover on the rigging. Winter is hurrying upon us. The poppies are quite wilted.

"Examined ice with Mr. Bonsall and determined to enter the broken land-ices by warping; not that there is the slightest probability of getting through, but it affords moral aid and comfort to the men and officers: it looks as if we were doing something."

AUGUST 17, THURSDAY. "Warped one hundred yards into the trash, and, after a long day of labor, have turned in, hoping to recommence at 5:00 A.M. tomorrow.

"In five days the spring tides come back: should we fail in passing with them, I think our fortunes are fixed. The young ice bore a man this morning: it had a bad look, this man supporting August ice! The temperature never falls below twenty-eight degrees but it is cold o'nights with no fire."

AUGUST 18, FRIDAY. "Reduced our allowance of wood to six pounds a meal. This, among eighteen mouths, is one-third of a pound of fuel for each. It allows us coffee twice a day and soup once. Our fare besides this is cold pork boiled in quantity and eaten as required. This sort of thing works badly; but I must save coal for other emergencies. I see 'darkness ahead.'

"I inspected the ice again today. Bad! bad!—I must face another winter. While we have a chance ahead, it is my first duty to have all things in readiness to meet it. It is *horrible*—yes, that is the word—to look forward to another year of disease and darkness to be met without fresh food and without fuel. I should meet it with a more tempered sadness if I had not comrades to think for and protect."

AUGUST 20, SUNDAY. "Rest for all hands. The daily prayer is no longer 'Lord, accept our gratitude and bless our undertaking,' but 'Lord, accept our gratitude and restore us to our homes.' The ice shows no change: after a boat and foot journey around the entire southeastern curve of the bay, no signs!"

* * * *

The birds had left their colonies. The water streams from the bergs and of the shore were freezing up rapidly. The young ice made the water surface impassable even to a whaleboat. It was clear to me that without an absolute change of circumstances, such as it was vain to look for any longer, to leave the ship would be to enter upon a wilderness destitute of resources, and from which it would be difficult, if not impracticable, to return.

Everything before us was involved in gloomy doubt.

Hopeful as I had been, it was impossible not to feel that we were finally and inevitably near the climax of the expedition.

I determined to place upon the Observatory Island a large signal beacon or cairn, and to bury under it documents which, in case of disaster to our party, would convey to any who might seek us intelligence of our proceedings and our fate. The memory of the first winter quarters of Sir John Franklin, and the painful feelings with which, while standing by the graves of his dead, I had five years before sought for written signs pointing to the fate of the living, made me careful to avoid a similar neglect.

A conspicuous spot was selected upon a cliff looking out upon the icy desert, and on a broad face of rock the words

ADVANCE,

A.D. 1853–54

were painted in letters which could be read at a distance. A pyramid of heavy stones, perched above it, was marked with the Christian symbol of the cross. It was not without a holier sentiment than that of mere utility that I placed under this the coffins of our two poor comrades. It was our beacon and their gravestone.

Near this a hole was worked into the rock and a paper, enclosed in glass, sealed in with melted lead. It read as follows:

"Brig *Advance,* August 14, 1854.

"E.K. Kane, with his comrades Henry Brooks, John Wall Wilson, James McGary, I.I. Hayes, Christian Ohlsen, Amos Bonsall, Henry Goodfellow, August Sontag, William Morton, J. Carl Petersen, George Stephenson, Jefferson Temple Baker, George Riley, Peter Schubert, George Whipple, John Blake, Thomas Hickey, William Godfrey, and Hans Christian, members of the Second Grinnell Expedition in search of Sir John Franklin and the missing crews of the *Erebus* and *Terror,* were forced into this harbor while endeavoring to bore the ice to the north and east.

"They were frozen in on the 8th of September, 1853, and liberated— — — —

"During this period the labors of the expedition have delineated nine hundred and sixty miles of coastline, without developing any traces of the missing ships or the slightest information bearing upon their fate. The amount of travel to effect this exploration exceeded two thousand miles, all of which was upon foot or by the aid of dogs.

"Greenland has been traced to its northern face, whence it is connected with the farther north of the opposite coast by a great glacier. This coast has been charted as high as latitude 82°27′. Smith's Sound expands into a capacious bay: it has been surveyed throughout its entire extent. From its northern and eastern corner, in latitude 80°10′, longitude 66°, a channel has been discovered and followed until farther progress was checked by water free from ice. This channel trended nearly due north, and expanded into an apparently open sea, which abounded with birds and bears and marine life.

"The death of the dogs during the winter threw the travel essential to the above discoveries upon the personal efforts of the officers and men. The summer finds them much broken in health and strength.

"Jefferson Temple Baker and Peter Schubert died from injuries received from cold while in manly performance of their duty. Their remains are deposited under a cairn at the north point of Observatory Island.

"The site of the observatory is seventy-six English feet from the northernmost salient point of this island, in a direction S 14°E. Its position is in latitude 78°37′10″, longitude 70°40′. The mean tidal level is twenty-nine feet below the highest point upon this island. Both of these sites are further designated by copper bolts sealed with melted lead into holes upon the rocks.

"On the 12th of August, 1854, the brig warped from her position, and, after passing inside the group of islands, fastened to the outer floe about a mile to the northwest, where she is now awaiting further changes in the ice.

Signed,

"E. K. Kane
"Commanding Expedition
"Fox-Trap Point, August 14, 1854"

Some hours later, the following note was added.

"The young ice having formed between the brig and this island, and prospects of a gale showing themselves, the date of departure is left unfilled. If possible, a second visit will be made to insert our dates, our final escape being still dependent upon the course of the season.

E. K. Kane"

And now came the question of the second winter:

How to look our enemy in the face, and how to meet him. Anything was better than inaction; and, in spite of the uncertainty which yet attended our plans, a host of expedients were to be resorted to, and much Robinson Crusoe labor ahead. Moss was to be gathered for eking out our winter fuel, and willow stems and stonecrops and sorrel, as antiscorbutics, collected and buried in the snow. But while all these were in progress came other and graver questions.

Some of my party had entertained the idea that an escape to the south was still practicable; and this opinion was supported by Mr. Petersen, our Danish interpreter, who had once accompanied the Searching Expedition of Captain Penny, and had a matured experience in the changes of Arctic ice. They even thought that the safety of all would be promoted by a withdrawal from the brig.

AUGUST 21, MONDAY. "The question of detaching a party was in my mind some time ago; but the more I thought it over, the more I was convinced that it would be neither right in itself nor practically safe. For myself personally, it is a simple duty of honor to remain by the brig: I could not think of leaving her till I had proved the effect of the later tides; and after that, as I have known all along, it would be too late. Come what may, I share her fortunes.

"But it is a different question with my associates. I cannot expect them to adopt my impulses; and I am sure that I ought to hold them bound by my conclusions. Have I the *moral right*? for, as to nautical rules, they do not fit the circumstances. For example, among the whalers, when a ship is hopelessly beset, the master's authority gives way, and the crew take counsel for themselves whether to go or stay by her. My party is subordinate and well disposed; but if the restlessness of suffering makes some of them anxious to brave the chances, they may certainly plead that a second winter in the ice was no part of the cruise they had ever bargained for.

"But what presses on me is of another character. I cannot disguise it from myself that we are wretchedly prepared for another winter on board. We are a set of scurvy riddled, broken down men; our provisions are sorely reduced in quantity, and are altogether unsuited to our condition. My only hope of maintaining or restoring such a degree of health among us as is indispensable to our escape in the spring has been and must be in a wholesome elastic tone of feeling among the men: a reluctant, brooding, disheartened spirit would sweep our decks like a pestilence. I fear the bane of depressing example.

"I know all this as a medical man and an officer; and I feel that we might be wearing away the hearts and energies, if not the lives of all, by forcing those who were reluctant to remain. With half a dozen confiding resolute men, I have no fears of ultimate safety.

"I will make a thorough inspection of the ice tomorrow, and decide finally the prospects of our liberation."

AUGUST 23, WEDNESDAY. "The brig cannot escape.

I got an eligible position with my sledge to review the floes, and returned this morning at two o'clock. There is no possibility of our release, unless by some extreme intervention of the incoming tides. I doubt whether a boat could be forced as far as the Southern Water. When I think of the extraordinary way in which the ice was impacted last winter, how very little it has yielded through the summer, and how early another winter is making its onset upon us, I am very doubtful, indeed, whether our brig can get away at all. It would be inexpedient to attempt leaving her now in boats; the water streams closing, the pack nearly fast again, and the young ice almost impenetrable.

"I shall call the officers and crew together, and tell them very fully how things look, and what hazards must attend such an effort as has been proposed among them. They shall have my views unequivocally expressed. I will then give them twenty-four hours to deliberate; and at the end of that time all who determine to go shall say so in writing, with a full exposition of the circumstances of the case. They shall have the best outfit I can give, an abundant share of our remaining stores, and my goodbye blessing."

AUGUST 24, THURSDAY. "At noon today I had all hands called and explained to them frankly the considerations that have determined me to remain where we are. I endeavored to show them that an escape to open water could not succeed, and that the effort must be exceedingly hazardous: I alluded to our duties to the ship: in a word, I advised them strenuously to

forego the project. I then told them that I should freely
give my permission to such as were desirous of making the attempt, but that I should require them to place
themselves under the command of officers selected
by them before setting out, and to renounce in writing all claims upon myself and the rest who were resolved to staying with the vessel. Having done this, I
directed the roll to be called, and each man to answer
for himself."

In the result, eight out of the seventeen survivors of
my party resolved to stand by the brig. It is just that I
should record their names for posterity. They were
Henry Brooks, James McGary, J.W. Wilson, Henry
Goodfellow, William Morton, Christian Ohlsen,
Thomas Hickey, Hans Christian.

I divided to the others their portion of our resources
justly and even liberally; and they left us on Monday,
the twenty-eighth, with every appliance our narrow
circumstances could furnish to speed and guard them.
One of them, George Riley, returned a few days afterward; but weary months went by before we saw the
rest again. They carried with them a written assurance of a brother's welcome should they be driven
back; and this assurance was redeemed when hard trials had prepared them to share again our fortunes.

XV

After Seal

THE PARTY moved off with the elastic step of men confident in their purpose, and were out of sight in a few hours. As we lost them among the hummocks, the stern realities of our condition pressed themselves upon us anew. The reduced numbers of our party; the helplessness of many; the waning efficiency of all; the impending winter with its cold, dark night; our penury of resources; the dreary sense of increased isolation—these made the staple of our thoughts. For a time, Sir John Franklin and his party, our daily topic through so many months, gave place to the question of our own fortunes—how we were to escape, how to live. The summer had gone, the harvest was ended, and—we did not care to finish the sentence.

Following close on this gloomy train and, in fact blending with it, came the more important discussion of our duties. We were like men driven to the wall, quickened, not depressed. Our plans were formed at once: there is nothing like emergency to speed, if not to instruct, the energies.

It was my first resolve that, come what might, our organization and its routine of observances should be adhered to strictly. It is the experience of every man who has either combated difficulties himself or who attempted to guide others through them, that the controlling law shall be systematic action. Nothing depresses and demoralizes so much as a surrender of the approved and habitual forms of life. I resolved that all should go on as it had done. The arrangement of hours, the distribution and details of duty, the religious exercises, the ceremonials of the table, the fires, the lights, the watch, even the labors of the observatory and the notation of the tides and the sky—nothing should be intermitted that had contributed to make up the day.

My next was to practice on the lessons we had learned from the Esquimaux. I had studied them carefully and determined that their form of habitations and their peculiarities of diet, without their unthrift and filth, were the safest and best to which the necessity of our circumstances invited us.

My journal tells how these resolves were carried out:

SEPTEMBER 6, WEDNESDAY. "We are at it, all hands, sick and well, each man according to his measure, working at our winter's home. We are none of us in condition to brave the frost, and our fuel is nearly out. I have determined to borrow a lesson from our Esquimaux neighbors, and am turning the brig into an igloo.

"The sledge is to bring us moss and turf from wherever the men can scrape it. This is an excellent non-conductor; and when we get the quarterdeck well padded with it we shall have a nearly cold-proof covering. Down below we will enclose a space some eighteen feet square, and pack it from floor to ceiling with inner walls of the same material. The floor itself we are caulking carefully with plaster of Paris and common paste, and will cover it when we have done with Manilla oakum a couple of inches deep, and a canvas carpet. The entrance is to be from the hold, by a low moss-lined tunnel, the *tossut* of the native huts, with as many doors and curtains to close it up as our ingenuity can devise. This is to be our apartment of all uses—not a very large one, but we are only ten to stow away, and the closer the warmer."

SEPTEMBER 9, SATURDAY. "All hands but the carpenter and Morton are out 'mossing.' Though it has a very May day sound, this mossing is a frightfully wintry operation. The mixed turf of willows, heaths, grasses, and moss is frozen solid. We cannot cut it out from the beds of the snow streams any longer, and are obliged to seek for it on the ledges of the rocks, quarrying it with crowbars and carrying it to the ship like so much stone. I would escape this labor if I could, for our party have all of them more or less scurvy in their systems, and the thermometer is often below zero. But there is no help for it. I have some eight sledge loads more to collect before our little home can be called wind proof: and then, if we only have snow enough to bank up against the brig's sides, I shall have no fear either for height or uniformity of temperature."

SEPTEMBER 10, SUNDAY. " 'The work goes bravely on.' We have got moss enough for our roof, and some to spare for below. Tomorrow we begin to strip off the outer deck planking of the brig, and to stack it for firewood. It is cold work, hatches open and no fires going; but we saved time enough for our Sunday's exercises, though we forego its rest.

"It is twelve months today since I returned from the weary foot tramp that determined me to try the winter search. Things have changed since then, and the prospect ahead is less cheery. But I close my pilgrim experience of the year with devout gratitude for the blessings it has registered, and an earnest faith in the support it pledges for the times to come."

SEPTEMBER 11, MONDAY. "Our stock of game is down to a mere mouthful—six long-tailed ducks not larger than a partridge and three ptarmigan. The rabbits have not yet come to us, and the foxes seem tired of touching our trap baits.

"I determined last Saturday to try a novel expedient for catching seal. Not more than ten miles to seaward the icebergs keep up a rude stream of broken ice and water, and the seals resort there in scanty numbers to breathe. I drove out with my dogs, taking Hans along; but we found the spot so hemmed in by loose and fragile ice that there was no approaching it. The thermometer was eight degrees, and a light breeze increased my difficulties.

"*Deo volente*, I will be more lucky tomorrow. I am going to take my long Kentucky rifle, the kayack, an Esquimaux harpoon with its attached line and bladder, and a pair of large snowshoes to boot. My plan this time is to kneel where the ice is unsafe, resting my weight on the broad surface of the snowshoes, Hans following astride of his kayack, as a sort of life preserver in case of breaking in. If I am fortunate enough to stalk within gun range, Hans will take to the water and secure the game before it sinks. We will be gone for some days probably, tenting it in the open air; but our sick men—that is to say, all of us—are languishing for fresh meat."

I started with Hans and five dogs, all we could muster from our disabled pack, and reached the "Pinnacly Berg" in a single hour's run. But where was the water? where were the seals? The floes had closed, and the crushed ice was all that told of our intended hunting ground.

Ascending a berg, however, we could see to the north and west the dark cloud stratus which betokens water. It ran through our old battleground, the "Bergy Belt,"—the labyrinth of our wanderings after the frozen party of last winter. I had not been over it since, and the feeling it gave me was anything but joyous.

But in a couple of hours we emerged upon a plain unlimited to the eye and smooth as a billiard table. Feathers of young frosting gave a plush like nap to its surface, and toward the horizon dark columns of frost smoke pointed clearly to the open water. This ice was firm enough: our experience satisfied us that it was not a recent freezing. We pushed on without hesitation, cheering ourselves with the expectation of coming upon the seals. We passed a second ice-growth.

It was not so strong as the one we had just come over, but it was still safe for a party like ours. On we went, at a brisker gallop, maybe for another mile, when Hans sang out at the top of his voice, "Pusey! puseymut! seal, seal!" At the same instant the dogs bounded forward, and, as I looked up, I saw crowds of gray netsik, the rough or hispid seal of the whalers, disporting in an open sea of water.

I had hardly welcomed the spectacle when I saw that we had passed upon a new belt of ice that was obviously unsafe. To the right and left and front was one great expanse of snow-flowered ice. The nearest solid floe was a mere lump, which stood like an island in the white level. To turn was impossible: we had to keep up our gait. We urged on the dogs with whip and voice, the ice rolling like leather beneath the sledge runners. It was more than a mile to the lump of solid ice. Fear gave to the poor beasts their utmost speed, and our voices were soon hushed to silence.

The suspense, unrelieved by action or effort, was intolerable: we knew that there was no remedy but to reach the floe, and that everything depended upon our dogs, and our dogs alone. A moment's check would plunge the whole concern into the rapid tideway: no presence of mind could avail us. The seals— for we were now near enough to see their expressive faces—were looking at us with that strange curiosity that seems to be their characteristic expression: we must have passed some fifty of them, breast-high out of water, mocking us by their self-complacency.

This desperate race against fate could not last: the rolling of the tough salt water ice terrified our dogs; and within fifty paces from the floe they paused. The left hand runner went through: Our leader "Toodlamick" followed, and in one second the entire left of the sledge was submerged. My first thought was to liberate the dogs. I leaned forward to cut poor Tood's traces, and the next minute was swimming in a little circle of pasty ice and water alongside him. Hans, dear good fellow, drew near to help me, uttering piteous expressions in broken English; but I ordered him to throw himself on his belly, with his hands and legs extended, and to make for the island.

I succeeded in cutting poor Tood's lines and letting him scramble to the ice, for the poor fellow was drowning me with his piteous caresses, and made my way for the sledge; but I found that it would not buoy me, and that I had no resource but to try the circumference of the hole. Around this I paddled faithfully, the miserable ice always yielding when my hopes of a lodgement were greatest. During this process I enlarged my circle of operations to a very uncomfortable diameter, and was beginning to feel weaker after every effort. Hans meanwhile had reached the firm ice, and was on his knees, like a good Moravian, praying incoherently in English and Esquimaux; at every fresh crushing in of the ice he would ejaculate "God!" and when I recommenced my paddling, he recommenced praying.

I was nearly gone. My knife had been lost in cutting out the dogs; and a spare one that I carried in my trousers pocket was so enveloped in the wet skins that I could not reach it. I owed my extrication at last to a newly broken team dog, which was still fast to the sledge and in struggling carried one of the runners chock against the edge of the circle. All my previous attempts to use the sledge as a bridge had failed, for it broke through, to the much greater injury of the ice. I felt that it was a last chance. I threw myself on my back, so as to lessen as much as possible my weight, and placed the nape of my neck against the rim or edge of the ice; then with caution slowly bent my leg, and placing the ball of my moccasined foot against the sledge, I pressed steadily against the runner.

Presently I felt that my head was pillowed by the ice, and that my wet fur jumper was sliding up the surface. Next came my shoulders; they were fairly on. One more decided push, and I was launched up on the ice and safe. I reached the ice-floe, and was frictioned by Hans with frightful zeal. We saved all the dogs; but the sledge, kayack, tent, guns, snowshoes, and everything besides, were left behind. The thermometer at eight degrees will keep them frozen fast in the sledge till we can come and cut them out.

On reaching the ship, after a twelve-mile trot, I found so much of comfort and warm welcome that I forgot my failure. The fire was lit up, and one of our few birds slaughtered forthwith. It is with real gratitude that I look back upon my escape, and bless the great presiding Goodness for the very many resources which remain to us.

XVI

A Theft and Then a Treaty

IT IS, I suppose the fortune of everyone who affects to register the story of an active life, that his record becomes briefer and more imperfect in proportion as the incidents press upon each other more rapidly and with increased excitement. The narrative is arrested as soon as the faculties are claimed for action, and the memory brings back reluctantly afterward those details which, though interesting at the moment, have not reflected themselves in the result. I find that my journal is exceedingly meager for the period of our anxious preparations to meet the winter, and that I have mentioned the course of circumstances that led us, step by step, into communication with the Esquimaux.

My last notice of this strange people, whose fortunes became afterward so closely connected with our own, was at the time of Myouk's escape from imprisonment on board the brig. Although during my absence on the attempted visit to Beechey Island, the men I had left behind had frequent and unrestrained intercourse with them, I myself did not see any natives in Rensselaer Bay until immediately after the departure of Petersen and his companions. Just then, by a coincidence that convinced me how closely we had been under surveillance, a party of three made their appearance, as if to note for themselves our condition and resources.

Times had indeed altered with us. We had parted with half our provisions, half our boats and sledges, and more than half our able-bodied men. It looked very much as if we were to lie ensconced in our ice-battered citadel, rarely venturing out for exploration or supplies. We feared nothing of course but the want of fresh meat, and it was much less important that our neighbors should fear us than that we should secure from them offices of kindness. They were overbearing sometimes, and needed the instruction of rebuke; but I treated them with carefully regulated hospitality.

When the three visitors came to us near the end of August, I established them in a tent below deck, with a copper lamp, a cooking basin, and a liberal supply of slush for fuel. I left them under guard when I went to bed at two in the morning, contentedly eating and cooking and eating again without the promise of an intermission. An American or a European would have slept after such a debauch till the recognized hour for hock and seltzer water. But our guests managed to elude the officer of the deck and escape unsearched. They repaid my liberality by stealing not only the lamp, boiler, and cooking pot they had used for the feast, but Nannook also, my best dog. If the rest of my team had not been worn down by travel, no doubt they would have taken them all. Besides this, we discovered the next morning that they had found the buffalo robes and India rubber cloth McGary had left a few days before on the ice-foot near Six-Mile Ravine, and had added the whole to the spoils of their visit.

The theft of these articles was an embarrassment to me. I was indisposed to take it as an act of hostility. Their pilferings before this had been conducted with such a superb simplicity, the detection followed by such honest explosions of laughter, that I could not help thinking they had some law of general appropriation. But it was plain at least that we were now too few to watch our property as we had done, and that our gentleness was to some extent misunderstood.

I was puzzled how to inflict punishment, but saw that I must act vigorously. I despatched my two best walkers, Morton and Riley, as soon as I heard of the theft of the stores, with orders to make all speed to Anoatok and overtake the thieves, who, I thought, would probably halt there to rest. They found young Myouk making himself quite comfortable in the hut, in company with Sievu, the wife of Metek; and Aningna, the wife of Marsinga; and my buffalo robes already tailored into kapetahs on their backs.

A continued search of the premises recovered the cooking utensils, and a number of other things of greater or less value that we had not missed from the brig. With the prompt ceremonial outraged law delights in among the officials of the police everywhere, the women were stripped and tied; and then, laden with their stolen goods and as much walrus beef besides from their own stores as would pay for their board, they were marched on the instant back to the brig to redeposit the stolen booty and settle amidst it.

The thirty miles was quite a hard walk for them; but they did not complain, nor did their constabulary guardians, who had marched thirty miles already to apprehend them. It was hardly twenty-four hours since they left the brig with their booty before they were prisoners in the hold, with a dreadful white man for keeper, who never addressed to them a word that had not all the terrors of an unintelligible reproof, and whose scowl, I flatter myself, exhibited a well-arranged variety of menacing and demoniacal expressions.

They had not even the companionship of Myouk. Him I had despatched to Metek, "headman of Etah, and others," with the message of a melodramatic tyrant, to negotiate for their ransom. For five long days the women had to sigh and sing and cry in solitary converse—their appetite continued to be excellent, it should be remarked, though mourning the while a rightfully impending doom. At last the great Metek arrived. He brought with him Ootuniah, another man of elevated social position, and a sledge-load of knives, tin cups, and other stolen goods, refuse of wood and scraps of iron, the sinful prizes of many covetings.

I may pass over our peace conferences and the indirect advantages I of course derived from having the opposing powers represented in my own capital. But the splendors of our Arctic center of civilization, with its wonders of art and science—our "fire death" ordnance included—could not all of them impress Metek so much as the intimations he had received of our superior physical endowments. Nomads as they are, these people know better than all the world besides what endurance and energy it requires to brave the moving ice and snowdrifts. Metek thought, no doubt, that our strength was gone with the withdrawing party: but the fact that within ten hours after the loss of our buffalo skins we had marched to their hut, seized three of their culprits, and marched them back to the brig as prisoners—such a sixty miles' achievement as this they thoroughly understood.

The protocol was arranged without much difficulty, though not without the accustomed number of adjournments for festivity and repose. It abounded in protestations of power, fearlessness, and goodwill by each of the contracting parties, which meant as much as such protestations usually do on both sides of the Arctic Circle. I could give a summary of it without invading the privacy of a diplomatic bureau, for I have notes of it that were taken by a subordinate; but I prefer passing at once to the reciprocal engagements in which it resulted.

On the part of the *Inuit*, the Esquimaux, they were after this fashion:

"We promise that we will not steal. We promise we will bring you fresh meat. We promise we will sell or lend you dogs. We will keep you company whenever you want us, and show you where to find the game."

On the part of the *Kablunah*, the white men, the stipulation was of this ample equivalent:

"We promise that we will not visit you with death

or sorcery, nor do you any hurt or mischief whatsoever. We will shoot for you on our hunts. You shall be made welcome aboard ship. We will give you presents of needles, pins, two kinds of knife, a hoop, three bits of hard wood, some fat, an awl, and some sewing thread; and we will trade with you of these and everything else you want for walrus and seal meat of the first quality."

And the closing formula might have read, if the Esquimaux political system had included reading among its qualifications for diplomacy, in this time consecrated and, in civilized regions, veracious assurance:

"We, the high contracting parties, pledge ourselves now and forever brothers and friends."

This treaty—which, though I have spoken of it jocosely, was really an affair of much interest to us—was ratified, with Hans and Morton as my accredited representatives, by a full assembly of the people at Etah. All our future intercourse was conducted under it. It was not solemnized by an oath; but it was never broken. We went to and fro between the villages and the brig, paid our visits of courtesy and necessity on both sides, met each other in hunting parties on the floe and the ice-foot, organized a general community of interests, and really established some personal attachments deserving of the name. As long as we remained prisoners of the ice, we were indebted to them for invaluable counsel in relation to our hunting expeditions and in the joint hunt we shared alike, according to their own laws. Our dogs were in one sense common property; and often have they robbed themselves to offer supplies of food to our starving teams. They gave us supplies of meat at critical periods: we were able to do as much for them. They learned to look on us only as benefactors; and, I know, mourned our departure bitterly. The greeting which they gave my brother John, when he came out after me to Etah with the rescue expedition, should be of itself enough to satisfy me of this. I should be glad to borrow from his ingenuous narrative the story of his meeting with Myouk and Metek and Ootuniah, and of the almost affectionate confidence with which the maimed and sick invited his professional succor, as the representative of the elder "Docto Kayen."

SEPTEMBER 17, SUNDAY. "It is a strange life we are leading. We are absolutely nomads, so far as there can be anything of pastoral life in this region; and our wild encounter with the elements seems to agree with us all. Our table talk at supper was as merry as a marriage ball. One party was just in from a seventy-four miles' trip with the dogs; another from a foot journey of 160, with five nights on the floe."

SEPTEMBER 20, WEDNESDAY. "The natives are really acting up to contract. They are on board the brig today, and I have been off with a party of them on a hunt inland. We had no great luck; the weather was against us, and there are signs of a gale. The thermometer has been two degrees below zero for the entire twenty-four hours. This is September with a vengeance!"

SEPTEMBER 22, FRIDAY. "I am off for the walrus

grounds with our wild allies. It will be my sixth trip. I know the country and its landmarks now as well as any of them, and can name every rock and chasm and watercourse, in night or fog, just as I could the familiar spots about the dear Old Mills where I passed my childhood.

"The weather does not promise well; but the state of our larder makes the jaunt necessary."

Metek

XVII

Provisioning

Sᴇᴘᴛᴇᴍʙᴇʀ 29, Fʀɪᴅᴀʏ. "I returned last night from Anoatok, after a journey of much risk and exposure, that I should have avoided but for the insuperable obstinacy of our savage friends.

"I set out for the walrus grounds at noon, by the track of the 'Wind Point' of Anoatok, known to us as Esquimaux Point. I took the light sledge and, in addition to the five of my available team, harnessed in two animals that belonged to the Esquimaux. Ootuniah, Myouk, and the dark stranger accompanied me, with Morton and Hans.

"Our sledge was overladen: I could not persuade the Esquimaux to reduce its weight; and the consequence was that we failed to reach Force Bay in time for a daylight crossing. To follow the indentations of the land was to make the travel long and dangerous. We trusted to the tracks of our former journeys, and pushed out on the ice. But the darkness came on us rapidly, and the snow began to drift before a heavy north wind.

"At a about 10:00 ᴘ.ᴍ. we had lost the land, and, while driving the dogs rapidly, all of us running alongside of them, we took a wrong direction, and traveled out toward the floating ice of the sound. There was no guide to the points of the compass; our Esquimaux were completely at fault; and the alarm of the dogs, which became every moment more manifest, extended itself to our party. The instinct of a sledge dog makes him perfectly aware of unsafe ice, and I know nothing more subduing to a man than the warnings of an unseen peril conveyed by the instinctive fears of the lower animals.

"We had to keep moving, for we could not camp in the gale that blew around us so fiercely that we could scarcely hold down the sledge. But we moved with caution, feeling our way with the tent poles, which I distributed among the party for the purpose. A murmur had reached my ear for some time in the cadences of the storm, steadier and deeper, I thought, than the tone of the wind: on a sudden it struck me that I heard the noise of waves, and that we must be coming close on the open water. I had hardly time for the hurried order, 'Turn the dogs,' before a wreath of wet frost smoke swept over us, and the sea showed itself, with a great fringe foam, hardly a quarter of a mile ahead. We could now guess our position and its dangers. The ice was breaking up before the storm, and it was not certain that even a direct retreat in the face of the gale would extricate us. I determined to run to the south for Godsend Island. The floes were heavy in that direction, and less likely to give way in a northerly gale. It was at best a dreary venture.

"The surf line kept encroaching on us till we could feel the ice undulating under our feet. Very soon it began to give way. Lines of hummocks rose before us, and we had to run the gauntlet between them as they closed. Escaping these, we toiled over the crushed fragments that lay between them and the shore, stumbling over the projecting crags, or sinking in the water that rose among them. It was too dark to see the island which we were steering for; but the black loom of a lofty cape broke the line of the horizon and served as a landmark. The dogs, relieved from the burden of carrying us, moved with more spirit. We began to draw near the shore, the ice storm still raging behind us. But our difficulties were only reaching their climax. We knew as ice-men that the access to the land-ice from the floe was, under the most favoring circumstances, both toilsome and dangerous. The rise and fall of the tides always breaks up the ice at the margin of the ice-belt in a tangle of irregular, half floating masses; and these were now surging under the energies of the gale. It was pitchy dark. I persuaded Ootuniah, the eldest of the Esquimaux, to have a tent pole lashed horizontally across his shoulders. I gave him the end of a line, which I fastened at the other end round my waist. The rest of the party followed him.

"As I moved ahead, feeling round me for a practicable way, Ootuniah followed; and when a table of ice was found large enough, the others would urge forward the dogs, pushing the sledge themselves or clinging to it as the moment prompted. We had accidents of course, some of them menacing for the time but none to be remembered for their consequences; and at last one after another succeeded in clambering after me upon the ice-foot, driving the dogs before them.

"Providence had been our guide. The shore on which we landed was Anoatok, not four hundred yards from the familiar Esquimaux homestead. With a shout of joy, each man in his own dialect, we hastened to the 'wind loved spot'; and in less than an hour, our lamps burning cheerfully, we were discussing a famous stew of walrus steaks, none the less relished for an unbroken ice walk of forty-eight miles and twenty haltless hours.

"When I reached the hut, our stranger Esquimaux, whose name we found to be Awahtok, or 'Seal bladder float,' was striking a fire from two stones, one a plain piece of angular milky quartz held in the right hand, the other apparently an oxide of iron. He struck them together after the true tinder box fashion, throwing a scanty supply of sparks on a tinder composed of the silky down of the willow catkins (*S. lanata*), which he held on a lump of dried moss.

"The hut or igloo at Anoatok was a single rude elliptical apartment, built not unskillfully of stone, the outside lined with sods. At its farther end a rude platform, also of stone, was lifted about a foot above the entering floor. The roof formed something of a curve: it was composed of flat stones, remarkably large and heavy, arranged so as to overlap each other, but apparently without any intelligent application of the principle of the arch. The height of this cave-like abode barely permitted one to sit upright. Its length was eight feet, its breadth seven feet, and an expansion of the tunneled entrance made an appendage of perhaps two feet more.

"The true winter entrance is called the *tossut*. It is a walled tunnel, ten feet long and so narrow that a man can hardly crawl along it. It opens outside below the level of the igloo, into which it leads by a gradual ascent.

"Time had done its work on the igloo of Anoatok, as among the palatial structures of more southern deserts. The entire front of the dome had fallen in, closing up the *tossut*, and forcing us to enter at the solitary window above it. The breach was large enough to admit a sledge team; but our Arctic comrades showed no anxiety to close it up. Their clothes saturated with the freezing water of the floes, these iron men gathered themselves round the blubber fire and steamed away in apparent comfort. The only departure from their practiced routine, which the bleak night and open roof seemed to suggest to them, was that they did not strip themselves naked before coming into the hut, and hang up their vestments in the air to dry, like a votive offering to the god of the sea.

"Their kitchen implements were even more simple than our own. A rude saucer-shaped cup of sealskin, to gather and hold water in, was the solitary utensil that could be dignified as table furniture. A flat stone just above the shoulder blade of an old walrus—the stone slightly inclined, the cavity of the bone large enough to hold a moss wick and some blubber; a square block of snow was placed on the stone, and, as the hot smoke circled round it, the sealskin saucer caught the water that dripped from the edge. They had no vessel for boiling; what they did not eat raw they baked upon a hot stone. A solitary coil of walrus line, fastened to a movable lance head (noon-ghak) with the well-worn and well-soaked clothes on their backs, completed the inventory of their effects.

"We felt that we were more civilized than our poor cousins, as we fell to work making ourselves comfortable after our own fashion. The dais was scraped and its accumulated filth of years removed; a canvas tent was folded double over the dry, frozen stones, our buffalo bag spread over this, and dry socks and moccasins were drawn from under our wet clothes. My copper lamp, invaluable for short journeys, soon flamed with a cheerful fire. The soup pot, the walrus steak, and the hot coffee were the next things to be thought of; and, while these were getting ready, an India rubber floor cloth was fastened over the gaping entrance of the cave.

"During our long march and its series of ice-fights we had taken care to manifest no weariness, and had, indeed, borne both Ootuniah and Myouk at times upon our shoulders. We showed no signs either of cold; so that all this preparation and right store of appliances could not be attributed by the Esquimaux to effeminacy or inferior power. I could see that they were profoundly impressed with a conviction of our superiority, the last feeling which the egotistical self-conceit of savage life admits as a final show of resolve.

"I felt sure now that they were our more than sworn friends. They sang 'Amna Ayah' for us, their rude monotonous song, till our ears cracked with the discord; and improvised a special eulogistic chant, which they repeated over and over again with laughable gravity of utterance, subsiding always into the refrain of 'Nalegak! nalegak! nalegak-soak!' 'Captain! captain! great captain!' They nicknamed and adopted all of us as members of their fraternity, with grave and abundant form; reminding me through all their mummery, solemn and ludicrous at once, of the analogous ceremonies of our North American Indians.

"The chant and the feed and the ceremony all completed, Hans, Morton, and myself crawled feet first into our buffalo bag and Ootuniah, Awahtok, and Myouk flung themselves outside the skin between us and the last I heard of them or anything else was the renewed chorus of 'Nalegak! nalegak! nalegak-soak!' mingling itself sleepily in my dreams with schoolboy memories of Aristophanes and The Frogs. I slept for eleven hours.

"They were up long before us, and had breakfasted on raw meat cut from a large joint, which lay, without regard to cleanliness, among the deposits on the floor of the igloo. Their mode of eating was ingeniously active. They cut the meat in long strips, introduced one end into the mouth, swallowed it as far as the powers of deglutition would allow, and then, cutting of the protruding portion close to the lips, prepared for yet a second mouthful. It was really a feat of address: those who tried it failed awkwardly; and yet I have seen infants in the mother's hood, not two years old, who managed to perform it without accident."

I pass over the story of the hunt that followed. It had nothing to distinguish it from many others, and I find in my journal of a few days later the fresh narrative of Morton, after he had seen one for the first time.

My next extracts show the progress of our winter arrangements.

September 30, Saturday. "We have been clearing up on the ice. Our system for the winter has not the dignity of a year ago. We have no Butler Storehouse, no Medary, no Fern Rock with their appliances. We are ten men in a casemate, with all our energies concentrated against the enemy outside.

"Our beef house is now a pile of barrels holding our water-soaked beef and pork. Flour, beans, and dried apples make a quadrangular blockhouse on the floe: from one corner of it rises our flagstaff, lighting up the dusky gray with its red and white ensign, only on Sunday giving place to the Henry Grinnell flag, of happy memories.

"From this, along an avenue that opens abeam of the brig—New London Avenue, named after McGary's town at home—are our boats and square cordage. Outside of all these is a magnificent hut of barrel frames and snow, to accommodate our Esquimaux visitors; the only thing about it exposed to hazard being the tempting woodwork. What remains to complete our camp plot is the rope barrier that is to mark out our little curtilage around the vessel: this, when finished, is to be the dividing line between us and the rest of mankind.

"There is something in the simplicity of all this, which might commend itself to the most rigorous taste. Nothing is wasted on ornament."

OCTOBER 4, WEDNESDAY. "I sent Hans and Hickey two days ago out to the hunting ice, to see if the natives have had any luck with the walrus. They are back tonight with bad news—no meat, no Esquimaux. These strange children of the snow have made a mysterious flitting. Where or how, it is hard to guess, for they have no sledges. They cannot have traveled very far; and yet they have such unquiet impulses, that, once on the track, no civilized man can say where they will bring up.

"Ohlsen had just completed a sledge, fashioned like the Smith Sound kommetik, with an improved curvature of the runners. It weighs only twenty-four pounds, and, though I think it too short for light draught, it is just the article our Etah neighbors would delight in for their land portages. I intended it for them, as a great price for a great stock of walrus meat: but the other parties to the bargain have flown."

OCTOBER 5, THURSDAY. "We are nearly out of fresh meat again, one rabbit and three ducks being our sum total. We have been on short allowance for several days. What vegetables we have—the dried apples and peaches, and pickled cabbage—have lost much of their antiscorbutic virtue by constant use. Our spices are all gone. Except four small bottles of horseradish, our carte is comprised in three lines—bread, beef, pork.

"I must be off after these Esquimaux. They certainly have meat, and wherever they have gone we can follow. Once upon their trail, our hungry instincts will not risk being baffled. I will stay only long enough to complete my latest rootbeer brewage. Its basis is the big crawling willow, the miniature giant of our Arctic forests, of which we laid in a stock some weeks ago. It is quite pleasantly bitter, and I hope to get it fermenting in the deck house without extra fuel, by heat from below."

October 7, Saturday. "Lively sensation, as they say in the land of olives and champagne. 'Nannook, nannook!'—'A bear, a bear!'—Hans and Morton in a breath!

"To the scandal of our domestic regulations, the guns were all impracticable. While the men were loading and capping anew, I seized my pillow companion six-shooter and ran on deck. A medium-sized bear, with a four months' cub, was in active warfare with our dogs. They were hanging on her skirts, and she with wonderful alertness was picking out one victim after another, snatching him by the nape of the neck, and flinging him many feet or rather yards, by a barely perceptible movement of her head.

"Tudla, our master dog, was already *hors de combat*: he had been tossed twice. Jenny, just as I emerged from the hatch, was making an extraordinary somerset of some eight fathoms, and alighted senseless. Old Whitey, stanch but not bear wise, had been the first in the battle: he was yelping in helplessness on the snow.

"It seemed as if the controversy was adjourned: and Nannook evidently thought so; for she turned off to our beef barrels, and began in the most unconcerned manner to turn them over and nose out their fatness. She was apparently as devoid of fear as any of the bears in the stories of old Barentz and the Spitzbergen voyagers.[1]

"I lodged a pistol ball in the side of the cub. At once the mother placed her little one between her hind legs, and, shoving it along, made her way behind the beef house. Mr. Ohlsen wounded her as she went with my Webster rifle; but she scarcely noticed it. She tore down by single efforts of her forearms the barrels of frozen beef that made the triple walls of the store-house, mounted the rubbish, and, snatching up a half barrel of herrings, carried it down by her teeth, and was making off. It was time to close, I thought. Going up within half pistol range, I gave her six buckshot. She dropped, but instantly rose, and, getting her cub into its former position, moved off once more.

"This time she would have escaped but for the ad-mirable tactics of our new recruits from the Es-quimaux. The dogs of Smith's Sound are educated more thoroughly than any of their more southern brethren. Next to the walrus, the bear is the staple of

[1] See Chapter xxviii pages [385–386] for description of the ill-fated Barentz voyage.

diet to the north, and, except the fox, supplies the most important element of the wardrobe. Unlike the dogs we had brought with us from Baffin's Bay, these were trained not to attack, but to embarrass. They ran in circles round the bear, and when pursued would keep ahead with regulated gait, their comrades effecting a diversion at the critical moment by a nip at her hind quarters. This was done so systematically and with so little seeming excitement as to strike everyone on board. I have seen bear-dogs elsewhere that had been drilled to relieve each other in the *melée* and avoid the direct assault; but here, two dogs without even a demonstration of attack would put themselves before the path of the animal, and, retreating right and left, lead him into a profitless pursuit that checked his advance completely.

"The poor animal was still backing out, yet still fighting, carrying along her wounded cub, embarrassed by the dogs yet gaining distance from the brig, when Hans and myself threw in the odds in the shape of a couple of rifle balls. She staggered in front of her young one, faced us in death-like defiance, and only sank when pierced by six more bullets.

"We found nine balls in skinning her body. She was of medium size, very lean, and without a particle of food in her stomach. Hunger must have caused her boldness. The net weight of the cleansed carcass was 300 pounds; that of the entire animal, 650; her length, but seven feet eight inches.

"Bears in this lean condition are much the most

palatable food. The impregnation of fatty oil through the cellular tissue makes a well-fed bear nearly uneatable. The flesh of a famished beast, although less nutritious as a fuel diet, is rather sweet and tender than otherwise.

"The little cub is larger than the adjective implies. She was taller than a dog, and weighs 114 pounds. Like Morton's bear in Kennedy's Channel she sprang upon the corpse of her mother and raised a woeful lamentation over her wounds. She repelled my efforts to noose her with great ferocity; but at last, completely muzzled with a line fastened by a running knot between her jaws and the back of her head, she moved off to the brig amid the clamor of the dogs. We have her now chained alongside, but snarling and snapping constantly, evidently suffering from her wound.

"Of the eight dogs who took part in this passage of arms, only one—'Sneak,' as the men call him, 'Young Whitey,' as he figures in this journal—lost a flower from his chaplet. But two of the rest escaped without a grip.

"Strange to say, in spite of the powerful flings they were subjected to in the fight, not a dog suffers seriously. I expected, from my knowledge of the hugging propensity of the plantigrades, that the animal would rear, or at least use her forearm; but she invariably seized the dogs with her teeth, and, after disposing of them for the time, abstained from following up the advantage. The Esquimaux assert that this is the habit of the hunted bear. One of our Smith Sound dogs, 'Jack,' made no struggle when he was seized, but was flung, with all his muscles relaxed, I hardly dare to say how far: the next instant he rose and renewed the attack. The Esquimaux both of Proven and of this country say that the dogs soon learn this 'possum-playing' habit. Jack was an old bear dog.

"The bear seems to be more ferocious as he increases his latitude, or more probably as he recedes from the hunting fields.

"At Oominak, last winter (1852) an Esquimaux and his son were nearly killed by a bear that had housed himself in an iceberg. They attacked him with the lance, but he turned on them and worsted them badly before making his escape.

"But the continued pursuit of man seems to have exerted already a modifying influence upon the ursine character in South Greenland; at all events, the bears there never attack, and even in self defense seldom inflict injury upon the hunter. Many instances have occurred where they have defended themselves and even charged after being wounded, but in none of them was life lost. I have myself shot as many as a dozen bears near at hand, and never but once received a charge in return."

October 8, Sunday. "When I was out in the *Advance* with Captain De Haven, I satisfied myself that it was a vulgar prejudice to regard the liver of the bear as poisonous. I ate of it freely myself and succeeded in making it a favorite dish with the mess. But I find to my cost that it may sometimes be more savory than safe. The cub's liver was my supper last night, and today I have symptoms of poison in full measure—vertigo, diarrhea, and their concomitants."[2]

Another article of diet, less inviting at first, but which I found more innocuous, was the rat. We had failed to exterminate this animal by our varied and perilous efforts of the year before, and a well-justified fear forbade our renewing the crusade. It was marvelous, in a region apparently so unfavorable to reproduction, what a perfect warren we soon had on board. Their impudence and address increased with their numbers. It became impossible to stow anything below decks. Furs, woolens, shoes, specimens of natural history, everything we did not want to lose, however little valuable to them, was gnawed into and destroyed. They harbored among the men's bedding in the forecastle, and showed such boldness in fight and such dexterity in dodging missiles that they were tolerated at last as inevitable nuisances. Before the winter ended, I avenged our griefs by decimating them for my private table. I find in my journal of the tenth of October an anecdote that illustrates their boldness:

"We have moved everything movable out upon the ice, and, besides our dividing moss wall between our sanctum and the forecastle, we have built up a rude barrier of our iron sheathing to prevent these abominable rats from gnawing through. It is all in vain. They

[2]Polar bear livers have a high content of Vitamin A and can be poisonous. Richard C. Davids, *Lords of the Arctic: A Journey Among the Polar Bears* (New York, 1982), p. 84.

are everywhere already, under the stove, in the steward's lockers, in our cushions, about our beds. If I was asked what, after darkness and cold and scurvy, are the three besetting curses of our Arctic sojourn, I should say RATS, RATS, RATS. A mother rat bit my finger to the bone last Friday, as I was intruding my hand into a bear skin mitten she had chosen as a homestead for her little family. I withdrew it of course with instinctive courtesy; but among them they carried off the mitten before I could suck the finger."

Before I pass from these intrepid and pertinacious visitors, let me add that on the whole I am personally much their debtor. Through the long winter night, Hans used to beguile his lonely hours of watch by shooting them with the bow and arrow. The repugnance of my associates to share the table luxury of "such small deer"[3] gave me the frequent advantage of a fresh meat soup, which contributed no doubt to my comparative immunity from scurvy. I had only one competitor in the dispensation of this *entremet*, or rather one companion; for there was an abundance for both. It was a fox: we caught and domesticated him late in the winter; but the scantiness of our resources, and of course his own, soon instructed him in all the antipathies of a terrier. He had only one fault as a rat catcher: he would never catch a second till he had eaten the first.

At the date of these entries the Arctic hares had not

[3] Alludes to *King Lear,* Act III, sc. iv. Edgar, disguising himself as Poor Tom, says he eats "mice and rats, and such small deer."

ceased to be numerous about our harbor. They were very beautiful, as white as swans' down, with a crescent of black marking the ear tips. They feed on the bark and catkins of the willow, and affect the stony sides of the worn-down rocks, where they find protection from the wind and snowdrifts. They do not burrow like our hares at home, but squat in crevices or under large stones. Their average weight is about nine pounds. They would have entered largely into our diet list but for our Esquimaux dogs, who regarded them with relishing appetite.

OCTOBER 11, WEDNESDAY. "There is no need of looking at the thermometer and comparing registers to show how far this season has advanced beyond its fellow of last year. The ice-foot is more easily read, and quite as certain.

"The under part of it is covered now with long stalactitic columns of ice, unlike the ordinary icicle in shape, for they have the characteristic bulge of the carbonate of lime stalactite. They look like the fantastic columns hanging from the roof of a frozen temple, the dark recess behind them giving all the effect of a grotto. There is one that brings back to me saddened memories of Elephanta[4] and the merry friends that bore me company under its rock-chiselled portico. The fig trees and the palms and the gallant major's curries

---

[4] In 1843–44 Kane was the doctor aboard the naval frigate *Brandywine* on a cruise to China. Apparently he took time from the ship to visit the cave temples on the island of Elephanta in the Arabian Sea.

and his old India ale are wanting in the picture. Sometimes again it is a canopy fringed with gems in the moonlight. Nothing can be purer or more beautiful.

"The ice has begun to fasten on our brig: I have called a consultation of officers to determine how she may be best secured."

OCTOBER 14, SATURDAY. "Mr. Wilson and Hickey reported last night a wolf at the meat house. Now, the meat house is a thing of too much worth to be left to casualty, and a wolf might incidentally add some freshness of flavor to its contents. So I went out in all haste with the Marston rifle, but without my mittens and with only a single cartridge. The metal burnt my hands, as metal is apt to do at fifty degrees below the point of freezing; but I got a somewhat rapid shot. I hit—one of our dogs, a truant from Morton's team; luckily a flesh wound only, for he is too good a beast to lose. I could have sworn he was a wolf."

OCTOBER 9, THURSDAY. "We have been completing our arrangements for raising the brig. The heavy masses of ice that adhere to her in the winter make her condition dangerous at seasons of low tide. Her frame could not sustain the pressure of such a weight. Our object, therefore, has been to lift her mechanically above her line of flotation, and let her freeze in on a sort of ice-dock; so that the ice around her as it sinks may take the bottom and hold her up clear of the danger. We have detached four of the massive beams that were intended to resist the lateral pressure of nips, and have placed them as shores, two on each side of the vessel, opposite the channels. Brooks has rigged a crab or capstan on the floe, and has passed the chain cable under the keel at four bearing points. As these are hauled in by the crab and the vessel rises, the shores are made to take hold under heavy cleats spiked below the bulwarks, and in this manner to sustain her weight.

"We made our first trial of the apparatus today. The chains held perfectly, and had raised the brig nearly three feet, when away went one of our chain slings, and she fell back to her more familiar bearings. We will repeat the experiment tomorrow, using six chains, two at each line of stress."

OCTOBER 21, SATURDAY. "Hard at it still, slinging chains and planting shores. The thermometer is too near zero for work like this. We swaddle our feet in old cloth and guard our hands with fur mits; but the cold iron bites through them all.

"6:30 P.M.—Morton and Hans have come back, after tracking the Esquimaux to the lower settlement of Etah. I cannot give their report tonight: the poor fellows are completely knocked up by the hardships of their march. Hans, who is always careless of powder and firearms, exploded his powder flask while attempting to kindle a tinder fire. The explosion has risked his hand. I have dressed it, extracting several pieces of foreign matter and poulticing it in yeast and charcoal. Morton has frostbitten both his heels; I hope not too severely, for the indurated skin of the heel makes it a bad region for suppuration. But they bring us 270 pounds of walrus meat and a couple of foxes.

This supply, with what we have remaining of our two bears, must last us till the return of daylight allows us to join the natives in their hunts.

"The light is fast leaving us. The sun has ceased to reach the vessel. The northeastern headlands or their southern faces up the fiords have still a warm yellow tint, and the pinnacles of the icebergs far out on the floes are lighted up at noonday: but all else is dark shadow."

The brig in her second winter

The Rescue *in Her Arctic Dry Dock*
Oil, James Hamilton

Courtesy Seneca Falls Historical Society

ARCTIC OCEAN

Lincoln Sea

ARCTIC ARCHIPELAGO

Ellesmere Island

Kane Basin

Rensselaer Harbor (the *Advance* became ice-b...)

WEST

Wilcox Poin...

Jones Sound

Beechey I.

Melville Bay

Baffin

Upernavik

Bay

Disco I.

Baffin Island

GREE...

Gulf of Boothia

King William I.

Davis Strait

Sukker...

Fi...

SO...

Foxe Basin

M'Clintock Channel

G...

CANADA

Hudson Strait

Labrador

Hudson

Sea

Bay

NORTH

AMERICA

Newfoundland

St. John...

UNITED STATES

New York

Gulf of Mexico

105°W   90°W   75°W   60°W

Greenland

Spitzbergen
Sea

Spitzbergen
Islands

75°N

Greenland
Sea

N

eenland

Norwegian

ARCTIC CIRCLE

Sea

Denmark Strait

Iceland

ND

60°N

vell

North
Sea

Baltic
Sea

NORTH

ATLANTIC

OCEAN

Bay of
Biscay

EUROPE

45°N

or settlement

rinnell expedition, 1850-1851

Mediterranean Sea

rinnell expedition: initial year, 1853

p

30°N

er

AFRICA

30°W   15°W   0°   15°E

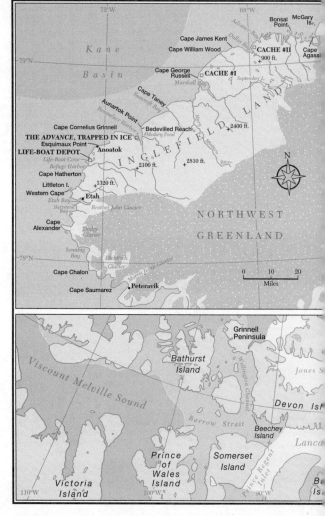

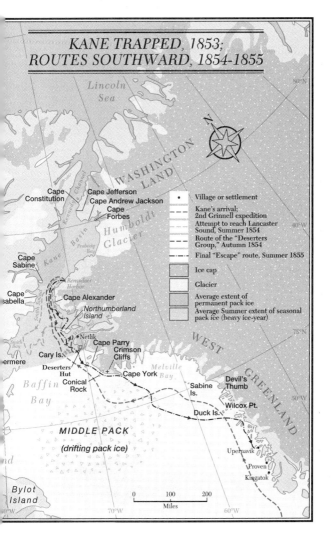

KANE TRAPPED, 1853;
ROUTES SOUTHWARD, 1854-1855

Lincoln
Sea

80°N

WASHINGTON LAND

Cape
Constitution

Cape Jefferson
Cape Andrew Jackson
Cape
Forbes

Humboldt
Glacier

40°W

Peabody
Bay

Cape
Sabine

Kane
Basin

Rensselaer
Harbor

Smith Sound

Cape
Isabella

Cape Alexander

Northumberland
Island

South
Bay

•Netlik

Cape Parry
Crimson
Cliffs

ermere

Cary Is.

Deserters
Hut

Conical
Rock

Cape York

Melville
Bay

WEST GREENLAND

75°N

Sabine
Is.

Devil's
Thumb

50°W

Baffin
Bay

Wilcox Pt.

Duck Is.

MIDDLE PACK

(drifting pack ice)

Upernavik

Proven

Bylot
Island

Kingatok

	Village or settlement
	Kane's arrival; 2nd Grinnell expedition
	Attempt to reach Lancaster Sound, Summer 1854
	Route of the "Deserters Group," Autumn 1854
	Final "Escape" route, Summer 1855
	Ice cap
	Glacier
	Average extent of permanent pack ice
	Average Summer extent of seasonal pack ice (heavy ice-year)

0   100   200
Miles

70°W   60°W

Breaking Up of an Iceberg in Melville Bay
Oil, James Hamilton

Greenland Fjord, Watercolor, James Hamilton

235

Dr. Kane's Arctic Brig, Advance
D. J. Kennedy

236

Crimson Cliffs of Beverly, Watercolor, James Hamilton

Courtesy The Library Company of Philadelphia

237

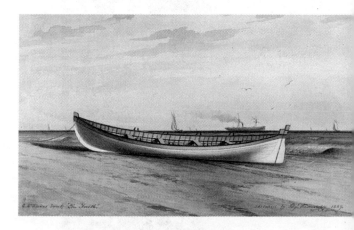

Two views of Dr. Kane's boat, Faith
D. J. Kennedy

Courtesy Historical Society of Pennsylvania

238

XVIII

Desolation Descends

OCTOBER 24, TUESDAY. "We are at work that makes us realize how short handed we are. The brig was lifted for the third time today, with double chains passed under her at low tide, both astern and amid ships. Her bows were already raised three feet above the water, and nothing seemed wanting to our complete success, when at the critical moment one of the after shores parted, and she fell over about five streaks to starboard. The slings were hove to by the crab, and luckily held her from going farther, so that she now stands about three feet above her flotation line, drawing four feet forward, but four and a half aft. She has righted a little with the return of tide, and now awaits the freezing in of her winter cradle. She is well out of water; and, if the chains only hold, we shall have the spectacle of a brig, high and dry, spending an Arctic winter over an Arctic ice-bed.

"We shall be engaged now at the hold and with the housing on deck. From our lodge room to the forward timbers everything is clear already. We have moved the carpenter's bench into our little dormitorium: everywhere else it is too cold for handling tools.

"9:00 P.M.—"A true and unbroken auroral arch: the first we have seen in Smith's Sound. It was colorless, but extremely bright. There was no pendant from the lower curve of the arc; but from its outer, an active wavy movement, dissipating itself into barely perceptible cirrhus, was broken here and there by rays nearly perpendicular, with a slight inclination to the east. The atmosphere was beautifully clear."

OCTOBER 25, THURSDAY. "The thermometer at thirty-four degrees below zero, but fortunately no wind blowing. We go on with the outdoor work. The gangway of ice is finished, and we have passed wooden steam tubes through the deck house to carry off the vapors of our cooking stove and the lighter impurities of the crowded cabin.

"We burn but seventy pounds of fuel a day, most of it in the galley; the fire being allowed to go out between meals. We go without fire altogether for four hours of the night; yet such is the excellence of our moss walls, and the air proof of our *tossut*, that the thermometer indoors never indicates less than forty-five degrees above zero, with the outside air at thirty degrees below. When our housing is arranged and the main hatch secured with a proper weather-tight screen of canvas, we shall be able, I hope, to meet the extreme cold of February and March without fear.

"Darkness is the worst enemy we have to face; but we will strive against the scurvy in spite of him, till the light days of sun and vegetation. The spring hunt will open in March, though it will avail us very little till late in April.

"Wilson and Brooks are my principal subjects of

anxiety; for, although Morton and Hans are on their backs, making four of our ten, I can see strength of system in their cheerfulness of heart. The best prophylactic is a hopeful, sanguine temperament; the best cure, moral resistance, that spirit of combat against every trial which is alone true bravery."

OCTOBER 27, FRIDAY. "The work is going on: we are ripping off the extra planking of our deck for fuel during the winter. The cold increases fast, verging now upon forty degrees below zero; and in spite of all my efforts we will have to burn largely into the brig. I prepared for this two months ago, and satisfied myself, after a consultation with the carpenter, that we may cut away some seven or eight tons of fuel without absolutely destroying her seaworthiness.

"We had then but thirty buckets of coal remaining, and had already burnt up the bulkheads. Since then we have made some additional inroads on our stock; but, unless there is an error in the estimate, we can go on at the rate of seventy pounds a day. Close housekeeping this; but we cannot do better. We must remodel our heating arrangements. The scurvy exacts a comfortable temperature and a drying one. Our mean thus far has been forty-seven degrees—decidedly too low; and by the clogging of our worn-out pipe it is now reduced to forty-two degrees.

"The ice-belt, sorry chronicler of winter progress, has begun to widen with the rise and fall of the sludgy water."

OCTOBER 31, TUESDAY. "We have had a scene on

board. We play many parts on this Arctic stage of ours and can hardly be expected to be at home in all of them.

"Today was appropriated to the reformation of the stoves, and there was demand, of course, for all our ingenuity both as tinkers and chimney sweeps. Of my company of nine, Hans had the good luck to be out on the hunt, and Brooks, Morton, Wilson, and Goodfellow were scurvy-ridden in their bunks. The other four and the commanding officer made up the detail of duty. First, we were to give the smoke tubes of the stove a thorough cleansing, the first they have had for now seventeen months; next, to reduce our effete snow melter to its elements of imperfect pipes and pans; and, last, to combine the practicable remains of the two into one efficient system for warming and melting.

"Of these, the first has been executed most gallantly. 'Glory enough for one day!' The work with the scrapers on the heated pipes—for the accumulation inside of them was as hard as the iron itself till we melted it down—was decidedly unpleasant to our gentle senses; and we were glad when it had advanced far enough to authorize a resort to the good old-fashioned country custom of firing. But we had not calculated the quantity of the gases, combustible and incombustible, which this process was to evolve, with duly scientific reference to the size of their outlet. In a word, they were smothering us, and, in a fit of desperation, we threw open our apartment to the atmosphere outside. This made short work of the smoky flocculi; the dormitory decked itself on the instant with a frosty forest of feathers, and it now rejoices in a drapery as gray as a cygnet's breast.

"It was cold work reorganizing the stove for the nonce; but we have got it going again, as red as a cherry, and my well-worn dog skin suit is drying before it. The blackened water is just beginning to drip, drip, drop from the walls and ceiling, and the bed clothes and the table on which I write."

My narrative has reached a period at which everything like progress was suspended. The increasing cold and brightening stars, the labors and anxieties and sickness that pressed upon us—these almost engross the pages of my journal. Now and then I find some marvel of Petersen's about the fox's dexterity as a hunter; and Hans tells me of domestic life in South Greenland, or of a seal hunt and a wrecked kayack; or perhaps McGary repeats his thrice-told tale of humor; but the night has closed down upon us, and we are hibernating through it.

Yet some of these were topics of interest. The intense beauty of the Arctic firmament can hardly be imagined. It looked close above our heads, with its stars magnified in glory and the very planets twinkling so much as to baffle the observations of our astonomer. I am afraid to speak of some of these night scenes. I have trodden the deck and the floes when the life of earth seemed suspended, its movements, its sounds, its coloring, its companionships; and as I looked on this radiant hemisphere, circling up above me as if rendering worship to the unseen light Centre, I have said in humility of spirit, "Lord, what is man that thou art mindful of him?" And then I have thought of the kindly world we had left, with its revolving sunshine and shadow, and the other stars that gladden it in their changes, and the hearts that warmed to us there; till I lost myself in memories of those who are not—and they bore me back to the stars again."

November 15, Wednesday. "The last forty-eight hours should have given us the annual meteoric shower. We were fully prepared to observe it; but it would not come off. It would have been a godsend variety. In eight hours that I helped to watch, from nine of last night until five this morning, there were fifty-one shooting stars. I have seen as many between the same hours in December and February of last winter.

"Our traps have been empty for ten days past: but for the pittance of excitement which the visit to them gives, we might as well be without them.

"The men are getting nervous and depressed. McGary paced the deck all last Sunday in a fit of homesickness, without eating a meal. I do my best to cheer them; but it is hard work to hide one's own trials for the sake of others who have not as many. I am glad of my professional drill and its companion influence over the sick and toil worn. I could not get along at all unless I combined the offices of physician and commander. You cannot punish sick men."

November 20, Monday. "I was out today looking over the empty traps with Hans, and when about two miles off the brig—luckily not more—I heard what I thought was the bellow of a walrus on the floe-ice. 'Hark there, Hans!' The words were scarcely uttered before we had a second roar, altogether unmistakable. No walrus at all: a bear, a bear! We had jumped to the ice-foot already. The day was just thirty minutes past the hour of noon; but, practiced as we all are to see through the darkness, it was impossible to make out an object two hundred yards off. What to do?—we had no arms.

"We were both afraid to run, for we knew that the sight of a runner would be the signal for a chase; and, besides, it went to our hearts to lose such a providential accession to our means of life. A second roar, well pitched and abundant in volume, assured us that the game was coming nearer, and that he was large and of no doubt corresponding flavor. 'Run for the brig, Hans,'—he is a noble runner—'and I will play decoy.' Off went Hans like a deer. Another roar; but he was already out of sight.

"I may confess it to these well worn pages: there was something not altogether pleasant in the silent communings of the next few minutes; but they were silent ones.

"I had no stimulus to loquacity, and the bear had ceased to be communicative. The floe was about three-quarters of a tide; some ten feet it may be, lower than the ice-foot on which I lay. The bear was of course below my horizon. I began after a while to think over the reality of what I had heard, and to doubt whether it might not be after all a creature of the brain. It was very cold on that ice-foot. I resolved to crawl to the edge of it and peer under my hands into the dark shadow of the hummock ridges.

"I did so. One look: nothing. A second: no bear after all. A third: what is that long rounded shade? stained ice? Yes: stained ice. The stained ice gave a gross menagerie roar and charged on the instant for my position. I had not even a knife, and did not wait to think what would have been appropriate if I had had one. I ran—ran as I never expect these scurvy-stiffened knees to run again—throwing off first one mitten and then its fellow to avoid pursuit. I gained the brig, and the bear my mittens. I got back one of them an hour afterward, but the other was carried off as a trophy in spite of all the rifles we could bring to the rescue."

DECEMBER 2, SATURDAY. "Had to put Mr. McGary and Riley under active treatment for scurvy. Gums retracted, ankles swollen, and lumbago. Mr. Wilson's case, a still worse one, has now been brought under. Morton's is a saddening one: I cannot afford to lose him. He is not only one of my most intelligent men, but he is daring, cool, and every way trustworthy. His tendon Achilles has been completely perforated, and the surface of the heel bone exposed. An operation in cold, darkness, and privation, would probably bring on locked jaw. Brooks grows discouraged: the poor fellow has scurvy in his stump, and his leg is drawn up by the contraction of the flexors at the knee joint. This is the third case on board—the fourth if I include my own—of contracted tendons. I pray none worsen."

December 3, Sunday. "I have now on hand twenty-four hundred pounds of chopped wood, a store collected with great difficulty; and yet how inadequate a provision for the sickness and accident we must look for through the rest of the dark days! It requires the most vigorous effort of what we call a healthy man to tear from the oak ribs of our stout little vessel a single day's firewood. We have but three left who can manage even this; and we cannot spare more than one for the daily duty. Two thousand pounds will barely carry us to the end of January, and the two severest months of the Arctic year, February and March, will still be ahead of us.

"To carry us over these, our days of greatest anticipated trial, we have the outside oak sheathing—or trebling, as the carpenters call it—a sort of extra skin to protect the brig against the shocks of the ice. Although nearly three inches thick, it is only spiked to her sides, and carpenter Ohlsen is sure that its removal will not interfere with her seaworthiness. Cut the trebling only to the water line, and it will give me at least $2\frac{1}{2}$ tons; and with this—God willing—I may get through this awful winter, and save the brig besides!"

December 4, Monday. "That stove is smoking so that three of our party are down with acute inflammation of the eyes. I fear I must increase the diameter of our smoke pipes for the pitch pine that we burn, to save up our oak for the greater cold, is redundantly charged with turpentine. Yet we also do not want an increased draught to consume our seventy pounds; the fiat 'No more wood' comes soon enough.

"Then for the nightwatch. I have generally something on hand to occupy me, and can volunteer for the hours before my regular term. Everything is closed tight; I muffle myself in furs, and write; or, if the cold denies me that pleasure, I read, or at least think. Thank heaven, even an Arctic temperature leaves the mind unchilled. But in truth, though our hourly observations in the air range between minus forty-six degrees and minus thirty degrees, we seldom register less than thirty-six degrees below zero."

DECEMBER 5, TUESDAY. "McGary is no better, but happily has no notion how bad he is. I have to give him a grating of our treasured potatoes.[1] He and Brooks will doubtless finish the two I have got out, and then there will be left twelve. They are now three years old, poor old frozen memorials of the dear land they grew in. They are worth more than their weight in gold."

[1]Potatoes contain vitamin C, so were effective against scurvy. But value could be lost in cooking or processing; there were also problems of rotting in storage. See Carpenter, *The History of Scurvy & Vitamin C*.

XIX

Fire in the Brig!

I WAS ASLEEP in the forenoon of the seventh, after the fatigue of an extra nightwatch, when I was called to the deck by the report of "Esquimaux sledges." They came on rapidly, five sledges with teams of six dogs each, most of the drivers were strangers to us; and in a few minutes they arrived at the brig. Their errand was of charity: they were bringing back to us Bonsall and Petersen, two of the party that left us on the twenty-eighth of August.

The party had many adventures and much suffering to tell of. They had verified by painful and perilous experience all I had anticipated for them. But the most stirring of their announcements was the condition they had left their associates in, two hundred miles off, divided in their counsels, their energies broken, and their provisions nearly gone. I reserve for another page the history of their wanderings. My first thought was of the means of rescuing and relieving them.

I resolved to despatch the Esquimaux escort at once with such supplies as our miserably imperfect store allowed, they giving their pledge to carry them with all speed, and, what I felt to be much less certain, with all honesty. But neither of the gentlemen who had come with them felt in any condition to repeat the journey.

Mr. Bonsall was evidently broken down, and Petersen, never too reliable in emergency, was for postponing the time of setting out. Of our own party—those who had stayed with the brig—McGary, Hans, and myself were the only ones able to move, and of these McGary was now fairly on the sick list. We could not be absent for a single day without jeopardizing the lives of the rest."

December 8, Friday. "I am much afraid these provisions will never reach the wanderers. We were very busy every hour since Bonsall arrived getting them ready. We cleaned and boiled and packed a hundred pounds of pork, and sewed up smaller packages of meat biscuit, bread dust, and tea; and despatched some 350 pounds, by the returning convoy. But I have no faith in an Esquimaux under temptation, and I almost regret that I did not accompany them myself. It might have been wiser. But I will set Hans on the track in the morning; and, if I do not hear within four days, that the stores are fairly on their way, *coûte qui coûte,*[1] I will be off to the lower bay and hold the whole tribe as hostages for the absent party.

"Brooks is wasting with night sweats; and my iron man, McGary, has been suffering for two days with anomalous cramps from exposure.

"The Esquimaux left us some walrus beef; and poor little Myouk, who is unabated in his affection for me, made me a special present of half a liver. These go, of course, to the hospital. God knows they are needed

[1]*Coute qui coute:* at all costs.

there and will also raise all our spirits immeasurably!"

DECEMBER 9, SATURDAY. "The superabundant life of Northumberland Island has impressed Petersen as much as it did me. I cannot think of it without recurring to the fortunes of Franklin's party. Our own sickness I attribute to our civilized diet; had we plenty of frozen walrus I would laugh at the scurvy. And it was only because I was looking to other objects—summer researches and explorations in the fall with the single view to escape—that I failed to secure an abundance of fresh food. Even in August I could have gathered a winter's supply of birds and cochlearia.

"From May to August we lived on seal, twenty-five before the middle of July, all brought in by one man: a more assiduous and better-organized hunt would have swelled the number without a limit. A few boat parties in June would have stocked us with enough eider eggs for winter use, three thousand to the trip; and the snowdrifts would have kept them fresh for the breakfast table. I loaded my boat with ducks in three hours, as late as the middle of July and not more than thirty-five miles from our anchorage. And even now, here are these Esquimaux, sleek and oily with their walrus blubber, only seventy miles off. It is not a region for starvation, nor ought it to be for scurvy."

DECEMBER 12, TUESDAY. "Brooks awoke me at three this morning with the cry of 'Esquimaux again!' I dressed hastily, and, groping my way over the pile of boxes that leads up from the hold into the darkness above, made out a group of human figures, masked by the hooded jumpers of the natives. They stopped at the gangway, and, as I was about to challenge, one of them sprang forward and grasped my hand. It was Doctor Hayes. A few words, dictated by suffering, certainly not by any anxiety as to his reception, and at his bidding the whole party came upon deck. Poor fellows! I could only grasp their hands and give them a brother's welcome.

"The thermometer was at minus fifty degrees; they were covered with rime and snow, and were fainting with hunger. It was necessary to use caution in taking them below; for, after an exposure of such fearful intensity and duration as they had gone through, the warmth of the cabin would have prostrated them completely. They had journeyed 350 miles; and their last run from the bay near Etah, some seventy miles in a right line, was through the hummocks at this appalling temperature.

"One by one they all came in and were housed. Poor fellows! As they threw their Esquimaux garments by the stove, how they relished the scanty luxuries we had to offer them! The coffee and the meat biscuit soup, and the molasses and the wheat bread, even the salt pork, which our scurvy forbade the rest of us to touch[2]—how they relished it all! For more than two months they had lived on frozen seal and walrus meat.

[2]Salted meat was erroneously thought to cause scurvy. What it does is greatly reduce the quantity of vitamin C. See Kenneth Carpenter, *The History of Scurvy & Vitamin C*, and Pierre Berton, *The Arctic Grail*, p.431.

"They are almost all of them in danger of collapse, but I have no apprehension of life unless from tetanus. Stephenson is prostrate with pericarditis.[3] I resigned my own bunk to Dr. Hayes, who is much prostrated: he will probably lose two of his toes, perhaps a third. The rest have no special injury.

"I cannot crowd the details of their journey into my diary. I have noted some of them from Dr. Hayes's words; but he has promised me a written report, and I wait for it. It was providential that they did not stop for Petersen's return or rely on the engagements his Esquimaux attendants had made to them as well as to us. The sledges that carried our relief of provisions passed through the Etah settlement empty, on some furtive project, we know not what."

DECEMBER 13, WEDNESDAY. "The Esquimaux who accompanied the returning party are nearly all of them well-known friends. They were engaged from different settlements, but, as they neared the brig, volunteers added themselves to the escort till they numbered six drivers and as many as forty-two dogs. Whatever may have been their motive, their conduct to our poor friends was certainly full of humanity. They drove at flying speed; every hut gave its welcome as they halted; the women were ready without invitation to dry and chafe their worn-out guests.

"I found, however, that there were other objects connected with their visit to the brig. Suffering and a sense of necessity had involved some of our foot-worn

[3]Inflammation of the membrane that encloses the heart.

absentees in a breach of hospitality. While resting at Kalutunah's hut, they had found opportunity of appropriating to their own use certain articles of clothing, fox skins, and the like, under circumstances which admitted of justification only by the law of the more sagacious and the stronger. It was apparent that our savage friends had their plaint to make, or, it might be, to avenge.

"My first attention, after ministering to the immediate wants of all, was turned to the office of conciliating our Esquimaux benefactors. Though they wore their habitual faces of smiling satisfaction, I could read them too well to be deceived. Policy as well as moral duty have made me anxious always to deserve their respect; but I had seen enough of mankind in its varied relations not to know that respect is little else than a tribute to superiority either real or supposed—and that among the rude at least, one of its elements is fear.

"I therefore called them together in stern and cheerless conference on the deck, as if to inquire into the truth of transactions that I had heard of, leaving it doubtful from my manner which was the party I proposed to implicate. Then, by the intervention of Petersen, I called on Kalutunah for his story and went through a full train of questionings on both sides. It was not difficult to satisfy them that it was my purpose to do justice all round. The subject of controversy was set out fully, and in such a manner as to convince me that an appeal to kind feeling might have been substituted with all effect for the resort to artifice or force. I therefore, to the immense satisfaction of our stranger guests, assured them of my approval, and pulled their hair all around.

"They were introduced into the oriental recess of our dormitory—hitherto an unsolved mystery. There, seated on a red blanket, with four pork fat lamps, throwing an illumination over old worsted damask curtains, hunting knives, rifles, beer barrels, galley stove, and chronometers, I dealt out to each man five needles, a file, and a stick of wood. To Kalutunah and Shunghu I gave knives and other extras; and in conclusion spread out our one remaining buffalo close to the stove, built a roaring fire, cooked a hearty supper, and by noonday they were sleeping away in a state of thorough content. I explained to them further that my people did not steal; that the fox jumpers and boots and sledges were only taken to save their lives; and I thereupon returned them.

"The party took a sound sleep, and a second or rather a continuous feed, and left again on their return through the hummocks with apparent confidence and good humor. Of course they prigged a few knives and forks."

DECEMBER 23, SATURDAY. "This uncalculated accession of numbers makes our little room too crowded to be wholesome: I have to guard its ventilation with all the severity that would befit a surgical ward of our Blockley Hospital. We are using the Esquimaux lamp as an accessory to our stove: it helps out with the cooking and water making, without encroaching upon our rigorously meted stock of wood. But the odor of pork fat, our only oil, we have found to be injurious; and our lamps are therefore placed outside the *tossut*.

"This new arrangement gave rise yesterday to a nearly fatal disaster. A watch was stationed in charge of the lamp, with the usual order of 'No uncovered lights.' He deserted his post. Soon afterward, Hans found the cooking room on fire. It was a horrible crisis; for no less than eight of our party were absolutely nailed to their beds, and there was nothing but a bulkhead between them and the fire. I gave short but instant orders, stationing a line between the tide-hole and the main hatch, detailing two men to work with me, and ordering all the rest who could move to their quarters. Dr. Hayes with his maimed foot, Mr. Brooks with his contracted legs, and poor Morton, otherwise among our best men, could do nothing.

"Before we reached the fire, the entire bulkhead was in a blaze, as well as the dry timbers and skin of the brig. Our moss walls, with their own tinder-like material and their light casing of inflammable wood, were entirely hidden by the flames.

"The water now began to pass down; but with the discharge of the first bucketful the smoke overcame me. As I found myself going, I pushed for the hatchway, knowing that the bucket line would *feel* me. Seeing was impossible; but, striking Ohlsen's legs as I fell, I was passed up to the deck, *minus* beard, eyebrows, and forelock *plus* two burns on the forehead and one on each palm.

Life in the brig, second winter
From left: Bonsall, Brooks, Dr. Kane, Dr. Hayes, Morton

"In about three minutes after making way with the canvas, the fire was got under, and in less than half an hour all was safe again. But the transition, for even the shortest time, from the fiery Shadrachian furnace temperature below, to forty-six degrees below zero above, was intolerably trying. Every man suffered, and only a few escaped without frostbitten fingers.

"The remembrance of the danger and its horrible results almost miraculously averted shocks us all. Had we lost our brig, not a man could have survived: without shelter, clothing, or food, the thermometer almost eighty degrees below the freezing point, and a brisk wind stirring, what hope could we have on the open ice-field?"

DECEMBER 25, CHRISTMAS, MONDAY. "All together again, the returned and the steadfast, we sat down to our Christmas dinner. There was more love than with the stalled ox of former times; but of herbs none. We forgot our discomforts in the blessings that adhered to us still; and when we thought of the long road ahead of us, we thought of it hopefully. I pledged myself to give them their next Christmas with their homes; and each of us drank his 'absent friends' with ferocious zest over one-eighteenth part of a bottle of sillery—the last of its hamper, and alas! no longer *mousseux*.

"But if this solitary relic of festival days had lost its sparkle, we had not. We passed around merrily our turkeys roast and boiled, roast beef, onions, potatoes and cucumbers, watermelons, and God knows what other cravings of the scurvy-sickened palate, with entire exclusion of the fact that each of these was variously represented by pork and beans. Even Lord Peter was not more cordial in his dispensation of plum pudding, mutton, and custard to his unbelieving brothers.

"So much for the Merrie Christmas. What portion of its mirth was genuine with the rest I cannot tell, for we are practiced actors some of us; but there was no heart in my share of it. My thoughts were with those far off, who are thinking, I know, of me. I could bear my own troubles as I do my eiderdown coverlet; for I can see myself as I am, and feel sustained by the knowledge that I have fought my battle well. But there is no one to tell of this at the home table. Pertinacity, unwise daring, calamity—any of these may come up unbidden, as my name circles round, to explain why I am still away."

This fruitless adventure closed the year 1854.

XX

Searching for Food

JANUARY 6, SATURDAY. "If this journal ever gets to be inspected by other eyes, the color of its pages will tell of the atmosphere it is written in. We have been emulating the Esquimaux for some time in everything else; and now, last of all, this intolerable temperature and our want of fuel have driven us to rely on our lamps for heat. Counting those which I have added since the wanderers came back, we have twelve constantly going, with the grease and soot everywhere in proportion.

"Fearing the effect of this on the health of everyone, crowded as we are, and inhaling so much insoluble foreign matter without intermission, I have today reduced the number of lights to four; two of them stationary, and communicating by tin funnels with our chimney, so as to carry away their soot."

JANUARY 13, SATURDAY. "I am feeding up my few remaining dogs very carefully; but I have no meat for them except the carcasses of their late companions. These have to be boiled; for in their frozen state they act as caustics, and, to dogs famishing as ours have been, frozen food often proves fatal, abrading the stomach and esophagus. One of these poor creatures had been a child's pet among the Esquimaux. Last night I found her in nearly a dying state at the mouth of our *tossut,* wistfully eyeing the crevices of the door as they emitted their forbidden treasures of light and heat. She could not move, but, completely subdued, licked my hand—the first time I ever had such a civilized greeting from an Esquimaux dog. I carried her in among the glories of the moderate paradise she aspired to and cooked her a dead puppy soup. She is now slowly gaining strength but can barely stand.

"I want all my scanty dog force for another attempt to communicate with the bay settlements. I am confident we will find Esquimaux there alive, and they *shall* help us. I am not satisfied with Petersen, the companion of my last journey: he is too cautious for the emergency. The occasion is one that calls for every risk short of the final one that man can encounter. My mind is made up, should wind and ice point to its successful accomplishment, to try the thing with Hans. Hans is completely subject to my will, careful and attached to me, and by temperament daring and adventurous.

"Counting my greatest possible number of dogs, we have but five at all to be depended on, and these far from being in condition for the journey. Toodla, Jenny—at this moment officiating as wet nurse—and Rhina are the relics of my South Greenland teams; little Whitey is the solitary Newfoundlander; one big yellow and one feeble little black, all that are left of the powerful recruits we obtained from our Esquimaux brethren.

"It is a fearful thing to attempt a dog trot of near one

hundred miles, where your dogs may drop at any moment and leave you without protection from fifty degrees below zero. As to riding, I do not look to it: we must run alongside of the sledge, as we do on shorter journeys. Our dogs cannot carry more than our scanty provisions, our sleeping bags and guns.

"At home one would fear to encounter such spitting, snarling beasts as the Esquimaux dogs of Peabody Bay. But, wolves as they are, they are far from dangerous: the slightest appearance of a missile or cudgel subdues them at once. Indispensable to the very life of their masters, they are treated, of course, with studied care and kindness; but they are taught from the earliest days of puppy life a savory fear that makes them altogether safe companions even for the children. But they are absolutely ravenous of everything below the human grade. Old Yellow, who goes about with arched back, gliding through the darkness more like a hyena than a dog, made a pounce the other day as I was feeding Jenny, and, almost before I could turn, had gobbled down one of her pups. As none of the litter will ever be of sledging use, I have taken the hint and refreshed Old Yellow with a daily morning puppy. The two last of the family, who will then, I hope, be tolerably milk fed, I shall reserve for my own eating."

JANUARY 14, SUNDAY. "Our sick are all about the same; Wilson, Brooks, Morton, McGary, and Riley unserviceable, Dr. Hayes getting better rapidly. How grateful I ought to be that I, the weakling of a year ago, am a well and helping man! Renewed, I focus on plans.

"At noonday, in spite of the mist, I can see the horizon gap of Charlotte Wood Fiord, between Bessie Mountain and the other hills to the southeast, growing lighter; its twilight is decidedly less doubtful. In four or five days we will have our noonday sun not more than eight degrees below the horizon. This depression, which was Parry's lowest, enabled him by turning the paper toward the south to read diamond type. We are looking forward to this more penumbral darkness as an era. It has now been fifty-two days since we could read such type, even after climbing the dreary hills. One hundred and twenty-four days with the sun below the horizon! One hundred and forty before he reaches the rocky shadowing of our brig!

"I found an overlooked godsend this morning—a bear's head, put away for a specimen, but completely frozen. There is no inconsiderable quantity of meat adhering to it, and I serve it out raw to Brooks, Wilson, and Riley.

"I do not know that my journal anywhere mentions our habituation to raw meats, nor does it dwell upon their strange adaptation to scorbutic disease. Our journeys have taught us the wisdom of the Esquimaux appetite, and there are few among us who do not relish a slice of raw blubber or a chunk of frozen walrus beef. The liver of a walrus *(awuktanuk)* eaten with little slices of his fat—of a verity it is a delicious morsel. Fire would ruin the curt, pithy expression of vitality that belongs to its uncooked juices. Charles Lamb's roast pig[1] was nothing to *awuktanuk*. I wonder that raw beef is not eaten at home. Deprived of extraneous fiber, it is neither indigestible nor difficult to masticate. With acids and condiments, it makes a salad an educated palate cannot help relishing; and as a powerful and condensed heat-making and antiscorbutic food, it has no rival.

"My plans for sledging, simple as I once thought them, and simple certainly as compared with those of the English parties, have completely changed. Give me an eight-pound reindeer fur bag to sleep in, an Esquimaux lamp with a lump of moss, a sheet iron snow melter or a copper soup pot with a tin cylinder to slip over it and defend it from the wind, a good *pièce de résistance* of raw walrus beef; and I want nothing more for a long journey, if the thermometer will keep itself as high as minus thirty degrees. Give me a bear skin bag and coffee to boot; and with the clothes on my back I am ready for minus sixty degrees—but no wind."

JANUARY 17, WEDNESDAY. "There is no evading it any longer: it has been evident for the past ten days that the 'present state of things cannot last.' We require meat and cannot get along without it. Our sick have finished the bear's head and are now eating the condemned abscessed liver of the animal, including some intestines that were not given to the dogs. We have about three days' allowance; thin chips of raw frozen meat, not exceeding four ounces in weight for

[1] Famous essay by Charles Lamb.

each man per diem. Our poor fellows eat it with zest; but it is lamentably little.

"Although I was unsuccessful in my last attempt to reach the huts with the dogs, I am far from sure that with a proper equipment it could not be managed by walking. The thought weighs upon me. A foot travel does not seem to have occurred to my comrades; and at first sight the idea of making for a point seventy-five miles by the shortest line from our brig, with this awfully cold darkness on, is gloomy enough.

"But I propose walking at first only as far as the broken hut at Anoatok (the 'wind-loved spot') and giving our poor dogs a chance of refreshing there. After this, Hans and myself will force them forward as far as we can, with nothing but our sleeping gear, and spend the second night wherever they happen to break down. After that, we can manage the rest of the journey without any luggage but our personal clothing.

"It seems hard to sacrifice the dogs, not to speak of the rest of the party; but the necessity is too palpable and urgent. As we are now, a very few deaths would break us up entirely. Still, the emergency would not move me if I did not feel, after careful, painful thought that the thing can be accomplished. If by the blessing of the Great Ruler it should prove successful, the result will secure the safety of all hands. No one knows as yet of my intention except Hans himself. I am quietly preparing a special outfit, and will leave with the first return of moonlight.

"McGary, my relief, calls me: he has foraged out

some raw cabbage and spiced it up with curry powder, our only remaining pepper. This, with a piece of corn bread—no bad article either—he wants me to share with him. True to my old times habitude, I hasten to the cabbage—cold roast beef, Worcester sauce, a head of endive, and a bottle—not one drop less—of Preston ale (I never drink any other). McGary, 'bring on de beans!' "

JANUARY 22, MONDAY. "Busy preparing for my trip to the lower Esquimaux settlement. The barometer remains at the extraordinary height of 30°85′,—a bad prelude to a journey!

"Petersen caught another providential fox. We divided him into nine portions, three for each of our scurvied patients. I am off."

* * * *

JANUARY 29, MONDAY. "The dogs carried us to the lower curve of the reach before breaking down. I was just beginning to hope for an easy voyage when Toodla and the Big Yellow gave way nearly together; the latter frightfully contorted by convulsions. There was no remedy for it: the moon went down, and the wretched night was upon us. We groped along the ice-foot and, after fourteen hours' painful walking, reached the old hut.

"A dark water-sky extended in a wedge from Littleton to a point north of the cape. The height of the barometer continued as we left it at the brig, and our own sensations of warmth convinced us that we were about to have a snowstorm. The mist was rising around us.

"We hardly expected to meet the Esquimaux here, and were not disappointed. Hans set to work at once to cut out blocks of snow to close up the entrance to the hut. I carried in our blubber lamp, food, and bedding, unharnessed the dogs, and took them into the same shelter. We were barely housed before the storm broke upon us.

"Here, completely excluded from the knowledge of things without, we spent many miserable hours. We could keep no note of time, and, except by the whirring of the drift against the roof of our kennel, had no information of the state of the weather. We slept and cooked coffee, and drank coffee, and slept and cooked coffee, and drank again; and when our tired instincts told us that twelve hours had passed, we treated ourselves to a meal—that is to say, we divided impartial bites out of the raw hind leg of a fox to give zest to our biscuits spread with frozen tallow.

"We then turned in to sleep again, no longer heedful of the storm, for it buried us deep in with the snow.

"But in the meantime, although the storm continued, the temperatures underwent an extraordinary change. I was awakened by the dropping of water from the roof above me; and, upon turning back my sleeping bag, found it saturated by the melting of its previously condensed hoar frost. My eiderdown was like a wet swab. I found afterward that the phenomenon of the warm southeast had come unexpectedly upon us. The thermometers at the brig indicated a temperature of twenty six degrees above zero; and, closer as we were to the water, the weather was probably above the freezing point.

"When we left the brig—how long before it was we did not know—the temperature was minus forty-four degrees. It had risen at least seventy degrees. I defy the strongest man not to suffer from such a change. A close, oppressive sensation attacked both Hans and myself. We both suffered from cardiac symptoms, and are up to this moment under anxious treatment by our comrades. Mr. Wilson, I find, has had spasmodic asthma from it here, and Brooks has a renewal of his old dyspnoea.

"In the morning—that is to say, when the combined light of the noonday dawn and the circumpolar moon permitted our escape—I found, by comparing the time as indicated by the Great Bear with the present increased altitude of the moon, that we had been pent up nearly two days. Under these circumstances we made directly for the hummocks, *en route* for the bay. But here was a disastrous change. The snow had accumulated under the windward sides of the inclined tables to a height so excessive that we buried sledge, dogs, and drivers in the effort to work through. It was all in vain that Hans and I harnessed ourselves to, or lifted, levered, twisted, and pulled. Utterly exhausted and sick, I was obliged to give it up. The darkness closed in again, and with difficulty we regained our igloo.

"The ensuing night then brought a return to hard

freezing temperatures. Our soft, downy coverlet was a stiff, clotted lump of ice. In spite of our double lamp, it was a miserable halt. Our provisions grew short; the snow kept on falling, and we had still forty-six miles between us and the Esquimaux.

"I determined to try the land-ice (ice-foot) by Fog Inlet; and we worked four hours upon this without a breathing spell, utterly in vain. My poor Esquimaux, Hans, adventurous and buoyant as he was, began to cry like a child. Sick, worn out, strength gone, dogs fast and floundering, I am not ashamed to admit that, as I thought of the sick men on board, my own equanimity also was at fault.

"We had not been able to get the dogs out, when the big moon appeared above the water-smoke. A familiar hill, 'Old Beacon Knob,' was near. I scrambled to its top and reconnoitered the coast around it. The ridge about Cape Hatherton seemed to jut out of a perfect chaos of broken ice. The water—that inexplicable North Water—was there, a long black wedge, overhung by wreaths of smoke, running to the northward and eastward. Better than all yet—could I be deceived?—a trough through the hummock ridges and level plains of ice stretching to the south!

"Hans heard my halloo, and came up to confirm me. But for our disabled dogs and the waning moonlight, we could easily have made our journey. It was with a rejoiced heart that I made my way back to our miserable little cavern, and restuffed its gaping entrance with the snow. We had no blubber and, of course, no fire; but I knew that we could gain the brig, and that, after refreshing the dogs and ourselves we could now assuredly reach the settlements.

"We took the back track next morning over Bedevilled Reach upon the mid-ice floes, and reached the brig by 4:00 P.M. on Friday; since when I have been so stiff and scorbutic, so utterly used up, that today gives me a first return to my journal."

JANUARY 30, TUESDAY. "My companions on board felt all my disappointment at bringing back no meat; but infinite gladness took the place of regret when they heard the great news of a passage through the hummocks. Petersen began at once to busy himself with his wardrobe; and an eight-day party was organized almost before we turned in, to start as soon as the tempestuous weather subsides and the drifts settle down. It is four days since, but as yet we dare not venture out.

"That there is no time for delay, this health table will show:

"Henry Brooks: Unable any longer to go on deck: we carry him with difficulty from his berth to a cushioned locker.

"McGary: Less helpless; but off duty and saturated with articular scurvy.

"Mr. Wilson: In bed. Severe purpuric blotches, and nodes in limbs. Cannot move.

"George Riley: Abed; limbs less stiff, gums better, unable to do duty.

"Thomas Hickey, (our cook): Cannot keep his legs

many days more; already swelled and badly blistered.

"William Morton: Down with a frozen heel; the bone exfoliating.

"Henry Goodfellow: Scurvied gums, but generally well.

"Dr. Hayes is prostrate with his amputated toes— Sontag just able to hobble. In a word, our effective force is reduced to five—Mr. Ohlsen, Mr. Bonsall, Petersen, Hans, and the Commander; and even of these some might, perhaps, be rightfully transferred to the other list. We have the whole burden of the hourly observations and the routine of our domestic life, even to the cooking, which we take in rotation.

"Still this remarkable temperature; the barometer slowly librating between 29°20 and the old 30°40. Snow falling: wind from the southwest, hauling by the west to north: yet the thermometer at minus ten degrees and three degrees above zero. We long anxiously for weather to enable our meat party to start. The past two days our sick have been entirely out of meat: the foxes seem to avoid our traps. I gave Wilson one raw meal from the masseter muscle[2], which adhered to another old bear's head I was keeping for a specimen. But otherwise we have had no antiscorbutic for three days.

"Among other remedies which I oppose to the distemper, I have commenced making sundry salts of iron; among them the citrate and a chlorohydrated

[2] Powerful muscle that is connected to and helps raise the lower jaw, as in chewing.

tincture. We have but one bottle of brandy left: my applying a half pint of it to the tincture shows the high value I set upon this noble chalybeate.[3] My nose bled today, and I was struck with the fluid brickdusty poverty of the blood. I use iron much among my people: as a single remedy it exceeds all others, except only the specific of raw meat: potash for its own action is well enough to meet some conditions of the disease. We were in the habit of using freely an extemporaneous citrate prepared from our lime juice;[4] but, as our cases became more reduced and complicated with hemorrhages, iron was our one great remedy."

FEBRUARY 2, FRIDAY. "The weather clears, the full moon shows herself, the sledge is packed, and Petersen will start tomorrow."

FEBRUARY 3, SATURDAY. "He is gone with Hans. A bad time with Brooks, in a swoon from exhaustion!"

FEBRUARY 4, SUNDAY. "Ohlsen breaks down: the scurvy is in his knee, and he cannot walk. This day, too, Thomas Hickey, our acting cook, gives way completely. I can hardly realize that among these strong men I alone should be the borne up man—the only one, except Mr. Bonsall, on his legs. It sometimes makes me tremble when I think of how necessary I am

[3] Impregnated with compounds of iron, as mineral water.
[4] Lime juice was considered an important ascorbic acid, but later research showed that lemons were far stronger in vitamin C. Also the early methods of storing and processing of lime or lemon juice reduced its vitamin C potency, especially if there was any contact with copper. See Carpenter, *The History of Scurvy & Vitamin C*, p. 117.

to sustain this state of things. It is a Sunday thought, that it must be for some wise and good end I am thus supported."

* * * *

FEBRUARY 6, TUESDAY. "At ten, last evening, not long after my journal record, I heard voices outside. Petersen and Hans had returned. I met them silently on deck, and heard from poor Petersen how he had broken down. The snows had been increasing since my own last trial—his strength had left him; the scurvy had entered his chest; in a word, he had failed.

"But today our fortunes are on the mend. It has been beautifully clear; and for the first time a shade of bronzed yellow has warmed our noon horizon, with a gentle violet running into rich brown clouds, unlike our night skies. Hans and I started for a hunt—one to explore new grounds, the other to follow tracks in the recent snow. The result was two rabbits, the first fruits of the coming light, and the promise of more in the numerous feeding traces among the rocks of Charlotte Wood Fiord. The meat, our first for ten days, was distributed raw. By keeping the rabbits carefully covered up, they reached the ship sufficiently unfrozen to give us about a pint of raw blood. It was a grateful cordial to Brooks, Wilson, and Riley."

FEBRUARY 9, FRIDAY. "Still no supplies. Three of us have been out all day, without getting a shot. Hans thinks he saw a couple of reindeer at a distance; and his eyes rarely deceive him. He will try for them tomorrow. I have fitted out for him a tent and a sleeping bag on the second table land; and the thermometer is now so little below zero that he will be able to keep the field for a steady hunt. Our sick are sinking for want of fresh food. It is the only specific: I dislike to use the unphilosophical term; but in our case it is the true one. In large quantities it dissipates the disease; in ordinary rations it prevents its occurrence; in small doses it checks it while sustaining the patient. We have learned its value too well to waste it; every part of every animal is used. The skin makes the basis of a soup, and the claws can be boiled to a jelly. Lungs, larynx, stomach, and entrails, all are available. I have not permitted myself to taste more than an occasional entrail of our last rabbits. Not that I am free from symptoms of the universal pest. I am conscious of a stiffness in the tendons, a shortness of breath, and a weariness of the bones that should naturally attend the eruption that covers my body. But I have none of the more fearful signs. I can walk with energy after I get warmed up, I have no bleeding of the gums, and, better than all, I am without that horrible despondency which the disease nourishes and feeds on. I sleep sound and dream pleasantly—generally about successes in the hunt or a double ration of reindeer or ptarmigan."

FEBRUARY 12, MONDAY. "Hans is off for his hunting lodge, 'over the hills and far away,'[5] beyond Charlotte Wood Fiord. I have sent Godfrey with him; for I fear the boy has got the taint like the rest of us and he may

[5] Alfred Lord Tennyson, "The Day Dream," 1842.

suffer from exposure. He thinks he can bring back a deer, and the chances are worth the trial. We can manage the small hunt, Petersen and I, till he comes back, unless we break down too. But I do not like these symptoms of mine, and Petersen is very far from the man he was. We had a tramp today, both of us, after an imaginary deer—a *bennisoak*[6] that has been supposed for the last three days to be hunting the neighborhood of the water pools of the big fiord, and have come back jaded and sad. If Hans gives way, God help us!"

It is hardly worthwhile to inflict on the reader a succession of journal records like these. They tell of nothing but the varying symptoms of sick men, dreary, profitless hunts, relieved now and then by the signalized incident of a killed rabbit or a deer seen, and the longed for advent of the solar light. My memorandum went on:

"We have three months before us of intense cold. We have a large and laborious outfit to arrange, boats, sledges, provisions, and accoutrements for a journey of alternating ice and water of more than thirteen hundred miles. Our carpenter is among the worst of our invalids. Supposing all our men able to move, four of them must be carried by the rest, three in consequence of amputation and one from frost wounds; and our boats must be sledged over some sixty or perhaps ninety miles of terrible ice before launching and loading them. Finally, a part of our force, whatever it may be, must be detailed to guard our property from the

[6] A great reindeer or bull caribou. "Soak" meant "great."

Esquimaux while the other detachments are making their successive trips to the open water. So much for the shadow of the picture!

"But it has two sides; and, whether from constitutional temperament or well-reasoned argument, I find our state far from desperate. I cheer my comrades after this fashion:

"1. I am convinced, from a careful analysis of our disease, that under its present aspects it is not beyond control. If, with the aid of our present hunting resources or by any providential accession to them, I can keep the cases from rapid depression, next month ought to give us a bear, and in the meantime Hans may find a deer; and, with a good stock of fresh meat even for a few days, I can venture away from the vessel to draw supplies from the Esquimaux at Etah. I should have been there before this, if I could have been spared for forty-eight hours. We want nothing but meat.

"2. The coming of the sun will open appliances of moral help to the sick, and give energy to the hygienic resorts which I am arranging at this moment. Our miserable little kennel, where eighteen are crowded into the space of ten, is thoroughly begrimed with lamp-black from the inevitable smoke of our fuel. The weather has prevented our drying and airing the sleeping gear. The floor is damp from the conducted warmth of the seawater under us, melting the ice that has condensed everywhere below. Sunshine and dry weather will cure all this. I have window sash ready to fix over the roof and southern side of the galley house; and our useless daguerreotype plates, tacked over wooden screens, make admirable mirrors to transfer the sun rays into the cabin. I have manufactured a full draught pipe for our smokey stove. Chloride of sodium must do the rest.

"3. While we live we will stick together: one fate shall belong to us all, be it what it may.

"There is comfort in this review; and, please God in his beneficent providence to spare us for the work, I will yet give one more manly tug to search the shores of Kennedy Channel for memorials of the lost; and then, our duties over here, and the brig still prison bound, enter trustingly upon the task of our escape."

Section of winter apartment

XXI

Hanging On and a Deserter

FEBRUARY 22, THURSDAY. "Washington's birthday: all our colors flying in the new sunlight. A day of good omen, even to the sojourners among the ice. Hans comes in with great news. He has had a shot at our bennesoak, a long shot; but it reached him. The animal made off at a slow run, but we are sure of him now. This same deer has been hanging round the lake at the fiord through all the dim returning twilight; and so many stories were told of his appearance and movements that he had almost grown into a myth. Tomorrow we shall desire his better acquaintance."

FEBRUARY 23, FRIDAY. "Hans was out early this morning on the trail of the wounded deer. Rhina, the least barbarous of our sledge dogs, assisted him. He was back by noon, with the joyful news, 'The tukkuk dead only two miles up big fiord!' The cry found its way through the hatch, and came back in a broken huzza from the sick men.

"We are so badly off for strong arms that our reindeer threatened to be as great an embarrassment to us as the auction-drawn elephant was to his lucky master. We had hard work with our dogs carrying him to the brig, and still harder, worn down as we were, in getting him over the ship's side. But we succeeded, and were tumbling him down the hold, when we found ourselves in a dilemma like the Vicar of Wakefield[1] with his family picture. It was impossible to drag the prize into our little moss-lined dormitory; the *tossut* was not half big enough to let him pass: and it was equally impossible to skin him anywhere else without freezing our fingers in the operation. It was a happy escape from the embarrassments of our hungry little council to determine that the animal might be carved before skinning as well as he could be afterward; and in a very few minutes we proved our united wisdom by a feast on his quartered remains.

"It was a glorious meal, such as the compensations of Providence reserve for starving men alone. We ate, forgetful of the past, and almost heedless of the morrow; cleared away the offal wearily; and now, at 10:00 P.M., all hands have turned in to sleep, leaving to their commanding officer the solitary honor of an eight hours' vigil."

FEBRUARY 24, SATURDAY. "A bitter disappointment met us at our evening meal. The flesh of our deer was nearly uneatable from putrefaction; the liver and intestines, from which I had expected so much, utterly so. The rapidity of such a change, in a temperature so low as minus thirty-five degrees, seems curious; but the Greenlanders say that extreme cold is rather a promoter than otherwise of the putrefactive process. All the graminivorous[2] animals have the same tendency,

[1] Oliver Goldsmith's sentimental novel, *The Vicar of Wakefield*.
[2] *Graminivorous:* grass-eating.

Icebergs near Kosoak, Life-Boat Cove

James Hamilton, from a sketch by Dr. Kane

as is well known to the butchers. Our buffalo hunters, when they clean a carcass, do it at once; they have told me that the musk ox is sometimes tainted after five minutes' exposure. The Esquimaux, with whom there is no fastidious sensibility of palate, are in the practice at Yotlik and Horses' Head, in latitude 73°40′, even in the severest weather, of withdrawing the viscera immediately after death and filling the cavity with stones."

FEBRUARY 25, SUNDAY. "Today, blessed be the Great Author of Light! I have once more looked upon the sun. I was standing on deck, thinking over our prospects, when a familiar berg, which had been hid in shadow, flashed out in sun birth. I knew this berg well: it stood between Charlotte Wood Fiord and Little Willie's Monument. One year ago I traveled toward it from Fern Rock to catch the sunshine. Then I had to climb the hills beyond, to get the luxury of basking in its brightness; but now, though the sun is but a single degree above the horizon, it is so much elevated by refraction that the sheen stretched across the trough of the fiord like a flaming tongue. I could not resist the influence. It was a Sunday act of worship: I started off at an even run, and caught him as he rolled slowly along the horizon, and before he sank. I was the first of my party to rejoice and meditate in sunshine. It is the third sun I have seen rise for a moment above the long night of an Arctic winter."

FEBRUARY 28, WEDNESDAY. "February closes: thank God for the lapse of its twenty-eight days! Should the thirty-one of the coming March not drag us further downward, we may hope for a successful close to this dreary drama. By the tenth of April we should have seal; and when they come, if we remain to welcome them, we can call ourselves saved."

* * * *

My journal for the beginning of March is little else than a chronicle of sufferings. Our little party was quite broken down. Every man on board was tainted with scurvy, and it was not common to find more than three who could assist in caring for the rest. The greater number were in their bunks, absolutely unable to stir.

The circumstances were well fitted to bring out the character of individuals. Some were very grateful for every little act of kindness from their more fortunate messmates; some querulous; others desponding; others again wanted only strength to become mutinous. Brooks, my first officer, as stalwart a man-o'-war's man as ever faced an enemy, burst into tears when he first saw himself in the glass. On Sunday, the fourth, our last remnant of fresh meat had been doled out. Our invalids began to sink rapidly. The wounds of our amputated men opened afresh. The region about our harbor ceased to furnish its scanty contingent of game. One of our huntsmen, Petersen, never very reliable in anything, declared himself unfit for further duty. Hans was unsuccessful: he made several wide circuits, and saw deer twice; but they were beyond range.

I tried the hunt for a long morning myself, without

meeting a single thing of life, and was convinced, by the appearance of things on my return to the brig, that I should peril the morale, and with it the only hope, of my command by repeating the experiment.

I labored, of course, with all the ingenuity for a well-taxed mind to keep up the spirits of my comrades. I cooked for them all imaginable compounds of our un-varied diet list, and brewed up flaxseed and lime juice and quinine and willow stems into an abomination which was dignified as beer, and which some were persuaded for the time to believe such. But it was becoming more and more certain every hour that, unless we could renew our supplies of fresh meat, the days of the party were numbered.

I spare myself, as well as the readers of this hastily compiled volume, when I pass summarily over the details of our condition at this time.

I look back at it with recollections like those of a nightmare. Yet I was borne up wonderfully. I never doubted for an instant that the same Providence that had guarded us through the long darkness of winter was still watching over us for good, and that it was yet in reserve for us—for some; I dared not hope for all—to bear back the tidings of our rescue to a Christian land. But how I did not see.

On the sixth of the month I made the desperate venture of sending off my only trusted and effective huntsman on a sledge journey to find the Esquimaux of Etah.

"In clearing out Riley's bunk, we found that a rat

had built his nest in my insect box, destroying all our specimens. This is a grave loss; for, besides that they were light of carriage and might have accompanied us in the retreat which now seems inevitable, they comprised our entire collection, and, though few in numbers, were rich for this stinted region. I had many spiders and bees. He is welcome to the whole of them, however, if I only catch him the fatter for the ration."

MARCH 10, SATURDAY. "Hans has not yet returned so that he must have reached the settlement. His orders were, if no meat be obtained of the Esquimaux, to borrow their dogs and try for bears along the open water. In this resource I have confidence. The days are magnificent.

"I had hardly written the above, when 'Bim, bim, bim!' sounded from the deck, mixed with the chorus of our returning dogs. The next minute Hans and myself were shaking hands.

"He had much to tell us; to men in our condition Hans was as a man from cities. We of the wilderness flocked around him to hear the news. Sugar teats of raw meat are passed around. 'Speak loud, Hans, that they may hear in the bunks.'

"The 'wind-loved' Anoatok he had reached on the first night after leaving the brig: no Esquimaux there of course; and he slept not warmly at a temperature of fifty-three degrees below zero. On the evening of the next day he reached Etah Bay and was hailed with joyous welcome. But a new phase of Esquimaux life had come upon its indolent, happy, blubber-fed denizens. Instead of plump, greasy children and round-cheeked matrons, Hans saw around him lean figures of misery: the men looked hard and bony, and the children shrivelled in the hoods that cradled them at their mothers' backs. Famine had been among them; and the skin of a young sea unicorn, lately caught, was all that remained to them of food. It was the old story of improvidence and its miserable train. They had even eaten their reserve of blubber, and were seated in darkness and cold, waiting gloomily for the sun. Even their dogs, their main reliance for the hunt and for an escape to some more favored camping ground, had fallen a sacrifice to hunger. Only four remained out of thirty: the rest had been eaten.

"Hans behaved well, and carried out my orders in their full spirit. He proposed to aid them in the walrus hunt.

"I have not time to detail Hans's adventurous hunt, equally important to the scurvied sick of Rensselaer and the starving residents of Etah Bay. Metek (the eider-duck) speared a medium-sized walrus, and Hans gave him no less than five Marston balls before he gave up his struggles. The beast was carried back in triumph, and all hands fed as if they could never know famine again. It was a regular feast, and the kablunah interest was exalted to the skies.

"I had directed Hans to endeavor to engage Myouk, if he could, to assist him in hunting. A most timely thought: for the morning's work made them receive the invitation as a great favor. Hans got his share of the meat, and returned to the brig accompanied by the boy, who is now under my care on board. This imp—for he is full of the devil—has always had a relishing fancy for the kicks and cuffs with which I recall the forks and teaspoons when they get astray; and, to tell the truth, he always takes care to earn them. He is very happy, but so wasted by hunger that the work of fattening him will be a costly one. Poor little fellow! born to toil and necessity and peril; stern hunter as he already is, the lines of his face are still quite soft and childlike. I think we understand one another better than our incongruities would imply."

* * * *

MARCH 15, THURSDAY. "Today we have finished burning our last Manilla hawser for fuel, the temperature remaining at the extraordinary mean of minus 52 degrees. Our next resort must be to the trebling of the brig: Petersen—what remains of him, for the man's energies are gone—is now at work cutting it off. It is a hard trial for me. I have spared neither exertion, thought, nor suffering to save the seaworthiness of our little vessel, but all to no end: she can never bear us to the sea. Want of provisions alone, if nothing else, will drive us from her; for this solid case of nine-foot ice cannot possibly give way until the late changes of fall, nor then unless a hot summer and a retarded winter afterward allow the winds to break up its iron casing."

MARCH 16, FRIDAY. "We have just a scant two day's meat for the sick. Hans is doing his best; but there is nothing to be found on the hills: and I fear that a long hunting journey to the south is our only resource."

MARCH 17, SATURDAY. "I have been getting Hans ready for the settlement, with a five-sinnet line of Maury's sounding twine. The natives to the south have lost nearly all their *allunaks* or walrus lines by the accidents of December or January, and will be unable to replace them till the return of the seal. A good or even serviceable allunak requires a whole ussuk to cut it from. It is almost the only article whose manufacture seems to be conducted by the Esquimaux with any care and nicety of process. Our sounding line will be a valuable contribution to them, and may, like some more ostentatious charities, include the liberal givers among those whom it principally blesses."

MARCH 18, SUNDAY. "I have a couple of men on board whose former history I would give something to know—bad fellows both of them, but daring, energetic, and strong. They gave me trouble before we reached the coast of Greenland; and they keep me constantly on the watch at this moment, for it is clear to me that they have some secret object in view, involving probably a desertion and escape to the Esquimaux settlements. They are both feigning sickness this morning; and, from what I have overheard, it is with the view of getting thoroughly rested before a start. Hans's departure with the sledge and dogs would give them a fine chance, if they could only way-lay him, of securing all our facilities for travel; and I should not be surprised if they tried to compel him to go along with them. They cannot succeed in this except by force.

"I am acting very guardedly with them. I cannot punish till I have the evidence of an overt act. Nor can I trust the matter to other hands. It would not do to depress my sick party by disclosing a scheme which, if it could be carried out fully, might be fatal to the whole of us. All this adds to my other duties those of a detective policeman. I do not find them agreeable."

MARCH 19, MONDAY. "Hans got off at eleven. I have been all right in my suspicions about John and Bill. They were anxious to get together this morning, and I was equally resolved to prevent any communication between them. I did this so ingeniously that they did not suspect my motive, by devising some outside duty for one or the other of them and keeping his comrade in the plot at work under my own eye. Their impatience and cunning little resorts to procure the chance of a word in private were quite amusing. It might be very far otherwise if they could manage to rob us of our dogs and gain the Netlik settlements.

"I hope the danger is over now. I shall keep the whole thing to myself for even the frustration of a mutinous purpose had best be concealed from the party."

MARCH 20, TUESDAY. "This morning I received information from Stephenson that Bill had declared his intention of leaving the brig today at some time. John, being now really lame, could not accompany him. This Stephenson overheard in whispers during the night and, in faithful execution of his duty, conveyed it to me.

"I kept the news to myself; but there was no time to be lost. William, therefore, was awakened at 6:00 A.M. after my own night watch—and ordered to cook breakfast. Meantime I watched him. At first he appeared troubled and had several stealthily whispered interviews with John: finally his manner became more easy, and he cooked and served our breakfast meal. I now felt convinced that he would meet John outside as soon as he could leave the room, and that one or both would then desert. I therefore threw on my furs and armed myself, made Bonsall and Morton acquainted with my plans, and then, crawling out of our dark passage, concealed myself near its entrance. I had hardly waited half an hour—pretty cold work too—when John crawled out, limping and grunting. Once fairly out, he looked furtively round, and then, with a sigh of satisfaction, mounted our rickety steps entirely cured of his lameness. Within ten minutes after he had gained the deck the door opened again, and William made his appearance, booted for travel and clad in buffalo. As he emerged into the hold, I confronted him. He was ordered at once to the cabin; and Morton was despatched on deck to compel the presence of the third party, while Mr. Bonsall took his station at the door, allowing no one to pass out.

"In a very few minutes John crawled back again, as lame and exhausted as when he was last below, yet growing lamer rapidly as, recovering from the glare of the light, he saw the tableau. I then explained the state of things to the little company and detailed step by step to the principals in the scene every one of their plans.

"Bill was the first to confess. I had prepared myself for the emergency, and punished him on the spot. As he rose with some difficulty, I detailed from the log-book the offenses he had committed and adduced the proofs.

"The short-handed condition of the brig made me unable to confine him; therefore I deemed it best to re-move his handcuffs, to accept his protestations of re-form and put him again to work. He accepted my lenity with abundant thanks, went to duty, and in less than an hour deserted. I was hunting at the time, but the watch reported his having first been discovered on the ice-foot and out of presenting distance. His inten-tion undoubtedly is to reach Etah Bay, and, robbing Hans of sledge and dogs, proceed south to Netlik.

"Should he succeed, the result will be a heavy loss to us. The dogs are indispensable in the hunt and in transporting us to Anoatok. The step however is not likely to be successful. At all events, he is off, and I re-gret that duty prevents my rejoicing at his departure. John remains with us, closely watched, but apparently sincere in his protestations of absolute reform."

* * * *

MARCH 21, WEDNESDAY. "The day had been beautifully clear, and so mild that our midday thermometers gave but seven degrees above zero. This bears badly upon the desertion of Godfrey, for the probabilities are that he will find Hans's buffalo robe at the hut, and thus sleep and be refreshed. In that case, he can easily reach the Esquimaux of Etah Bay, and may easily seize upon the sledge dogs, rifle, and trading articles. The consequences of such an act would be very disastrous; nearly all my hopes of lifting the sick, and therefore of escaping in boats to the south, rest upon these dogs."

MARCH 22, THURSDAY. "Petersen's ptarmigan are all gone, (five of them) and of the rabbit, but two rations of eight ounces each remain. We three, Bonsall, Petersen, and myself, have made up our minds to walk up Mary River Ravine until we reach the deer plains, and there separate and close in upon them. Today is therefore a busy one, for we must prepare beforehand the entire daily requirements of the sick: the ice for melting water must be cut in blocks and laid near the stove; the wood, of which it requires one entire day to tear enough out for two days, must be chopped and piled within arm reach; the bread must be cooked and provisions arranged before we can leave our comrades. When we three leave the brig, there will not be a single able man on board. McGary is able to leave his bed and stump about a little; but this is all. Need the dear home folks, who may some day read this, wonder that I am a little careworn, and that I leave the brig with reluctance? Of we three God-supported men, each has his own heavy load of scurvy."

MARCH 23, FRIDAY. "We started this morning, overworked and limping, rather as men ending a journey than beginning one. After four hours of forced walking, we reached the reindeer feeding grounds, but were too late: the animals had left at least two hours before our arrival. We scouted it over the protruding syenites, and found a couple of ptarmigan and three hares: these we secured.

"My people had done well during my absence, and welcomed me back impressively."

MARCH 24, SATURDAY. "Our yesterday's ptarmigan gave the most sick a raw ration, and today we killed a second pair, which will serve them for tomorrow. To my great joy, they seem on that limited allowance to hold their ground.

"Bonsall and Petersen are now woodmen, preparing our daily fuel. My own pleasant duty consists in chopping from an iceberg six half-bushel bagfuls of frozen water, carrying it to the brig and passing it through the scuttle into our den; in emptying by three several jobs some twelve to fifteen bucketfuls from the slop barrel; in administering both as nurse and physician to fourteen sick men; in helping to pick eider-down from its soil as material for boat bedding; in writing this wretched daily record, eating my meals, sleeping my broken sleeps, and feeling that the days pass without congenial occupation.

"Hans has not returned. I give him two days more before I fall in with the opinion which some seem to entertain, that Godfrey has waylaid or seized upon his sledge. This wretched man has been the very bane of the cruise. My conscience tells me that almost any measure against him would be justified, but aversion to extreme measures binds my hands."

XXII

The Deserter Returns

MARCH 25, SUNDAY. "A hard-working, busy Sunday it has been—a cheerless, scurvy-breeding day; and now by the midnight, which is as it were the evening of its continued light, I read the thermometers unaided except by the crimson fires of the northern horizon. It is, moreover, cold again, minus thirty-seven degrees.

"Refraction with all its magic is back upon us; the 'Delectable Mountains' appear again; and, as the sun has now worked his way to the margin of the northwestern horizon, we can see the blaze stealing out from the black portals of these uplifted hills, as if there was truly beyond it a celestial gate."

MARCH 31, SATURDAY. "This month, badly as its daily record reads, is upon review a cheering one. We have managed to get enough game to revive the worst of our scurvy patients, and have kept in regular movement the domestic wheel of shipboard. Our troubles have been greater than at any time before; perhaps I ought to say they are greatest as the month closes: but, whatever of misery Bonsall and Petersen and myself may have endured, it seems nearly certain now that at least four men will soon be able to relieve us. Brooks, McGary, Riley, and Thomas have seen the crisis of their malady, and, if secured from relapse, will recover rapidly. Ohlsen also is better, but slow to regain his powers. But the rest of the crew are still down.

"The game season besides is drawing nearer; and, once able to shoot seal upon the ice, I have little fears for the recovery of the larger portion of our party. Perhaps I am too sanguine; for it is clear that those of us who have till now sustained the others are beginning to sink. Bonsall can barely walk in the morning, and his legs become stiffer daily; Petersen gives way at the ankles; and I suffer much from the eruption, a tormenting and anomalous symptom, which affects eight of our sick. It has many of the characteristics of exanthemata;[1] but is singularly persistent, varied in its phases, and possibly in its result dangerous.

"The moral value of this toilsome month to myself has been the lesson of sympathy it has taught me with the laboring man. The fatigue and disgust and secret trials of the overworked brain are bad enough, but not to me more severe than those which follow the sick and jaded body to a sleepless bed. I have realized the sweat of the brow, and can feel how painful his earnings must be to whom the grasshopper has become a burden."

APRIL 2, MONDAY. "At eleven o'clock this morning, Mr. Bonsall reported a man about a mile from the brig, apparently lurking on the ice-foot. I thought it was Hans, and we both went forward to meet him. As we drew closer we discovered our sledge and dog team

---

[1]*Exanthemata:* an eruption of the skin.

near where he stood; but the man turned and ran to the south.

"I pursued him, leaving Mr. Bonsall, who carried a Sharpe rifle, behind; and the man, whom I now recognized to be Godfrey, seeing me advance alone stopped and met me. He told me that he had been to the south as far as Northumberland Island; that Hans was lying sick at Etah, in consequence of exposure; that he himself had made up his mind to go back and spend the rest of his life with Kalutunah and the Esquimaux; and that neither persuasion nor force should divert him from this purpose.

"Upon my presenting a pistol, I succeeded in forcing him back to the gangway of the brig; but he refused to go farther; and, being loath to injure him, I left him under the guardianship of Mr. Bonsall's weapon while I went on board for irons; for both Bonsall and myself were barely able to walk, and utterly incapable of controlling him by manual force, and Petersen was out hunting: the rest, thirteen in all, are down with scurvy. I had just reached the deck when he turned to run. Mr. Bonsall's pistol failed at the cap. I jumped at once to the gun stand; but my first rifle, affected by the cold, went off in the act of cocking, and a second, aimed in haste at long but practicable distance, missed the fugitive. He made good his escape before we could lay hold of another weapon.

"I am now more anxious than ever about Hans. The past conduct of Godfrey on board, and his mutinous desertion, make me aware that he is capable of daring wrong as well as deception. Hans has been gone more than a fortnight: he has been used to making the same journey in less than a week. His sledge and dogs came back in the possession of the very man whom I suspected of an intention to waylay him; and this man, after being driven by menaces to the ship's side, perils his life rather than place himself in my power on board of her.

"Yet he came back to our neighborhood voluntarily, with sledge and dogs and walrus meat! Can it have been that John, his former partner in the plot, was on the lookout for him, and had engaged his aid to consummate their joint desertion?

"One thing is plain. This man at large and his comrade still on board, the safety of the whole company exacts the sternest observance of discipline. I have called all hands, and announced it as a standing order of the ship, and one to be observed inflexibly, that desertion, or the attempt to desert, shall be met at once by the sternest penalty. I have no alternative. By the body of my crew, sick, dependent, unable to move, and with everything to lose by the withdrawal of any portion of our efficient force, this announcement was received as a guarantee of their personal safety. But it was called for by other grave considerations. There is at this time on the part of all, men as well as officers, a warm feeling toward myself, and a strict, stanch fidelity to the expedition. But, for moral reasons which would control me, even if my impulse were different, I am constrained for the time to mingle among them

Crossing the ice-belt at Coffee Gorge

James Hamilton, from a sketch by Dr. Kane

without reserve, to act as a servant to their wants, to encourage colloquial equality and good humor; and, looking only a little way ahead to the juncture when a perfectly regulated subordination will become essential, I know that my present stand will be of value.

"This sledge load of Godfrey's meat, coming as it does, may well be called a Godsend: one may forgive the man in consideration of the good which it has done us all. We have had a regular feed all round, and exult to think we need no catering for the morrow. It has cheered our downhearted sick men wonderfully. Our brew of beer, too—the 'Arctic Linseed Mucilage Adaptation'—turns out excellent. Our grunts and growls are really beginning to have a good-natured twang. Our faces lessen as our shadows promise to increase. I think I see a change which points to the happier future.

"Our sick, however, are still nonoperatives, and our one room is like the convalescent ward of a hospital, with Bonsall and myself for the only nurses."

* * * *

APRIL 3, TUESDAY. "Today I detained Petersen from his hunt, and took a holiday rest myself—that is to say, went to bed and—sweated: tomorrow I promise as much for Bonsall."

APRIL 6, FRIDAY. "Our little family is growing more and more uneasy about Hans. William reported him sick at Etah; but we had no faith in this story, and looked on his absence as merely the result of fatigue from exposure. But there seems ground for serious apprehension now. My own fear is that William may have conveyed to him some false message, or some threat of reproof, using my name, and in this way deterred him from returning. Hans is very faithful; but he is entirely unaware of William's desertion, and he is besides both credulous and sensitive. I am attached to Hans: he has always been a sort of henchman, a bodyguard, the companion of my walks. He is a devout Moravian and when the party withdrew from the brig last fall he refused to accompany them on grounds of religious obligation. The boy has fixed, honorable principles. Petersen thinks that he ought to be sent for, but he has not thought out the question who is to be sent. Bonsall is too lame to travel; Petersen himself is infinitely the best fitted, but he shirks the duty, and today he takes to his bed: I alone am left.

"Clearly duty to this poor boy calls me to seek him, and clearly duty to these dependent men calls upon me to stay. Long and uncomfortably have I pondered over these opposing calls, but at last have come to a determination. Hans was faithful to me: the danger to him is imminent; the danger to those left behind only contingent upon my failure to return. With earnest trust in that same supervising Agency which has so often before in graver straits interfered to protect and carry me through, I have resolved to go after Hans.

"The orders are given. In three hours I will be equipped and ready to take advantage of the first practicable moment for the start. It makes me write gravely;

for I am far from well, very far from strong, and am obliged to drive our reduced team twice seventy miles. The latter half of the journey I shall have to do entirely on foot, and our lowest night temperatures are under minus forty degrees."

Portrait of Hans

XXIII

Maturing Plans

APRIL 10, TUESDAY. "I left the brig at 10:30 A.M., with but five dogs and a load so light as to be hardly felt.

"It requires some suggestive incident to show us how we have gradually become assimilated in our habits to the necessities of our peculiar life. Such an incident I find in my equipment. Compare it with similar sledge outfits of last winter, and you will see that we are now more than half Esquimaux. It consists of—

1. One small sledge, five feet six by two.
2. An extra jumper and sack pants for sleeping.
3. A ball of raw walrus meat. This is all.

"The sledge is portable, and adapted to jump over the chasms of the land-ice, and to overturn with impunity, save to the luckless driver. It has two standards, or "upstanders," which spring like elbows from its hinder extremity.

"They serve as handles, by which, running or walking behind, you guide the sledge, lift it over rugged places, or rest yourself and your dogs while in progress together.

"The extra jumper is a bear skin jacket, or shirt, which after being put on is overlapped at the waist by a large pair of footed trousers. No winter traveler should be without these: at temperatures below minus twenty-five or minus thirty degrees they are invaluable. Blanket bags are nearly useless below minus thirty degrees, in a gale of wind; it riddles through them.

"The ball of raw meat is made by chopping into inch pieces walrus or other meat, and pouring among it hot tallow, by which the pieces are prevented from freezing too hard, so that you can readily cut out your meal as it is required. A little butter, if you have some, will contribute to soften it: olive oil perhaps would be better; but without some such luxurious additions a man in too great a hurry for dinner might be apt to risk his teeth. In the present journey, having nothing but tallow, I made my meat ball like a twist loaf, and broke it with a stone.

"Faithful Hans! Dear good follower and friend! I was out on the floes just beyond the headlands of our old 'Refuge Harbor,' when I made out a black speck far in to shoreward. Refraction will deceive a novice on the ice; but we have learned to baffle refraction. By sighting the suspected object with your rifle at rest, you soon detect motion. It was a living animal—a man. Shoreward went the sledge; off sprang the dogs ten miles an hour, their driver yelling the familiar provocative to speed, 'Nannook! nannook!' 'A bear! a bear!' at the top of his lungs.

"There was no room for mistaking the methodical seal stalking gait of Hans. He hardly varied from it as we came near; but in about fifteen minutes we were shaking hands and jabbering, in a patois of Esquimaux and English, our mutual news. The poor fellow had been really ill: five days down with severe pains of limbs have left him still a 'little veek'; which means with Hans well used up. I stuck him on the sledge and carried him to Anoatok.

"Hans reached Etah with Myouk two days after leaving us, and at once commenced his hunt. In the course of five days of most hazardous ice-range, he killed two fine young animals; his three companions in the hunt killing only three. He had the great advantage of my powerful Marston rifle, but his tackle was very inferior. Our sinnet laid twine would not stand the powerful struggles of the beast, and on one occasion parted while fast in a large female. Still his success must have acquired for him the goodwill of these people, for in the 'flens' or hunting division of spoil they gained by his companionship.

"In the sickness that followed his long exposure, he tells me, he was waited on most carefully at the settlement. A young daughter of Shunghu elected herself his nurse, and her sympathies and smiles have, I fear, made an impression on his heart which a certain damsel near Upernavik might be sorry to hear of.

"Hans cached part of his meat at Littleton Island, after sending a load by William to the brig. He had no difficulty, I find, in penetrating this man's designs. He was indeed urged by him to agree that they should drive off together to the south and so leave us sledgeless. Upon Hans's refusal, he tried to obtain his rifle; but this of course was easily prevented. He consented at last to take up the meat, with a view of making terms with me and securing probably a companion. Baffled in this, as I have mentioned, he made his escape a second time to Etah. There I might be content to leave him, an unwelcome guest, and dependent upon the Esquimaux. Strong and healthy as he is, our daily work goes on better for his absence, and the ship seems better when purged by his desertion; but the example is disastrous; and, cost what it may, I must have him back."

APRIL 11, WEDNESDAY. "Hans started again to bring back the meat from Littleton Island cache. If he feels strengthened, I have given him a commission to which I attach the greatest importance.

"My hopes of again undertaking a spring journey to Kennedy Channel were strong in the early months of the winter; but, as our dogs died away a second time, and the scurvy crept in upon us, I became sad and distrustful as to the chance of our ever living to gain the open water. The return of the withdrawing party absorbed all my thoughts. They brought news of disaster, starvation, and loss of dogs, among the natives. Our prospects seemed at the lowest ebb. Still, I cherished a secret hope of making another journey, and had determined to undertake it alone with our poor remnant of four dogs, trusting to my rifle for provision. In fact, this continuation of my one great duty has been constantly before me, and I now think that I can manage it. Thus—the Esquimaux have left Northumberland Island, and are now near Cape

Alexander, as a better hunting ground. Kalutunah, the best and most provident man among them, has saved seven dogs. I have authorized Hans to negotiate *carte blanche,* if necessary, for four of these, even as a loan; promising as a final bait the contingent possession of my whole team when I reach the open water on my return. On this mission I send my 'fides Achates,'[1] and await his return with anxious hope.

"I have seen, almost from the first day of our imprisonment by the ice, the probability that we might never be able to liberate the ship. Elsewhere in this journal I have explained by what construction of my duty I urged the brig to the north, and why I deemed it impossible honorably to abandon her after a single season. The same train of reasoning now leads me to mature and organize everything for an early departure without her in case she cannot be released. My hopes of this release are very feeble; and I know that when it does occur, if ever, the season will, like the last, be too far advanced for me to carry my people home. All my experience, carefully reviewed from my notebooks and confirmed by consultation with Petersen, convinces me that I must start early, and govern my boat and sledges by the condition of the ice and hunting grounds.

"Whatever of executive ability I have picked up during this brain- and body-wearying cruise warns me against immature preparation or vacillating purposes.

---

[1] "The Faithful Achates," companion to Virgil's Aeneas, an ideal figure of faithfulness and loyalty.

I must have an exact discipline, a rigid routine, and a perfectly thought-out organization. For the past six weeks I have, in the intervals between my duty to the sick and the ship, arranged the schedule of our future course. Much of it is already underway. My journal shows what I have done, but what there is to do is appalling.

"I state all this to show how much I hazard and possibly sacrifice by my intended journey to the north, and to explain why I have so little time and mood for scientific observation or research. My feelings may be understood when I say that my carpenter and all the working men, save Bonsall, are still on their backs; and that a month's preliminary labor is needed before I can commence the heavy work of transporting my three boats over the ice to the anticipated water. At the moment of my writing this, the water is over eighty miles in a straight line from our brig."

APRIL 12, THURSDAY. "The wind still blowing as yesterday, from the southward and eastward. This is certainly favorable to the advance of open water. The long swell from the open spaces in Baffin's Bay has such a powerful effect upon the ice, that I should not wonder if the floes about Life-Boat Cove, off McGary Island, were broken up by the first of May.

"Our sick have been without fresh food since the fifth; but such is the stimulus imparted by our late supply that they as yet show no backward symptoms. McGary, Ohlsen, Brooks, and Riley sun themselves daily, and are able to do much useful jobbing. Thomas begins to relieve me in cooking, Riley to take a spell at the slops, Morton cooks breakfast, and, aided by McGary and Ohlsen, has already finished one worsted quilted camp blanket, with which I intend to cover our last remaining buffalo skins. Wilson comes on slowly; Dr. Hayes's toe begins to heal. Sontag is more cheery and with the exception of Goodfellow, John, and Whipple, I can feel that those of my little household are fast becoming men again."

APRIL 13, FRIDAY. "Our sick—which still means all hands except the cook, which means the captain—entered this morning on their eighth day of fasting from flesh. One or two have been softening about the gums again for some days past, and all feel weak with involuntary abstinence. The evening comes, and 'Bim! bim! bim!' sounds upon the deck: Hans is back with his dogs. Rabbit stew and walrus liver!—a supper for a king!

"This life of ours—for we have been living much in this way for nine months past—makes me more charitable than I used to be with our Esquimaux neighbors. The day provides for itself; or, if it does not, we trust in the morrow, and are happy till tomorrow disappoints us. Our smoke-dried cabin is a scene worth looking at: no man with his heart in the right place but would enjoy it. Every man is elbowed up on his platform, with a bowl of rich gravy soup between his knees and a stick of frozen liver at his side, gorging himself with the antiscorbutic luxuries, and laughing as if neither ice nor water was before him to traverse.

"Hans has brought Metek with him, and Metek's young nephew, a fine-looking boy of fourteen.

"I do not know whether I have mentioned that some little time before our treaty of alliance and mutual honesty Metek stole the gunwale of the *Red Eric*. He has been, of course, in something of uncertainty as to his political and personal relations, and his present visit to the nalegak with a noble sledge load of walrus meat is evidently intended as a propitiation for his wrong.

"They are welcome, the meat and Metek, abundantly. He is the chieftain of Etah, and, as such, a vassal of him of Aunatok, the 'Open Place,' which we have named Rensselaer Harbor. He speaks sadly, and so does Hans, of the fortunes of the winter.

"The Netelik settlement on Northumberland Island was already, when we heard of it last, the refuge of the natives from the south, even beyond Wolstenholme. It has always been a hunting stronghold; but as the winter darkness inevitably advanced, the pressure of numbers combined with their habitual improvidence to dissipate their supplies.

"It seems that the poor wretches suffered terribly—even more than our neighbors of Etah Bay. Their laws exact an equal division; and the success of the best hunters was dissipated by the crowds of starving claimants upon their spoils. At last the broken nature of the ice-margin and the freezing up of a large zone of ice prevented them from seeking walrus. The water was inaccessible, and the last resource pressed itself upon them. They killed their dogs. Fearful as it sounds when we think how indispensable the services of these animals are to their daily existence, they cannot now number more than twenty in the entire ownership of the tribe. From Glacier South to Glacier North, from Glacier East to the rude ice-bound coast which completed the circuit of their little world, this nation has but twenty dogs. What can they hope for without them?

"I can already count eight settlements, including about 140 souls. There are more, perhaps, but certainly not many. Out of these I can number five deaths since our arrival; and I am aware of hardships and disasters encountered by the survivors, which, repeated as they must be in the future, cannot fail to involve a larger mortality. Crime combines with disease and exposure to thin their numbers: I know of three murders within the past two years; and one infanticide occurred only a few months ago. These facts, which are open to my limited sources of information, cannot, of course, indicate the number of deaths correctly. They confirm, however, a fearful conclusion which these poor wretches have themselves communicated to us—that they are dying out; not lingeringly, like the American tribes, but so rapidly as to be able to mark within a generation their progress toward extinction. Nothing can be more saddening, measured by our own sensibilities, than such a conviction; but it seems to have no effect upon this remarkable people. Surrounded by the graves of their dead, by huts untenanted yet still recent in their memory as homesteads, even by caches of meat which, frozen under the snow by the dead of one year, are eaten by the living of the next, they show neither apprehension nor regret. Even Kalutunah—a man of fine instincts, and, I think, of heart—will retain his apathy of face as, by the aid of Petersen, our interpreter, I point out to him the certainty of their speedy extinction. He will smile in his efforts to count the years which must obliterate his nation, and break in with a laugh as his children shout out their 'Amna Ayah' and dance to the tap of his drum.

"How wonderful is all this! Rude as are their ideas of numbers, there are those among this merry-hearted people who can reckon up to the fate of their last man.

"After Netelik, the receptacle of these half-starved fugitives, had been obliged itself to capitulate with famine, the body corporate determined, as on like occasions it had often done before, to migrate to the seats of the more northern hunt.

"The movements of the walrus and the condition of the ice seem to be known to them by a kind of instinct; so, when the light came, they harnessed in their reserve of dogs and started for Cape Alexander.

"It could not, one might suppose, have been a very cheerful migration—women, children, and young babies thrusting themselves into a frozen wilderness at temperatures below minus thirty degrees, and sometimes verging on minus sixty degrees. But Hans, with a laugh that seemed to indicate some exquisite point of concealed appreciation of the ludicrous, said they traveled generally in squads, singing 'Amna Ayah,' and, when they reached any of the halting huts, ate the blubber and liver of the owners and danced all through the night. So at last they came to Utak-soak, the 'great caldron,' which we call Cape Alexander, and settled down at Peteravik, or the 'Welcome Halt.'

"At first game was scarce here also; but the season came soon when the female walrus is tending her calf on the ice, and then, but for the protracted exposure of the hunt, there was no drawback to its success. They are desperately merry now, and seem to have forgotten that a second winter is ahead of them. Hans said, with one of his quiet laughs, 'One half of them are sick and cannot hunt: these do nothing but eat, and sing.' "

APRIL 18, WEDNESDAY. "I am just off a two-hundred-mile journey, bringing back my deserter, and, what is perhaps quite as important, a sledge load of choice walrus cuts.

"I found from Hans that his negotiation for the dogs had failed, and that unless I could do something by individual persuasion I must give up my scheme of a closing exploration to the north. I learned too that Godfrey was playing the great man at Etah, defying recapture; and I was not willing to trust the influence he might exert on my relations with the tribe. I determined that he should return to the brig.

"I began by stratagem. I placed a pair of foot cuffs on Metek's sledge, and, after looking carefully to my body companion six-shooter, invited myself to ride back with him to Etah. His nephew remained on board in charge of Hans, and I disguised myself so well in my nessak that, as we moved off, I could easily have passed for the boy Paulik, whose place I had taken.

"As our eighty miles drew to an end, and that which we call the settlement came in view, its population streamed out to welcome their chief's return. Among the first and most prominent was the individual whom I desired to meet, waving his hand and shouting 'Tima!' as loudly as the choicest savage of them all. An instant later and I was at his ear, with a short phrase of salutation and its appropriate gesture. He yielded unconditionally at once, and, after walking and running by turns for some eighty miles before the sledge, with a short respite at Anoatok, is now a prisoner on board.

"My remaining errand was almost as successful."

Sledges

XXIV

Venturing Out

Etah is on the northeastern curve of Hartstene Bay, facing to the south and west. As you stretch from the south point of Littleton Island to the main, the broken character of the ice subsides into a traversable plain, and the shore scenery assumes a singular wildness. The bottom series of plutonics rises to grand and mountainous proportions, and in the background, soaring above these, are the escaladed greenstones of the more northern coast. At the very bottom of the bay are two perforations, one a fortress-mantled fiord, the other a sloping ravine: both are occupied by extensions of the same glacier.

The fiord points to Peteravik, where Kalutunah and his hungry southern corps have now taken up their quarters; the other is the oft-mentioned settlement of Etah. A snowdrift, rising at a forty-five degree angle till it mingles with the steep sides of a mountain, is dotted by two dark blemishes upon its pure white. Coming nearer, you see that the dirt spots are perforations of the snow: nearer still, you see above each opening a smaller one, and a covered roof connecting them. These are the doors and windows of the settlement; two huts and four families, but for these vent openings entirely buried in the snow.

The inmates of the burrows swarmed around me as I arrived. "Nalegak! nalegak! tima!" was yelled in chorus: never seemed people more anxious to propitiate, or more pleased with an unexpected visit. But they were airily clad, and it blew a northwester; and they soon crowded back into their ant hill. Meantime preparations were making for my indoor reception, and after a little while Metek and myself crawled in on hands and knees, through an extraordinary *tossut* thirty paces long. As I emerged on the inside, the salute of "nalegak" was repeated with an increase of energy that was anything but pleasant.

There were guests before me—six sturdy denizens of the neighboring settlement. They had been overtaken by the storm while hunting, and were already crowded upon the central dais of honor. They united in the yell of welcome, and I soon found myself gasping the ammoniacal steam of some fourteen vigorous, amply fed, unwashed, unclothed fellow lodgers. I had come somewhat exhausted by an eight miles' journey through the atmosphere of the floes: the thermometer inside was at ninety degrees above zero, and the vault measured fifteen feet by six. Such an amorphous mass of compounded humanity one could see nowhere else: men, women, children, with nothing but their native dirt to cover them, twined and dovetailed together like the worms in a fishing basket.

No hyperbole could exaggerate that which in serious earnest I have as the truth. The platform measured but seven feet in breadth by six in depth, the shape being semi-elliptical. Upon this, including children and excluding myself, were bestowed thirteen persons.

The kotluk of each matron was glowing with a flame sixteen inches long. A flipper-quarter of walrus, which lay frozen on the floor of the netek, was cut into steaks; and the kolopsuts began to smoke with a burden of ten or fifteen pounds apiece. Metek, with a little amateur aid from some of the sleepers, emptied these without my assistance. I had the most cordial invitation to precede them; but I had seen enough of the culinary regime to render it impossible. I broke my fast on a handful of frozen liver nuts that Bill brought me, and, bursting out into a profuse perspiration, I stripped like the rest, threw my well-tired carcass across Mrs. Eider-duck's extremities, put her left hand baby under my armpit, pillowed my head on Myouk's somewhat warm stomach, and thus, an honored guest and in the place of honor, fell asleep.

Next morning, the sun nearly at noonday height, I awoke: Mrs. Eider-duck had my breakfast very temptingly ready. It was forked on the end of a curved piece of bone—a lump of boiled blubber and a choice cut of meat. The preliminary cookery I had not seen: I am an old traveler, and do not intrude into the mysteries of the kitchen. My appetite was in its usual blessed redundance, and I was about to grasp the smiling proffer, when I saw the matron, who was manipulating as chief intendant of the other kotluk, performing an operation that arrested me. She had in her hand a coun-

terpart of the curved bone that supported my *déjeu-
ner*—indeed, it is the universal implement of an Esquimaux cuisine; and, as I turned my head, I saw her
quietly withdrawing it from beneath her dress, and
then plunging it into the soup pot before her, to bring
out the counterpart of my own smoking morsel. I
learned afterward that the utensil has its two recognized uses; and that, when not immediately wanted for
the purposes of pot or table, it ministers to the "royal
luxury" of the Scottish king. I dare not amplify this description.

Dirt or filth in our sense is not a conceived quality
with these Esquimaux. Incidentally, it may be an
annoyance or obstruction; but their nearest word,
"Eberk," expresses no more than this.

It is an ethnological trait of these ultra-northern nomads—so far as I know, a unique one; and must be attributed not alone to their predatory diet and peculiar
domestic system, but to the extreme cold, which by
rapid freezing resists putrefaction and prevents the
joint accumulation of the dogs and the household from
being intolerable. Their senses seem to take no cognizance of what all instinct and association make re-
volting to the sight and touch and smell of civilized
man.

My notebook proves this by exact and disgusting
details, the very mildest of which I cannot transfer to
these pages.

I spent some time at Etah in examining the glacier
and in making sketches of things about me. I met sev-

eral old friends. Among the rest was Awahtok, only now recovering from his severe frost bite, the effect of his fearful adventure with Myouk among the drifting ice. I gave him a piece of red flannel and powwowed him. He resides with Ootuniah in the second hut, a smaller one than Metek's, with his pretty wife, a sister of Kalutunah's.

* * * *

On the day of my arrival, four walrus were killed at Etah, and no doubt many more by Kalutak at Peteravik. The quantity of beef thus gained during a season of plenty, one might suppose, should put them beyond winter want; but there are other causes besides improvidence which make their supplies scanty. The poor creatures are not idle: they hunt indomitably without the loss of a day. When the storms prevent the use of the sledge, they still work in stowing away the carcasses of previous hunts. An excavation is made either on the mainland, or, what is preferred, upon an island inaccessible to foxes, and the jointed meat is stacked inside and covered with heavy stones. One such cache, which I met on a small island a short distance from Etah, contained the flesh of ten walrus.

The excessive consumption is the true explanation of the scarcity. By their ancient laws, all share with all; and, as they migrate in numbers as their necessities prompt, the tax on each particular settlement is excessive. The quantity that the members of a family consume, exorbitant as it seems to a stranger, is rather a necessity of their peculiar life and organization than the result of inconsiderate gluttony. In active exercise and constant exposure to cold the waste of carbon must be enormous.

When indoors and at rest, tinkering over their ivory harness rings, fowl nets, or other household gear, they eat as we often do in more civilized lands—for animal enjoyment and to pass away time. But when on the hunt they take but one meal a day, and that after the day's labor is over; they go out upon the ice without breakfast, and, except the "cold cuts," which I confess are numerous, eat nothing until their return. I would average the Esquimaux ration in a season of plenty— it is of course a mere estimate, but I believe a perfectly fair one—at eight or ten pounds a day, with soup and water to the extent of half a gallon.

At the moment of my visit, when returning plenty had just broken in upon their famine, it was not wonderful that they were hunting with avidity. The settlements of the South seek at this season the hunting ground above, and, until the seals begin to form their basking holes, some ten days later the walrus is the single spoil.

My departure from Etah Bay was hastened by news from the brig. Hans brought me a letter from Dr. Hayes, while I was out walrus hunting near Life-Boat Cove, which apprised me of the dangerous illness of Mr. McGary. I had a load of meat on my sledge and was therefore unable to make good speed with my four tired dogs; but I rode and ran by turns and reached the brig, after fifty miles' travel, in seven hours from the time of meeting Hans. I was thoroughly broken down by the effort, but had the satisfaction of finding that my second officer had passed the crisis of his attack.

I left Hans behind me with orders to go to Peteravik and persuade Kalutunah to come to the brig, sending him a capstan bar as a pledge of future largess—invaluable for its adaptation to harpoon shafts.

APRIL 19, THURSDAY. " The open water has not advanced from the south more than four miles within the past three weeks. It is still barely within Cape Alexander. It is a subject of serious anxiety to me.

"I will not leave the brig until it is absolutely certain that she cannot thaw out this season; but everything shall be matured for our instant departure as soon as her fate is decided. Every detail is arranged; and, if the sick go on as they have done, I do not doubt but that we may carry our boats some thirty or forty miles over the ice before finally deciding whether we must desert the brig.

APRIL 20, FRIDAY. "A relief watch of Riley, Morton, and Bonsall, are preparing to saw out sledge runners from our crossbeams. It is slow work. They are very weak, and the thermometer sinks at night to minus twenty-six degrees. Nearly all our beams have been used up for fuel; but I have saved enough to construct two long sledges of seventeen feet six inches each. I want a sledge sufficiently long to bring the weight of the whaleboat and her stowage within the line of the runner: this will prevent her rocking and pitching when crossing hummocked ice, and enable us to cradle her firmly to the sledge.

"They are at this moment breaking out our cabin bulkhead to extract the beam. Our cabin dormitory is full of cold vapor. Everything is comfortless: blankets make a sorry substitute for the moss-padded wall that protected us from minus sixty degrees."

* * * *

We continued toiling on with our complicated preparations till the evening of the twenty-fourth, when Hans came back well laden with walrus meat. Three of the Esquimaux accompanied him, each with his sledge and dog team fully equipped for a hunt. The leader of the party, Kalutunah, was a noble savage, greatly superior in everything to the others of this race. He greeted me with respectful courtesy, and, after a short interchange of salutations, seated himself in the post of honor at my side.

I waited of course till the company had fed and slept for, among savages especially, haste is indecorous, and, after distributing a few presents, then opened to them my project of a northern exploration. Kalutunah received his knife and needles with a "Kuyanaka," "I thank you": the first thanks I have heard from a native of this upper region. He called me his friend—"Asakaoteet," "I love you well"—and would be happy, he said, to join the "nalegak-soak" in a hunt.

The project was one that had engaged my thoughts

long before daylight had renewed the possibility of carrying it out. I felt that the farther shores beyond Kennedy Channel were still to be searched before our work could be considered finished; but we were without dogs, the indispensable means of travel. We had only four left out of sixty-two. Famine among the Esquimaux had been as disastrous as disease with us: they had killed all but thirty, and of these there were now sixteen picketed on the ice about the brig. The aid and influence of Kalutunah could secure my closing expedition.

I succeeded in making my arrangements with him, provisionally at least, and the morning after, we all set out. The party consisted of Kalutunah, Shanghu, and Tatterat with their three sledges. Hans, armed with the Marston rifle, was my only companion from the ship's company. The natives carried no arms but the long knife and their unicorn ivory lances. Our whole equipment was by no means cumbersome: except the clothes upon our back and raw walrus meat, we carried nothing. The walrus, both flesh and blubber, was cut into flat slabs half an inch thick and about as long and wide as a folio volume. These when frozen were laid directly upon the crossbars of the sledge, and served as a sort of floor. The rifle and the noonghak were placed on top, and the whole was covered by a well-rubbed bear skin, strapped down by a pliant cord of walrus hide.

Thus stowed, the sledge is wonderfully adapted to its wild travel. It may roll over and over, for it defies an upset; and its runners of the bones of the whale seem to bear with impunity the fierce shocks of the ice. The meat, as hard as a plank, is the driver's seat: it is secure from the dogs; and when it is wanted for a cold cut, which is not seldom, the sledge is turned upside down, and the layers of flesh are hacked away from between the crossbars.

We halted about thirty miles north of the brig, after edging along the coast about thirty miles to the eastward. Here Shanghu burrowed into a snow bank and slept, the thermometer standing at minus thirty degrees. The rest of us turned in to lunch; the sledge was turned over, and we were cutting away at the raw meat, each man for himself, when I heard an exclamation from Tatterat, an outlandish Esquimaux, who had his name from the Kittywake gull. He had found a tallow ball, which had been hid away without my knowledge by my comrades for my private use. Instantly his knife entered the prized recesses of my ball, and, as the lumps of liver and cooked muscle came tossing out in delicate succession, Kalutunah yielded to the temptation, and both of them picked the savory bits as we would the truffles of a "Perigord pâté." Of necessity I joined the group, and took my share; but Hans, poor fellow, too indignant at the liberty taken with my provender, refused to share in the work of demolishing it. My ten-pound ball vanished nevertheless in scarcely as many minutes.

The journey began again as the feast closed, and we should have accomplished my wishes had it not been

Bear hunt

for the untoward influence of sundry bears. The tracks of these animals were becoming more and more numerous as we rounded one iceberg after another; and we could see the beds they had worn in the snow while watching for seal. These swayed the dogs from their course: yet we kept edging onward; and when in sight of the northern coast, about thirty miles from the central peak of the "Three Brothers," I saw a deep band of stratus lying over the horizon in the direction of Kennedy Channel. This water-sky indicated the continued opening of the channel, and made me more deeply anxious to proceed. But at this moment our dogs encountered a large male bear in the act of devouring a seal. The impulse was irresistible: I lost all control over both dogs and drivers. They seemed dead to everything but the passion of pursuit. Off they sped with incredible swiftness; the Esquimaux clinging to their sledges and cheering their dogs with loud cries of "Nannook!" A mad, wild chase, wilder than German legend—the dogs, wolves; the drivers, devils. After a furious run, the animal was brought to bay; the lance and the rifle did their work and we halted for a general feed. The dogs gorged themselves, the drivers did as much, and we buried the remainder of the carcass in the snow. A second bear had been tracked by the party to a large iceberg north of Cape Russell; for we had now traveled to the neighborhood of the Great Glacier. But the dogs were too much distended by their abundant diet to move: their drivers were scarcely better. Rest was indispensable.

The next day I tried again to make my friends steer to the northward. But the bears were most numerous upon the Greenland side; and they determined to push on toward the glacier. They were sure, they said, of finding the game among the broken icebergs at the base of it. All my remonstrances and urgent entreaties were unavailing to make them resume their promised route. They said that to cross so high up as we then were was impossible, and I felt the truth of this when I remembered the fate of poor Baker and Schubert at this very passage. Kalutunah added, significantly, that the bear meat was absolutely necessary for the support of their families, and that Nalegak had no right to prevent him from providing for his household. It was a strong argument, and withal the argument of the strong.

I found now that my projected survey of the northern coast must be abandoned, at least for the time. My next wish was to get back to the brig, and to negotiate with Metek for a purchase or loan of his dogs as my last chance. But even this was not readily gratified. All of Saturday was spent in bear hunting. The natives, as indomitable as their dogs, made the entire circuit of Dallas Bay, and finally halted again under one of the islands that group themselves between the headlands of Advance Bay and at the base of the glacier.

Anxious as I was to press our return to the brig, I was well paid for my disappointment. I had not realized fully the spectacle of this stupendous monument of frost. I had seen it for some hours hanging over the ice like a white mist cloud, but now it rose up before me, clearly defined and almost precipitous. The whole horizon, so vague and shadowy before, was broken by long lines of icebergs; and as the dogs, cheered by the cries of their wild drivers, went on, losing themselves deeper and deeper in the labyrinth, it seemed like closing around us the walls of an icy world. They stopped at last; and I had time, while my companions rested and fed, to climb one of the highest bergs. The atmosphere favored me: the blue tops of Washington Land were in full view; and, losing itself in a dark water cloud, the noble headland of John Barrow.

The trend of this glacier is a few degrees to the west of north. We followed its face afterward, edging in for the Greenland coast, about the rocky archipelago which I have named after the *Advance.* From one of these rugged islets, the nearest to the glacier which could be approached with anything like safety, I could see another island larger and closer in shore, already half covered by the encroaching face of the glacier, and great masses of ice still detaching themselves and splintering as they fell upon that portion which protruded. Repose was not the characteristic of this solid mass; every feature indicated activity, energy, movement.

I have named this great glacier after Alexander Von Humboldt, and the cape which flanks it on the Greenland coast after Professor Agassiz.

The point at which this immense body of ice enters the Land of Washington gives even to a distant view impressive indications of its plastic or semisolid character. No one could resist the impression of fluidity conveyed by its peculiar markings. I have named it Cape Forbes, after the eminent crystallographer whose views it so abundantly confirms.

* * * *

Hans and myself crawled with Tatterat and his dogs into an impromptu snow hut, and, cheered by our aggregated warmth, slept comfortably. Our little dome, or rather burrow, for it was scooped out of a drift—fell down in the night; but we were so worn out that it did not wake us.

On rising from sleep in the open air, at a temperature of twelve degrees below zero, the hunt was resumed along the face of the glacier, with just enough of success to wear out the dogs and endanger my chances of return to the brig.

In spite of the grandeur of the scenery and the noble displays of force exhibited by the falling bergs, my thoughts wandered back to the party I had left; and I was glad when Kalutunah yielded to my renewed persuasion and turned his team toward the ice-belt of the southeastern shore.

The spot at which we landed I have called Cape James Kent. It was a lofty headland, and the land-ice that hugged its base was covered with rocks from the cliffs above. We followed the belt-ice, crossing only at the headlands of the bays, and arrived at the brig on the afternoon of Wednesday.

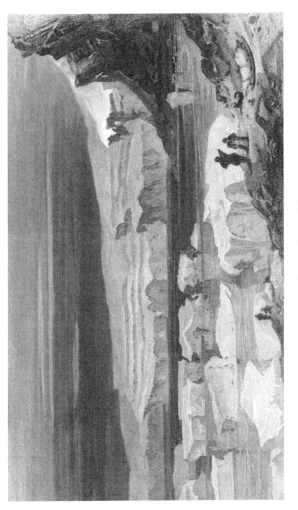

Great Glacier of Humboldt
James Hamilton, from a sketch by Dr. Kane

The month of May had come. Everything admonished me that the time was at hand when we must leave the brig and trust our fortunes to the floes. Our preparations were well advanced, and the crew so far restored to health that all but three or four could take some part in completing them.

Still I could not allow myself to pass away from our region of search without a last effort to visit the farther shores of the channel. Our communications with the Esquimaux and some successful hunts of our own had given us a stock of provisions for at least a week in advance. I conferred with my officers, made of full distribution of the work to be performed in my absence and set out once more with Morton for my only companion. We took with us the light sledge, adding the two borrowed dogs to our team, but traveling ourselves on foot. Our course was to be by the middle ice, and our hope that we might find it free enough from hummocks to permit us to pass.

My journal, written after our return, gives nothing but a series of observations going to verify and complete my charts. We struggled manfully to force our way through—days and nights of adventurous exposure and recurring disaster—and at last found our way back to the brig, Morton broken down anew, and my own energies just adequate to the duty of supervising our final departure. I had neither time nor strength to expend on my diary.

The operations of the search were closed.

XXV

Leaving the Brig

THE DETAILED preparations for our escape would have little interest for the general reader; but they were so arduous and so important that I cannot pass them by without a special notice. They had been begun from an early day of the fall, and had not been entirely intermitted during our severest winter trials. All who could work, even at picking over eider-down, found every moment of leisure fully appropriated. But since our party had begun to develop the stimulus of more liberal diet, our labors were more systematic and diversified.

The manufacture of clothing had made considerable progress. Canvas moccasins had been made for everyone of the party, and three dozen were added to meet emergencies. Three pairs of boots were allowed each man. These were generally of carpeting, with soles of walrus and seal hide; and when the supply of these gave out, the leather from the chafing gear of the brig for a time supplied their place. A much better substitute was found afterward in the gutta percha that had formed the speaking tube. This was softened by warm water, cut into lengths, and so made available to its new uses. Blankets were served out as the material for body clothing: every man was his own tailor.

For bedding, the woolen curtains that had formerly decorated our berths supplied us with a couple of large coverlets, which were abundantly quilted with eider-down. Two buffalo robes of the same size with the coverlets were arranged so as to button on them, forming sleeping sacks for the occasion, but easily detached for the purpose of drying or airing.

Our provision bags were of assorted sizes, to fit under the thwarts of the boats. They were of sailcloth made watertight by tar and pitch, which we kept from penetrating the canvas by first coating it with flour paste and plaster of Paris. The bread bags were double, the inner saturated with paste and plaster by boiling in the mixture, and the space between the two filled with pitch. Every bag was, in sailor phrase, roped and becketed; in ordinary parlance, well secured by cordage.

These different manufactures had all of them been going on through the winter, and more rapidly as the spring advanced. They had given employment to the thoughts of our sick men, and in this way had exerted a wholesome influence on their moral tone and assisted their convalescence. Other preparations had been begun more recently. The provisions for the descent were to be got ready and packed. The ship bread was powdered by beating it with a capstan bar, and pressed down into the bags which were to carry it. Pork fat and tallow were melted down, and poured into other bags to freeze. A stock of concentrated bean soup was cooked, and secured for carriage like the pork fat; and the flour and remaining meat biscuit were to be protected from moisture in double bags. These were the only provisions we were to carry with us. I knew I should be able to subsist the party for some time after their setting out by the food I could bring from the vessel by occasional trips with my dog team. For the rest we relied upon our guns.

Besides all this, we had our camp equipage to get in order, and the vitally important organization of our system of boats and sledges.

Our boats were three in number, all of them well battered by exposure to ice and storm, almost as destructive of their seaworthiness as the hot sun of other regions. Two of them were cypress whaleboats, twenty-six feet long, with seven feet beam and three feet deep. These were strengthened with oak bottom pieces and a long string piece bolted to the keel. A washboard of light cedar, about six inches high, served to strengthen the gunwale and give increased depth. A neat housing of light canvas was stretched upon a ridge line sustained fore and aft by stanchions, and hung down over the boat's sides, where it was fastened to a jack-stay. My last year's experience on the attempt to reach Beechey Island determined me to carry but one mast to each boat. It was stepped into an oaken thwart, made especially strong, as it was expected to carry sail over ice as well as water: the mast could be readily unshipped, and carried, with the oars, boat hooks, and ice-poles, alongside the boat. The third boat was my little *Red Eric*. We mounted her on the old sledge, the Faith, hardly relying on her for any purposes of navigation, but with the intention of cutting her up for firewood in case our guns should fail to give us a supply of blubber.

Indeed, in spite of all the ingenuity of our carpenter, Mr. Ohlsen, well seconded by the persevering labors of McGary and Bonsall, not one of our boats was positively seaworthy. The *Hope* would not even pass inspection, and we expected to burn her on reaching water. The planking of all of them was so dried up that it could hardly be made tight by caulking.

The three boats were mounted on sledges rigged with rue-raddies; the provisions stowed snugly under the thwarts; the chronometers, carefully boxed and padded, placed in the stern-sheets of the *Hope,* in charge of Mr. Sontag. With them were the instruments as we could venture to transport. They consisted of two Gambey sextants, with artificial horizon, our transit unifilar, and dip instruments. Our glasses, with a few of the smaller field instruments, we carried on our persons. Our fine theodolite we were alas forced to abandon.

Our powder and shot, upon which our very lives depended, were carefully distributed in bags and tin canisters. The percussion caps I took into my own possession, as more precious than gold. Mr. Bonsall had a general charge of the arms and ammunition. Places were arranged for the guns, and hunters appointed for each boat. Mr. Petersen took charge of the most important of our field equipage, our cooking gear. Petersen was our best tinker. All the old stove pipe, now none the better for two winters of Arctic fires, was called into requisition. Each boat was provided with two large iron cylinders, fourteen inches in diameter and eighteen high. Each of them held an iron saucer or lamp, in which we could place our melted pork fat or blubber, and, with the aid of spun yarn for a wick, make a roaring fire. I need not say that the fat and oil always froze when not ignited.

Into these cylinders, which were used merely to defend our lamp from the wind and our pots from contact with the cold air, we placed a couple of large tin vessels, suitable either for melting snow or making tea or soup. They were made out of cake canisters cut down. How many kindly festival associations hung by these now abused soup cans! One of them had, before the fire rubbed off its bright gilding, the wedding inscription of a large fruitcake.

We carried spare tins in case the others should burn out: it was well we did so. So completely had we exhausted our household furniture that we had neither cups nor plates, except crockery. This, of course, would not stand the travel, and our spare tin had to be saved for protecting the boats from ice. At this juncture we cut plates out of every imaginable and rejected piece of tinware. Borden's meat biscuit canisters furnished us with a splendid dinner; and some rightly feared tin jars, sporting ominous labels of Corrosive Sublimate and Arsenic, which once had belonged to our department of Natural History, were emptied, scoured, and then cut down into much-needed teacups.

Recognizing the importance of acting directly upon the men's minds, my first step now is to issue a general order appointing a certain day, the seventeenth of May, for setting out. Every man had twenty-four hours given him to select and get ready his eight pounds of personal effects. After that, his time was to cease to be his own for any purpose. The long indulged waywardness of our convalescents made them take this hardly. Some who were at work on articles of apparel that were really important to them threw them down unfinished, in a sick man's pet. I had these in some cases picked up quietly and finished by others. But I showed myself inexorable. It was necessary to brace up and concentrate every man's thoughts and energies upon the one great common object—our departure from the vessel on the seventeenth, not to return.

I tried my best also to fix and diffuse impressions that we were going home. But in this I was not always successful: I was displeased, indeed, with the moody indifference with which many went about the tasks to which I put them. The completeness of my preparations I know had its influence; but there were many doubters. Some were convinced that my only object was to move farther south, retaining the brig, however, as a home to retreat to. Others whispered that I wanted to transport the sick to the hunting grounds and other resources of the lower settlements, which I had such difficulty in preventing the mutinous from securing for themselves alone. A few of a more cheerful spirit thought I had resolved to make for some point of lookout, in the hope of a rescue by whalers or English expedition parties that were supposed to still be within the Arctic Circle. However, the number is unfortunately small of those human beings whom calamity elevates.

There was no sign or affectation of spirit or enthusiasm upon the memorable day when we first adjusted the boats to their cradles on the sledges and moved them off to the ice-foot. But the ice that was immediately around the vessel was smooth; and, as the boats had not received their lading, the first labor was an easy one. As the runners moved, the gloom of several countenances was perceptibly lightened. The croakers had protested that we could not stir an inch. These cheering remarks always reach a commander's ears, and I took good care of course to make the outset contradict them. By the time we reached the end of our little level, the tone had improved wonderfully, and we were prepared for the effort of crossing the lines of the belt-ice and forcing a way through the smashed material that interposed between us and the ice-foot.

This was a work of great difficulty, and sorrowfully exhausting to the poor fellows not yet accustomed to heave together. But in the end I had the satisfaction, before twenty-four hours were over, of seeing our little arks of safety hauled upon the higher plane of the ice-foot, in full trim for ornamental exhibition from the brig; their neat canvas housing rigged, tent fashion over the entire length of each; a jaunty little flag, made out of one of the commander's obsolete linen shirts, decorated in stripes from a disused article of stationery, the red ink bottle, and with a very little of the blue bag in the star-spangled corner. All hands after this returned on board: I had ready for them the best supper our supplies afforded; and they turned in with minds prepared for their departure next day.

They were nearly all of them invalids, unused to open air and exercise. It was necessary to train them very gradually. We made but two miles the first day, and with a single boat; and indeed for some time after this I took care that they should not be disheartened by overwork. They came back early to a hearty supper and warm beds, and I had the satisfaction of marching them back each recurring morning refreshed.

* * * *

Our last farewell to the brig was made with more solemnity. The entire ship's company was collected in our dismantled winter chamber to take part in the ceremonial. It was Sunday. Our moss walls had been torn down, and the wood that supported them burned. Our beds were off at the boats. The galley was unfurnished and cold. Everything about the little den of refuge was desolate.

We read prayers and a chapter of the Bible; and then, all standing silently round, I took Sir John Franklin's portrait from its frame and cased it in an India rubber scroll. I next read the reports of inspection and survey that had been made by the several commissions organized for the purpose, all of them testifying to the necessities under which I was about to act. I then addressed the party: I did not affect to disguise the difficulties that were before us; but I assured them that they could all be overcome by energy and subordination to command: and that the thirteen hundred miles of ice and water that lay between us and North Greenland could be traversed with safety for most of us and hope for all. I added that as men and messmates it was the duty of us all, to postpone every consideration of self to the protection of the wounded and sick; and that this must be regarded by every man and under all circumstances as a paramount order. In conclusion, I told them to think over the trials we had all of us gone through, and to remember each man for himself how often an unseen Power had rescued him in peril, and I admonished them still to place reliance on Him who could not change.

I was met with a right spirit. After a short conference, an engagement was drawn up by one of the officers, and brought to me with the signatures of all the company, without an exception. It read as follows:

"SECOND GRINNELL EXPEDITION,

"BRIG ADVANCE, MAY 20, 1855.

"The undersigned, being convinced of the impossibility of the liberation of the brig, and equally convinced of the impossibility of remaining in the ice a third winter, do fervently concur with the commander in his attempt to reach the South by means of boats.

Knowing the trials and hardships which are before us, and feeling the necessity of union, harmony, and discipline, we have determined to abide faithfully by the expedition and our sick comrades, and to do all that we can, as true men, to advance the objects in view.

Henry Brooks	J. Wall Wilson
James McGary	Amos Bonsall
George Riley	I.I. Hayes
William Morton	August Sontag
C. Ohlsen	&c. &c."

I had prepared a brief memorial of the considerations which justified our abandonment of the vessel, and had read it as part of my address. I now fixed it to a stanchion near the gangway, where it must attract the notice of any who might seek us hereafter, and stand with them as my vindication for the step, in case we should be overtaken by disaster. It closed with these words:

"I regard the abandonment of the brig as inevitable. We have by actual inspection but thirty-six days' provisions, and a careful survey shows that we cannot cut more firewood without rendering our craft unseaworthy. A third winter would force us, as the only means of escaping starvation, to resort to Esquimaux habits and give up all hope of remaining by the vessel and her resources. It would therefore in no manner advance the search after Sir John Franklin.

"Under any circumstances, to remain longer would be destructive to those of our little party who have already suffered from the extreme severity of the climate and its tendencies to disease. Scurvy has enfeebled more or less every man in the expedition, and an anomalous spasmodic disorder, allied to tetanus, has cost us the life of two of our most prized comrades.

"I hope, speaking on the part of my companions and myself, that we have done all that we ought to do to prove our tenacity of purpose and devotion to the cause which we have undertaken. This attempt to escape by crossing the southern ice on sledges is regarded by me as an imperative duty—the only means of saving ourselves and preserving the laboriously earned results of the expedition.

"E.K. KANE,
"Com. Grinnell Expedition.
"Advance, Rensselaer Bay, May 20, 1855."

We then went up on deck: the flags were hoisted and hauled down again, and our party walked once or twice around the brig, looking at her timbers and exchanging comments upon the scars which reminded them of every stage of her dismantling. Our figurehead—the fair Augusta, the little blue girl with pink cheeks, who had lost her breast by an iceberg and her nose by a nip off Bedevilled Reach—was taken from our bows and placed aboard the *Hope.*

No one thought of the mockery of cheers: we had no festival liquor to mislead our perception of the real state of things. When all hands were quite ready, we scrambled off over the ice together.

On reaching the boats, the party were regularly mustered and divided between the two. A rigid inspection took place and every article of personal equipment was examined. Each man had a woolen underdress and an Esquimaux suit of fur clothing— kapetah, nessak, and nannooke complete, with boots of our own make; that is to say, one pair of canvas faced with walrus hide and another inside made of the cabin Brussels carpet. In addition to this, each carried a rue-raddy adjusted to fit him comfortably, a pair of socks next his skin, and a pair of large goggles for snow blindness, made Esquimaux fashion by cutting a small slit in a piece of wood. Some of us had gutta percha masks fitting closely to the face, as large as an ordinary domino; but these were still less favorable to personal appearance than the goggles.

Excluding four sick men, who were unable to move, and myself, who had to drive the dog team and serve as common carrier and courier, we numbered but twelve men—which would have given six to a sledge, or too few to move it. It was therefore necessary to concentrate our entire force upon one sledge at a time. On the other hand, however, it was important to the efficiency of our organization that matters of cooking, sleeping, baggage, and rations should be regulated by separate messes.

The routine I established was the most precise: Daily prayers both morning and evening, all hands gathering round in a circle and standing uncovered during the short exercise; regulated hours; fixed duties and positions at the track lines and on the halt; the cooking to be taken by turns, the captains of the boats alone being excused. The charge of the log was confided to Dr. Hayes, and the running survey to Mr. Sontag. Though little could be expected from either of these gentlemen at this time, I deemed it best to keep up the appearance of ordinary voyaging; and after we left the first ices of Smith's Straits I was indebted to them for valuable results. The thermometer was observed every three hours.

To my faithful friend and first officer, boatswain Brooks, I assigned the command of the boats and sledges. I knew how well he was fitted for it; and when forced, as I was afterward during the descent, to be in constant motion between the sick station, the Esquimaux settlements, and the deserted brig, I felt safe in the assurance of his tried fidelity and indomitable resolution. The party under him was marshalled at the rue-raddies as a single gang; but the messes were arranged with reference to the two whale boats, and when we came afterward to the open water the crews were distributed in the same way:

To the *Faith:*	To the *Hope:*
James McGary	William Morton
Christian Ohlsen	August Sontag
Amos Bonsall	George Riley
Carl J. Petersen	John Blake
Thomas Hickey	William Godfrey

With this organization we set out on our march.

XXVI

Esquimaux Interlude

I HAD EMPLOYED myself and the team from an early day in furnishing out accommodations for the sick at Anoatok. I have already described this station as the halting place of our winter journeys. The hut was a low dome of heavy stones, more like a cave than a human habitation. It was perched on the very point of the rocky promontory I have named after Captain Inglefield, of the British Navy. Both to the north and south it commanded a view of the ice-expanse of the straits; and what little sunshine ever broke through the gorges by which it was environed encouraged a perceptible growth of flowering plants and coarse grasses on the level behind it. The ice-belt, now beautifully smooth, brought us almost to the edge of this little plain.

I had made up my mind from an early period that, in the event of our attempting to escape upon the ice, the "wind loved spot," as the Esquimaux poetically named it, would be well adapted to the purposes of an *entrepôt,* and had endeavored within the last few weeks to fit it up also as a resting place for our sick during the turmoil of removing from the brig. I had its broken outlet closed by a practicable door, and the roof perforated to receive a stovepipe. Still more recently the stone platform or dais had been thoroughly cleansed, and covered with shavings which Ohlsen had saved while working at his boats. Over these again were laid my best cushions; and two blankets, all that we could spare, were employed to tapestry the walls.

I made many journeys between the brig and Anoatok while the arrangements for our setting out were in progress, and after the sledges were underway. All of our invalids were housed there in safety, one or two of them occupying the dog sledge for the trip. Most of our provisions for the march and voyage had also been stacked in the neighborhood of the huts: eight hundred pounds out of fifteen hundred were already there. The remaining seven hundred I undertook to carry myself, as I had done most of the rest. It would have been folly to encumber my main body with anything more than their boats and sledges; they were barely able at first to carry even these. Our effort to escape would indeed have resulted in miserable failure had we been without our little Esquimaux dog team to move the sick, forward the intended lading of the boats, and keep up supplies along the line of march. I find by my notes that these six dogs, well worn by previous travel, carried me with a fully burdened sledge between seven and eight hundred miles during the first fortnight after leaving the brig—a mean travel of fifty-seven miles a day.

Up to the evening of the twenty-third, the progress had been a little more than a mile a day for one sledge: on the twenty-fourth, both sledges had reached First Ravine, a distance of seven miles, and the dog sledge had brought on to this station the buffalo bags and other sleeping appliances we had prepared during the winter. The condition of the party was such that it was essential they should sleep in comfort; and it was a rule therefore during the whole journey, never departed from unless in extreme emergency, never to begin a new day's labor till the party was refreshed from the exertions of the day before. Our halts were regulated by the condition of the men rather than by arbitrary hours, and sleep was meted out in proportion to the trials of the march. The thermometer still ranged below zero; but our housed boats, well crowded and fully stocked with sleeping gear, were hardly uncomfortable to weary men; besides which we slept by day when the sun was warmest, and traveled when we could avoid his greatest glare.

Mr. Morton, Ohlsen, and Petersen during this time performed a double duty. They took their turn at the sledges with the rest, but they were also engaged in preparing the *Red Eric* as a comrade boat. She was mounted on our good old sledge, the "Faith"—a sledge that, like her namesake our most reliable whaleboat, had been our very present help in many times of trouble. I believe every man felt, when he saw her brought out, that stout work was to be done, and under auspices of good.

In the meantime I had carried Mr. Goodfellow to the sick station with my dog sledge, and had managed to convey the rest one by one to the same spot. Mr. Wilson, whose stump was still unhealed, and who had suffered besides from scurvy; George Whipple, whose tendons were so contracted that he could not extend his legs; and poor Stephenson, barely able to keep the lamps burning and warm up food for the rest, were the other invalids, all incapable of moving without assistance. It is just that I should speak of the manly fortitude with which they bore up during this painful imprisonment. Dr. Hayes, though still disabled from his frozen foot, adhered manfully to the sledges.

I have already expressed my belief that this little refuge hut of Anoatok was the means of saving the lives of these four men. When they were first transported to it, they were all of them so drawn up with scurvy as to be unable to move. There was but one among them able to melt water for the rest. I attended them myself during the first week, at every interval that I could snatch from the duty of transporting our provisions. The temperature in which they lived was at first below zero; but, as the sun rose and the warmth increased, they gradually gained strength and were able to crawl out and breathe in the gladdening air.

Had I attempted to bring them down on our boat sledges, our progress would have been seriously impeded and their lives jeopardized. I cannot imagine a worse position for a sick and helpless man than some of those which I have described in our transit from the brig.

On the other hand, to have left them for the time behind us would have made it quite possible that they might not at last be reclaimed. Every day was making the ice-travel more difficult and full of hazard till we reached the open water; and they could not fail to know this as soon as they would look out on the floes.

Besides all this, there is something in the insidious disease which was their most dangerous enemy that is best combated by moral excitement. A change of scene, renewed or increased responsibilities, topics of active thought, incitements to physical effort are among the very best prescriptions for men suffering with the scurvy. I have had reason to feel, while tracing these pages, how reluctantly the system renews its energies under the pressure of a daily unvarying task.

The patients at our sick station no doubt suffered much, and for a while I never parted from them without anxiety. But their health improved under the stimulus of a new mode of life; and by the time that we called on them to rejoin us, their whole tone had undergone a happy change. I congratulate myself, as I write, that all who reached the open water with me are able now to bear a part in society and toil.

* * * *

I found that Mr. Brooks had succeeded in getting his boat and sledges as far as the floe off Bedevilled Reach. I stopped only long enough to point out to him an outside track, where I had found the ice quite smooth and free from snow, and pressed my dogs for the hut. I noticed to my great joy, too, that the health of his party seemed to be improving under our raw meat specific, and could not find fault with the extravagant use they were making of it. The invalids at the sick station were not as well as I could have wished: but I had only time to renew their stock of provision and give them a few cheering words. Our walrus meat was nearly exhausted.

I determined, therefore, as soon as I could secure the meat, which was my immediate errand, to make a requisition upon the Esquimaux for two of the four dogs which were still at Etah and, by their aid, to place the provisions in safety. The north cape of Littleton Island, afterward called Point Security, was selected for the purpose, and I left orders with the invalids at the sick station to be in readiness for instant removal. I pursued my journey alone.

It was quite late in the evening when I drew near Etah. It was verging on to our midnight, the sun being low in the heavens, and the air breathing that solemn stillness which belongs to the sleeping time of birds and plants. I had not quite reached the little settlement when loud sounds of laughter came to my ear; and, turning the cape, I burst suddenly upon an encampment of the inhabitants.

Some thirty men, women, and children were gathered together upon a little face of offal-stained rock. Except a bank of moss, which broke the wind draught from the fiord, they were entirely without protection from the weather, though the temperature was five degrees below zero. The huts were completely deserted, the snow *tossut* had fallen in, and the window was as free and open as summer to the purifying air. Every

Walrus hunt off Pikantlik

living thing about the settlement was out upon the bare rocks.

How they squalled, and laughed, and snored, and rolled about! Some were sucking bird skins, others were boiling incredible numbers of auks in huge soapstone pots, and two youngsters, crying, at the top of their voices, "Oopegsoak! Oopegsoak!" were fighting for an owl. It was the only specimen *(Strix nyctea)* that I had seen except on the wing; but, before I could secure it, they had torn it limb from limb and were eating its warm flesh and blood, their faces buried among its dishevelled feathers.

The fires were of peat-moss greased with the fat of the bird skins. They were used only for cooking, however; the people depending for comfort on the warmth of close contact. Old Kresut, the blind patriarch of the settlement, was the favored center, and around him, as a focus, was a coil of men, women, and children, as perplexing to unravel as a skein of eels. The children alone were toddling about and bringing in stores of moss, their faces smeared with blood and tidbits of raw liver between their teeth.

The scene was redolent of plenty and indolence— the *dolce far niente* of the short-lived Esquimaux summer. Provision for the dark winter was furthest from their thoughts; for, although the rocks were patched with sun-dried birds, a single hunting party from Peteravik could have eaten up their entire supplies in a night.

There was enough to make them improvident. The

little auks were breeding in the low cones of rubbish under the cliffs in such numbers that it cost them no more to get food than it does a cook to gather vegetables. A boy, ordered to climb the rocks with one of their purse nets of sealskin at the end of a narwhal's tusk, would return in a few minutes with as many as he could carry.

The dogs seemed as happy as their masters: they were tethered by sealskin thongs to prevent robbery but evidently fed to the full extent of their capacity.

Aningnah, wife of Marsumah was one of the presiding deities of the soup pot. She was a tall, well made woman, and, next to Mrs. Metek, had a larger influence than any female in the settlement.

During one of my visits to the settlement, I had relieved her from much suffering by opening a furuncle, and the kind creature never lost an opportunity of showing how she remembered it. Poor old Kresut was summarily banished from the central seat of honor, and the nalegak installed in his place. She stripped herself of her bird skin kapetah to make me a coverlet, and gave me her two-year-old baby for a pillow. There was a little commotion in the tangled mass of humanity as I crawled over them to accept these proffered hospitalities; but it was all of a welcoming sort. I had learned by this time to take kindly and condescendingly the privileges of my rank; and, with my inner man well refreshed with auk livers, I was soon asleep.

In the morning I left my own tired dogs in charge of Marsumah, quite confident that his wife would feed them faithfully, and took from them their only team in unequal exchange. Such had become our relations with these poor friends of ours, that such an act of authority would have gone unquestioned if it had cost them a much graver sacrifice. They saw the condition of my own travel-broken animals and were well aware of the sufferings of our party, so long their neighbors and allies. Old Nessark filled my sledge with walrus meat; and two of the young men joined me on foot to assist me through the broken ice between Littleton Island and the mainland.

* * * *

Before I left Etah on my return, I took an early stroll with Sip-su, "the handsome boy," to the lake back of my old traveled route directly under the face of the glacier.

He led me first to the playground where all his young friends of the settlement were busy in one of their sports. Each of them had a walrus rib for a *golph* or *shinny-stick,* and they were contending to drive a *hurley,* made out of the round knob of a flipper-joint, up a bank of frozen snow. Roars of laughter greeted the impatient striker as he missed his blow at the shining ball, and eager cries told how close the match was drawing to an end. They were counting on the fingers of both hands, Eight, eight, eight: the game is ten.

Strange—the thought intruded itself, but there was no wisdom in it—strange that these famine-pinched wanderers of the ice should rejoice in sports and games like the children of our own smiling sky, and that parents should fashion for them toy sledges and harpoons and nets, miniature emblems of a life of suffering and peril! how strange this merriment under the monitory shadow of these jagged ice-cliffs! My spirit was oppressed as I imagined the possibility of our tarrying longer in these frozen regions; but it was ordinary life with these other children of the same Creator, and they were playing as unconcerned as the birds that circled above. "Fear not, therefore: ye are of more value than many sparrows."

I do not wonder that the scene at the lake impressed my brother when he visited it on his errand of rescue: Captain Hartstene and he were the only white men, except myself, that have ever seen it.

A body of ice, resplendent in the sunshine, was enclosed between the lofty walls of black basalt; and from its base a great archway or tunnel poured out a dashing stream into the lake, disturbing its quiet surface with a horseshoe of foam. Birds flew about in myriads, and the green sloping banks were checkered with the purple lychnis and Arctic chickweeds.

I have named this lake after my brother, for it was near its shores that, led by Myouk, he stumbled on the summer tents of the natives and obtained the evidence of our departure south. I built a large cairn here, and placed within it a copper penny, on which was scratched the letter K; but, like many other such deposits, it never met the eyes for which it was intended.

XXVII

Making Progress

THE SLEDGE party under Mr. Brooks had advanced to within three miles of the hut when I reached them on my return. They had found the ice more practicable, and their health was improving. But their desire for food had increased proportionably; and, as it was a well-understood rule of our commissariat not to touch the reserved provision of the boats, it became necessary to draw additional supplies from the brig. The seven hundred pounds of bread dust, our entire stock, could not be reduced with safety.

But the dogs were wanted to advance the contents of our Anoatok storehouse to the stations farther south, and I resolved to take Tom Hickey with me and walk back for another baking exploit. It was more of an effort than I counted on: we were sixteen hours on the ice floe, and we had forgotten our gutta percha eyautick, or slit goggles. The glare of the sun as we entered the curve of our ice-cumbered harbor almost blinded us.

Tom had been a baker at home; but he assures me, with all the authority of an ancient member of the guild, that our achievement the day we came on board might be worthy of praise in the "old country": Tom knows no praise more expanded. We kneaded the dough in a large pickled cabbage cask, fired sundry volumes of the Penny Cyclopedia of Useful Knowledge, and converted, between duff and loaf, almost a whole barrel of flour into a strong likeness to the staff of life. It was the last of our stock; and "all the better too," said my improvident comrade, who retained some of the genius of blundering as well as the gallantry of his countrymen, "all the better, sir, since we'll have no more bread to bake."

Godfrey came on with the dogs three days after, to carry back the fruits of our labor; but an abrupt change of the weather gave us a howling gale outside, and we were all of us storm stayed. It was Sunday, and probably the last time that two or three would be gathered together in our dreary cabin. So I took a Bible from one of the bunks, and we went through the old times service. It was my closing act of official duty among my shipmates on board the poor little craft. I visited her afterward, but none of them were with me.

Tom and myself set out soon after, though the wind drove heavily from the south, leaving our companion to recover from his fatigue. We brought on our sledge load safely, and had forgotten our baking achievement, with things of minor note, in that dreamless sleep which rewards physical exhaustion, when Godfrey came in upon us. He had had a hard chase behind the sledge, and was unwilling to confess at first what had brought him after us so soon. He had tried to forget himself among the debris of a mattress on the cabin floor, when he heard Mr. Wilson's guitar, sad and flowing in all its unearthly harmonies. He was sure he was awake, for he ran for it on the instant, and the proof was, he had left his coat behind him. The harp of Aeolus had not been dreamed of in Bill's philosophy.

I was glad, when I reached the sick station, to find things so much better. Everybody was stronger, and, as a consequence, more cheerful. They had learned housekeeping, with its courtesies as well as comforts. Their kotluk was a credit to Aningnah herself: they had a dish of tea for us, and a lump of walrus; and they bestirred themselves real housewife fashion, to give us the warm place and make us comfortable. I was right sorry to leave them, for the snow outside was drifting with the gale; but after a little while the dogs struck the track of the sledges, and, following it with unerring instinct, did not slacken their pace till they had brought us to our companions on the floe.

They had wisely halted on account of the storm; and, with their three little boats drawn up side by side for mutual protection, had been lying to for the past two days, tightly housed, and moored fast by whale lines to the ice. But the drifts had almost buried the *Hope,* which was the windward boat; and when I saw the burly form of Brooks emerging from the snow-covered roof, I could have fancied it a walrus rising through the ice.

Six Esquimaux, three of them women—Nessark's wife, at the head of them—had come off to the boats for shelter from the gale. They seemed so entirely deferential, and to recognize with such simple trust our mutual relations of alliance, that I resolved to drive down to Etah with Petersen as interpreter and formally claim assistance, according to their own laws, on the ground of our established brotherhood. I had thought of this before; but both Marsumah and Metek had been so engrossed with their bird catching that I was loath to take them from their families.

Our dogs moved very slowly, and the discolored ice admonished me to make long circuits. As we neared Littleton Island, the wind blew so freshly from the southwest that I determined to take the inshore channel and attempt to make the settlements over land. But I was hardly under the lee of the island when there broke upon us one of the most fearful gales I have ever experienced. It had the character and the force of a cyclone. The dogs were literally blown from their harness, and it was only by throwing ourselves on our faces that we saved ourselves from being totally swept away: it seemed as if the ice must give way. We availed ourselves of a momentary lull to shoulder the sledge and, calling the affrighted dogs around us, made for the rocks of Eider Island, and, after the most exhausting exertions, succeeded in gaining terra firma.

We were now safe from the danger that had seemed most imminent; but our condition was not improved. We were out on a blank cliff, the wind eddying round us so furiously that we could not keep our feet, and the air so darkened with the snow wreaths that, although we were in the full daytime of the Arctic summer, we could neither see each other nor our dogs. There was

Traversing an open channel

Courtesy G. Trinetti Collection

not a cleft or a projecting knob that could give us refuge. I saw that we must move or die. It was impossible that the ice should continue to resist such a hurricane, and a bold channel separated us from the shore. Petersen indeed protested that the channel was already broken up and driving with the storm. We made the effort, and crossed.

We struck a headland on the main shore, where a dark hornblende rock, perhaps thirty feet high, had formed a barricade, behind which the drifts piled themselves; and into this mound of snow we had just strength enough left to dig a burrow. We knew it soon after as Cape Misery.

The dogs and sledge were dragged in, and Petersen and myself, reclining "spoon fashion," cowered among them. The snow piled over us all, and we were very soon so roofed in and quilted round that the storm seemed to rage far outside of us. We could only hear the wind droning like a great flywheel, except when a surge of greater malignity would sweep up over our burial place and sift the snow upon the surface like hail. Our greatest enemy here was warmth. Our fur jumpers had been literally torn off our backs by the wind; but the united respiration of dogs and men melted the snow around us, and we were soon wet to the skin. It was a noisome vapor bath, and we experienced its effects in an alarming tendency to syncope and loss of power.

Is it possible to imagine a juncture of more comic annoyance than that which now introduced itself among the terrors of our position? Toodla, our master dog, was seized with a violent fit, and, as their custom is, his companions indulged in a family conflict upon the occasion, which was only mediated, after much effort, at the sacrifice of all that remained of Petersen's pantaloons and drawers.

We had all the longing for repose that accompanies extreme prostration, and had been fearing every moment that the combatants would bring the snow down upon us. At last down came our whole canopy, and we were exposed in an instant to the fury of the elements. I do not think, often as I have gone up on deck from a close cabin in a gale at sea, that I was ever more struck with the extreme noise and tumult of a storm.

Once more snowed up—for the drift built its crystal palace rapidly about us—we remained cramped and seething till our appetites reminded us of the necessities of the inner man. To breast the gale was simply impossible; the alternative was to drive before it to the north and east. Forty miles of floundering travel brought us in twenty hours to the party on the floes.

They too had felt the force of the storm and had drawn up the boats with their prows to the wind, all hands housed, and wondering as much as we did that the ice still held.

* * * *

Petersen and myself gave up the sledge to Morton, Marsumah and Nessark, who set out at once to negotiate at Etah as I took my place with the sledge parties.

The ice, though not broken up by the storm, had been so much affected by it, as well as by the advancing season, that I felt we could not spare ourselves an hour's rest. The snow fields before us to the south were already saturated with wet. Around the bergs the black water came to the surface, and the whole area was spotted with pools. We summoned all our energies on the fifth for this dangerous traverse; but, although the boats were unladen and everything transported by sledge, it was impossible to prevent accidents. One of the sledges broke through, carrying six men into the water, and the *Hope* narrowly escaped being lost. Her stern went down, and she was extricated with great difficulty.

The sixth saw the same disheartening work. The ice was almost impassable. Both sick and well worked at the drag ropes alike, and hardly a man but was constantly wet to the skin. Fearing for the invalids at the sick station in case we should be cut off from them, I sent for Mr. Goodfellow at once, and gave orders for the rest to be in readiness for removal at a moment's notice.

The next day Morton returned from Etah. The natives had responded to the brotherly appeal of the nalegak; and they came down from the settlement, bringing a full supply of meat and blubber, and every sound dog that belonged to them. I had now once more a serviceable team. The comfort and security of such a possession to men in our critical position can hardly be realized. It was more than an addition of ten strong men to our party. I set off at once with Metek to glean from the brig her last remnant of slush (tallow) and to bring down the sick men from Anoatok.

As we traveled with our empty sledges along a sort of beaten track or road that led close under the cliffs, I realized very forcibly the influence of the coming summer upon the rocks above us. They were just released from the frost which had bound them so long and closely, and were rolling down the slopes of the debris with the din of a battlefield and absolutely clogging the ice-belt at the foot. Here and there, too, a large sheet of rocks and earth would leave its bed at once, and, gathering mass as it traveled, move downward like a cataract of ruins. The dogs were terrified by the clamor and could hardly be driven on till it intermitted.

Just beyond Six-Mile Ravine my sledge barely escaped destruction from one of these landslides. Happily Metek was behind, and warned me of the danger just in time to cut loose the traces and drag away the sledge.

Our visit to the brig was soon over: we had very few stores to remove. I trod her solitary deck for the last time, and returned with Metek to his sledge.

I had left the party on the floes with many apprehensions for their safety, and the result proved they were not without cause. While crossing a "tide-hole," one of the runners of the *Hope*'s sledge broke through, and, but for the strength and presence of mind of Ohlsen, the boat would have gone under. He saw the ice give way and, by a violent exercise of strength, passed a capstan bar under the sledge, and thus bore the load till it was hauled on to safer ice. He was a very powerful man, and might have done this without injuring himself; but it would seem his footing gave way under him, forcing him to make a still more desperate effort to extricate himself. It cost him his life: he died three days afterwards.

I was bringing down George Stephenson from the sick station, and, my sledge being heavily laden, I had just crossed, with some anxiety, near the spot at which the accident occurred. A little way beyond we met Mr. Ohlsen, seated upon a lump of ice, and very pale. He pointed to the camp about three miles farther on, and told us, in a faint voice, that he had not detained the party: he "had a little cramp in the small of the back," but would soon be better.

I put him at once in Stephenson's place, and drove him on to the *Faith*. Here he was placed in the stern sheets of the boat and well muffled-up in our best buffalo robes. That night he was assiduously attended by Dr. Hayes; but he sank rapidly. His symptoms had from the first a certain obscure but fatal resemblance to our winter's tetanus, which filled us with forebodings.

On Saturday, 6 June, after stowing away our disabled comrade in the *Faith,* we again set all hands at the drag ropes. The ice ahead of us bore the same character as the day before—no better: we were all perceptibly weaker and much disheartened.

We had been tugging in harness about two hours when a breeze set in from the northward, the first that we had felt since crossing Bedevilled Reach. We got out our long steering oar as a boom and made sail upon the boats. The wind freshened almost to a gale; and heading toward the depot on Little Island, we ran gallantly before it.

It was a new sensation to our footsore men, this sailing over solid ice. Levels which, under the slow labor of the drag ropes, would have delayed us for hours, were glided over without a halt. We thought it dangerous work at first, but the speed of the sledges made rotten ice nearly as available as sound. The men could see plainly that they were approaching new landmarks and leaving old ones behind. Their spirits rose; the sick mounted the thwarts; the well clung to the gunwale: and, for the first time for nearly a year broke out the sailor's chorus, "Storm along, my hearty boys!"

We must have made a greater distance in this single day than in the five that preceded it. We encamped at 5:00 P.M. near a small berg, which gave us plenty of fresh water, after a progress of at least eight miles.

As we were halting, I saw two Esquimaux on the ice toward Life-Boat Cove; and the well known "Huk! huuk!" a sort of Masonic signal among them, soon brought them to us. They turned out to be Sip-su and old Nessark. They were the bearers of good news: my dogs were refreshed and nearly able to travel again; and, as they volunteered to do me service, I harnessed up our united teams and dispatched Nessark to the hut to bring down Mr. Wilson and George Whipple.

We expected now to have our whole party together again, and the day would have been an active cheering one throughout but for the condition of poor Ohlsen, who was growing rapidly worse.

From this time we went on for some days aided by our sails, meeting with accidents occasionally—the giving way of a spar or the falling of some of the party through the spongy ice—and occasionally, when the floe was altogether too infirm, laboring our way with great difficulty upon the ice-belt. To mount this solid highway, or to descend from it, the axes were always in requisition. An inclined plane was to be cut, ten, fifteen, or even thirty feet long, and along this the sledges were to be pushed and guided by bars and levers with painful labor. These are light things, as I refer to them here; but in our circumstances, when the breaking of a stick of timber was in irreparable harm, and the delay of a day involved the peril of life, they were grave enough. Even on the floes the axe was often indispensable to carve our path through the hummocks; and many a weary and anxious hour have I looked on and toiled while the sledges were waiting for the way to open. Sometimes too, both on the land-ice and on the belt, we encountered heavy snowdrifts, which were to be shovelled away before we could get along; and within an hour, or perhaps even at the bottom of the drift, one of the sledge runners would cut through to the water.

Still passing slowly on day after day—I am reluctant to borrow from my journal the details of anxiety and embarrassment with which it abounds throughout this period—we came at last to the unmistakable neighborhood of the open water. We were off Pikantlik, the largest of the Littleton Island group, just opposite "Kosoak," the Great River. Here Mr. Wilson and George Whipple rejoined us, under the faithful charge of old Nessark. They had broken through twice on the road, but without any serious inconvenience in consequence. It was with truly thankful hearts we united in our prayers that evening.

One only was absent of all the party that remained on our rolls. Hans, the kind son and young lover of Fiskernaes, my trusted friend, had been missing for nearly two months. I am loath to tell the story as I believe it, for it may not be the true one after all, and I would not intimate an unwarranted doubt of the constancy of boyish love. But I must explain, as far as I can, why he was not with us when we first looked at the open water. Just before my departure for my April hunt, Hans came to me with a long face, asking permission to visit Peteravik: "he had no boots, and wanted to lay in a stock of walrus hide for soles: he did not need the dogs; he would rather walk." It was a long march, but he was well practiced in it, and I consented. Both Petersen and myself gave him commissions to execute, and he left us, intending to stop by the way at Etah.

In our labors of the next month we missed Hans

much. He had not yet returned, and the stories of him that came to us from Etah were the theme of much conversation and surmise among us. He had certainly called there as he promised, and given to Nessark's wife an order for a pair of boots, and he had then wended his way across the big headland to Peteravik, where Shang-hu and his pretty daughter had their home. This intimation was given with many an explanatory grin; for Hans was a favorite with all, the fair especially, and, as a match, one of the greatest men in the country. It required all my recollections of his "old love" to make me suspend my judgment; for the boots came, as if to confirm the scandal. I never failed in my efforts afterward to find his whereabouts and went out of our way to interrogate this and that settlement; for, independent of everything like duty, I was very fond of him. But the story was everywhere the same. Hans the faithful—yet, I fear, the faithless—was last seen upon a native sledge, driving south from Peteravik, with a maiden at his side, and professedly bound to a new principality at Uwarrow Suk-suk, high up Murchison's Sound. Alas for Hans, the married man!

Seal-skin cup

XXVIII

The Death of Ohlsen

THOUGH THE condition of the ice assured us that we were close to the end of our sledge journeys, it by no means diminished their difficulty or hazards. The part of the field near the open water is always abraded by the currents, while it remains apparently firm on the surface. In some places it was so transparent that we could even see the gurgling eddies below it; while in others it was worn into open holes that were already the resort of wild fowl. But in general it looked hard and plausible, though not more than a foot or even six inches in thickness.

This continued to be its character as long as we pursued the Littleton Island channel, and we were compelled, the whole way through, to sound ahead with the boat hook or narwhal horn. We learned this precaution from the Esquimaux, who always move in advance of their sledges when the ice is treacherous and test its strength before bringing on their teams. Our first warning impressed us with the policy of observing it. We were making wide circuits with the whaleboats to avoid the tide-holes when signals of distress from men scrambling on the ice announced to us that the *Red Eric* had disappeared. This unfortunate little craft contained all the dearly earned documents of the expedition. There was not a man who did not feel that the reputation of the party rested in a great degree upon their preservation. It had cost us many a pang to give up our collections of natural history, to which everyone had contributed his quota of labor and interest; but the destruction of the vouchers of the cruise—the logbooks, the meteorological registers, the surveys, and the journals—seemed to strike them all as an irreparable disaster.

When I reached the boat everything was in confusion. Blake, with a line passed round his waist, was standing up to his knees in sludge, groping for the document box, and Mr. Bonsall, dripping wet, was endeavoring to haul the provision bags to a place of safety. Happily the boat was our lightest one, and everything was saved. She was gradually lightened until she could bear a man, and her cargo was then passed out by a line and hauled upon the ice. In spite of the wet and the cold and our thoughts of poor Ohlsen, we greeted its safety with three cheers.

It was by great good fortune that no lives were lost. Stephenson was caught as he sank by one of the sledge runners, and Morton, while in the very act of drifting under the ice, was seized by the hair of the head by Mr. Bonsall and saved.

We were now close upon Life-Boat Cove, where nearly two years before we had made provision for just such a contingency as that which was now before us. Buried under the frozen soil, our stores had escaped even the keen scrutiny of our savage allies, and

The broken floes nearing Pikantlik

C. Schuessele & J. Hamilton, from a sketch by Dr. Kane

381

we now turned to them as essential to our relief. Mr. McGary was sent to the cache, with orders to bring everything except the salt beef. This had been so long a poison to us, that, tainted as we were by scurvy, I was afraid to bring it among those who might be tempted to indulge in it.

On the twelfth the boats and sledges came to a halt in the narrow passage between the islands opposite Cape Misery, the scene of our late snow storm. All of our cargo had been gathered together at this spot, and the rocks were covered with our stores. Out of the fourteen hundred pounds not an ounce had been sacrificed. All was cased in its waterproof covering, and as dry and perfect as when it had left the brig.

I ascended some eight hundred feet to the summit of Pikantlik and, looking out, beheld the open water, so long the goal of our struggles, spread out before me. It extended seemingly to Cape Alexander, and was nearer to the westward than the south of my position by some five or six miles. But the ice in the latter direction led into the curve of the bay, and was thus protected from the wind and swell. My jaded comrades pleaded anxiously in favor of the direct line to the water; but I knew that this ice would give us both safer and better travel. I determined to adopt the inshore route. Our position at Pikantlik, as we determine carefully by the mean of several observations, is in latitude 78°22′ 1″ and longitude 74°10′. We connected it with Cape Alexander and other determined stations to the north and west.

The channel between islands was much choked with upreared ice; but our dogs had now come back to us so much refreshed that I was able to call their services again into requisition. We carried one entire load to the main, which forms the northeast headland of Hartstene Bay and, the Esquimaux assisting us, deposited it safely on the inner side.

I was with the advance boat, trying to force a way through the channel, when the report came to me from Dr. Hayes that Ohlsen was no more. He had shown a short half hour before some signs of revival, and Petersen had gone out to kill a few birds in the hope of possibly sustaining him by a concentrated soup. But it was in vain: the poor fellow flushed up only to die a few minutes after.

We had no time to mourn the loss of our comrade, a tried and courageous man, who met his death in the gallant discharge of duty. It cast a gloom over the whole party; but the exigencies of the moment were upon us, and we knew not whose turn would come next, or how soon we might all of us follow him together.

I had carefully concealed Mr. Ohlsen's sickness from the Esquimaux, with everything else that could intimate our weakness; for, without reflecting at all upon their fidelity, I felt that with them, as with the rest of the world, pity was a less active provocative to good deeds than the deference which is exacted by power. I had therefore represented our abandonment of the brig as merely the absence of a general hunting party to the far south, and I was willing now to keep up the impression. I leave to moralists the discussion of the question how far I erred; but I now sent them to their village under pretext of obtaining birds and lent them our dogs to ensure their departure.

The body of Mr. Ohlsen was sewed up, while they were gone, in his own blankets and carried in procession to the head of a little gorge on the east face of Pikantlik where by hard labor we consigned his remains to a sort of trench, and covered them with rocks to protect them from the fox and bear. Without the knowledge of my comrades, I encroached on our little store of sheet lead, which we were husbanding to mend our leaky boats with, and, cutting on a small tablet his name and age—

CHRISTIAN OHLSEN,

Aged 36 Years,

laid it on his manly breast. The cape that looks down on him bears his name, a tribute to Mr. Ohlsen's bravery and contributions to our endeavor.

As we walked back to our camp upon the ice, the death of Ohlsen brought to my mind the strange parallel of our story with that of old William Barentz—a parallel which might verify that sad truth of history that human adventure repeats itself.

Two hundred and fifty-nine years ago, William Barentz, Chief Pilot of the States-General of Holland—the United States of that day—had wintered on the coast of Novaia Zemlia, exploring the northernmost region of the Old Continent, as we had that of the New. His men, seventeen in number, broke down during the trials of the winter and three died, just as of our eighteen three had gone. He abandoned his vessel as we had abandoned ours, took to his boats, and escaped along the Lapland coast to lands of Norwegian civilization. We had embarked with sledge and boat to attempt the same thing. We had the longer journey and the more difficult before us. He lost, as we had done, a cherished comrade by the wayside; and, as I thought of this closing resemblance in our fortunes also, my mind left but one part of the parallel incomplete—*Barentz himself perished.*

We gave two quiet hours to the memory of our dead brother, and then resumed our toilsome march. We kept up nearly the same routine as before; but as we neared the settlements, the Esquimaux came in flocks to our assistance. They volunteered to aid us at the drag ropes. They carried our sick upon hand sledges. They relieved us of all care for our supplies of daily food. The quantity of little auks that they brought us was enormous. They fed us and our dogs at the rate of eight thousand birds a week, all of them caught in their little hand nets. All anxiety left us for the time. The men broke out in their old forecastle songs; the sledges began to move merrily ahead, and laugh and jest drove out the old moody silence.

During one of our evening halts, when the congregation of natives had scattered away to their camp-fires, Metek and Nualik his wife came to me privately on a matter of grave consultation. They brought with them a fat, curious looking boy. "Accomodah," said they, "is our youngest son. His sleep at night is bad, and his nangah"—pointing to that protuberance which is supposed to represent aldermanic dignity—"is always round and hard. He eats ossuk (blubber) and no meat, and bleeds at the nose. Besides, he does not grow." They wanted me to, in my capacity of angekok-soak, charm or cure him.

I told them, with all the freedom from mystery that distinguishes the regulated practitioner from the empiric, what must be my mode of treatment: that I must dip my hand into the salt water where the ice cut against the sea, and lay it on the offending nangah; and that if they would bring to me their rotund little companion within three days, at that broad and deep Bethesda, I would signalize my consideration of the kindness of the tribe by a trial of my powers.

They went away very thankful, taking a preliminary prescription of a lump of brown soap, a silk shirt, and a taboo of all further eating of ossuk; and I had no doubt that their anxiety to have the boy duly pow-wowwed would urge forward our sledges and bring us early to the healing waters. We longed for them as much as Metek, and needed them more than Accomodah.

My little notebook closes for the week with this gratefully expanded record:

JUNE 16, SATURDAY. "Our boats are at the open water. We see its deep indigo horizon, and hear its roar against the icy beach. Its scent is in our nostrils and our hearts.

"Our camp is but three-quarters of a mile from the sea: it is at the northern curve of the North Baffin polynia. We must reach it at the southern sweep of Etah Bay, about three miles from Cape Alexander. A dark headland defines the spot. It is more marked than the southern entrance of Smith's Straits. How magnificently the surf beats against its sides! There are ridges of squeezed ice between us and it, and a broad zone of floating sludge is swelling and rolling sluggishly along its margin—formidable barriers to boats and sledges. But we have mastered worse obstacles, and by God's help we will master these."

Portrait of Ohlsen

XXIX

Farewell to Good Friends

WE HAD our boats to prepare now for a long and adventurous navigation. They were so small and heavily laden as hardly to justify much confidence in their buoyancy; but, besides this, they were split with frost and warped by sunshine, and fairly open at the seams. They were to be caulked and swelled and launched and stowed, before we could venture to embark in them. A rainy southwester too, which had met us on our arrival, was now spreading with its black nimbus over the bay, and it looked as if we were to be storm stayed on the precarious ice-beach. It was a time of anxiety, but to me personally of comparative rest. I resumed my journal:

JUNE 18, MONDAY. "The Esquimaux are camped by our side—the whole settlement of Etah congregated around the 'big caldron' of Cape Alexander to bid us goodbye. There are Metek, and Nualik his wife, our old acquaintance Mrs. Eider-duck, and their five children, commencing with Myouk, my bodyguard, and ending with the little Accomodah. There is Nessark and Anak his wife; and Tellerk the 'Right Arm,' and Amaunalik his wife; and Sip-su, and Marsumah and Aningnah. I can name them every one, and they know us as well. We have found brothers in a strange land.

"Each one has a knife, or a file, or a saw, or some such treasured keepsake; and the children have a lump of soap, the greatest of all great medicines. The merry little urchins break in upon me even now as I am writing: 'Kuyanake, kuyanake, Nalegak-soak!' 'Thank you, thank you, big chief!' While Myouk is crowding fresh presents of raw birds on me as if I could eat forever, and poor Aningnah is crying beside the tent curtain, wiping her eyes on a bird skin!

"My heart warms to these poor, dirty, miserable, yet happy beings, so long our neighbors, and of late so stanchly our friends. Theirs is no affectation of regret. There are twenty-two of them around me, all busy in good offices to the Docto Kayens; and there are only two women and the old blind patriarch Kresut, 'Driftwood,' left behind at the settlement.

"But see! more of them are coming up—boys ten years old pushing forward babies on their sledges. The whole nation is gypsying with us upon the icy meadows.

"We cook for them in our big camp kettle; they sleep in the *Red Eric;* a berg close at hand supplies them with water: and thus, rich in all that they value—sleep and food and drink and companionship—with their treasured short-lived summer sun above them, the *beau ideal* and sum of Esquimaux blessings, they seem supremely happy.

"Poor creatures! It is only six months ago that starvation was among them: many of the faces around me have not yet lost the lines of wasting suspense. The walrus season is again of doubtful productiveness, and they are cut off from their brethren to the south, at Netelik and Appah, until winter rebuilds the avenue of ice. With all this, no thoughts of the future cross them. Babies squall, and women chatter, and the men weave their long yarns with peals of rattling hearty laughter between.

"Ever since we reached Pikantlik, these friends of ours have considered us their guests. They have given us hand sledges for our baggage, and taken turn about in watches to carry us and it to the water's edge. But for them our dreary journey would have been pro-longed at least a fortnight, and we are so late even now that hours may measure our lives. Metek, Myouk, Nessark, Marsumah, Erkee, and the half grown boys have been our chief laborers; but women, children, and dogs are all bearing their part.

"Whatever were the faults of these Esquimaux heretofore, stealing was the only grave one. Treachery they may have conceived; and I have reason to believe that, under superstitious fears of an evil influence from our presence, they would at one time have been glad to destroy us. But the day of all this has passed away. When trouble came to us and to them, and we bent ourselves to their habits—when we looked to them to procure us fresh meat, and they found at our poor Oomiak-soak shelter and protection during their wild bear hunts—then we were so blended in our interests as well as modes of life that every trace of enmity wore away. God knows that since they professed friendship, albeit the imaginary powers of the angekok-soak and the marvelous six-shooter which attested them may have had their influence, never have friends been more true. Although, since Ohlsen's death, numberless articles of inestimable value to them have been scattered upon the ice unwatched, they have not stolen a nail. It was only yesterday that Metek, upon my alluding to the manner in which property of all sorts was exposed without pilfering, explained through Petersen, in these two short sentences, the argument of their morality:

" 'You have done us good. We are not hungry; we will not take (steal)—You have done us good; we want to help you: we are friends.' "

I made my last visit to Etah while we were waiting the issue of the storm. I saw old Kresut (Driftwood) the blind man, and listened to his long goodbye talk. I had passed with the Esquimaux as an angekok, in virtue of some simple exploits of natural magic; and it was one of the regular old times entertainments of our visitors at the brig, to see my hand terrible with blazing ether, while it lifted nails with a magnet. I tried now to communicate a portion of my wonder-working talent. I made a lens of ice before them, and "drew down the sun," so as to light the moss under their kolupsut. I did not quite understand old Kresut, and I was not quite sure he understood himself. But I trusted to the others to explain to him what I had done, and burned the back of his hand for a testimony in the most friendly manner. After all which, with a reputation for wisdom which I dare say will live in their short annals,

I slowly wended my way to the brig once more.

We had quite a scene, distributing our last presents. My amputating knives, the great gift of all, went to Metek and Nessark; but everyone had something as his special prize. Our dogs went to the community at large, as tenants in common, except Toodla-mik and Whitey, our representative dogs through very many trials. I could not part with them, the leaders of my team; I have them still.

But Nualik, the poor mother, had something still to remind me of. She had accompanied us throughout the transit of Etah Bay, with her boy Accomodah, waiting anxiously for the moment when the first salt water would enable me to fulfill my promised exorcisation of the demon in his stomach. There was no option but to fulfill the pledge with faithful ceremony. The boy was taken to the water's edge, and his exorbitant little nangah faithfully embrocated in the presence of both his parents. I could not speak my thanks in their language, but I contributed my scanty stock of silk shirts to the poor little sufferer—for such he was—and I blessed them for their humanity to us with a fervor of heart which from a better man might peradventure have carried a blessing along with it.

And now it only remained for us to make our farewell to these desolate and confiding people. I gathered them round me on the ice-beach, and talked to them as brothers for whose kindness I still needed to return. I told them what I knew of the tribes from which they were separated by the glacier and the sea, of the resources that abounded in those less ungenial regions not far off to the south, the greater duration of daylight, the lesser intensity of the cold, the facilities of the hunt, the frequent driftwood, the kayak and the fishing net. I tried to explain to them how, under bold and cautious guidance, they might reach there in a few seasons of patient march. I gave them drawings of the coast, with its headlands and hunting grounds, as far as Cape Shackleton, and its best camping stations from Red Head to the Danish settlements.

They listened with breathless interest, closing their circle round me; and, as Petersen described the big ussuk, the white whale, the bear, and the long open water hunts with the kayak and the rifle, they looked at each other with a significance not to be misunderstood. They would anxiously have had me promise that I would someday return and carry a load of them down to the settlements; and I shall not wonder if—guided perhaps by Hans—they hereafter attempt the journey without other aid.

This was our final parting. A letter which I addressed at the moment of reaching the settlements to the Lutheran Missions, the tutelary society of the Esquimaux of Greenland, will attest the sincerity of my professions and my willingness to assist in giving them effect.

It was in the soft subdued light of a Sunday evening, 17 June, that, after hauling our boats with much hard labor through the hummocks, we stood beside the open seaway. Before midnight we had launched the

Red Eric, and given three cheers for Henry Grinnell and "homeward bound," unfurling all our flags.

But we were not yet to embark; for the gale which had been long brooding now began to dash a heavy wind lipper against the floe, and obliged us to retreat before it, hauling our boats back with each fresh breakage of the ice. It rose more fiercely, and we were obliged to give way before it still more. Our goods, which had been stacked upon the ice, had to be carried farther inward. We worked our way back thus, step by step, before the breaking ice, for about two hundred yards. At last it became apparent that the men must sleep and rest, or sink; and, giving up for the present all thoughts of embarking, I hauled the boats at once nearly a mile from the water's edge, where a large iceberg was frozen tight in the floes.

But here we were still pursued. All the next night it blew fearfully, and at last our berg crashed away through the broken ice, and our asylum was destroyed. Again we fell to hauling back the boats; until, fearing that the continuance of the gale might induce a ground swell, which would have been fatal to us, I came to a halt near the slope of a low iceberg, on which I felt confident that we could haul up in case of the disruption of the floes. The entire area was already beginning to intersect with long cracks, and the surface began to show a perceptible undulation that was beneath our feet.

It was well for us I had not gratified the men by taking the outside track: we should certainly have been rafted off into the storm, and without an apparent possibility of escape.

I climbed to the summit of the berg; but it was impossible to penetrate the obscurity of mist and spray and cloud farther than a thousand yards. The sea tore the ice up almost to the very base of the berg, and all around it looked like one vast tumultuous caldron, the ice-tables crashing together in every possible position with deafening clamor.

Bidding good-bye

XXX

Moving to the South

T HE GALE died away to a calm, and the water became as tranquil as if the gale had never been. All
hands were called to prepare for embarking. The boats
were stowed, and the cargo divided between them
equally; the sledges unlashed and slung outside the
gunwales; and on Tuesday the nineteenth, at 4:00 P.M.,
with the bay as smooth as a garden lake, I put off in the
Faith. She was followed by the *Red Eric* on our quarter, and the *Hope* astern. In the *Faith* I had with me Mr.
McGary, and Petersen, Hickey, Stephenson, and
Whipple. Mr. Brooks was in the *Hope,* with Hayes,
Sontag, Morton, Goodfellow, and Blake. Bonsall,
Riley, and Godfrey made the crew of the *Eric.*

The wind freshened as we doubled the western-
most point of Cape Alexander, and, as we looked out
on the expanse of the sound, we saw the kittiwakes and
the ivory gulls and jagers dipping their wings in the
curling waves. They seemed the very same birds we
had left two years before screaming and catching fish
in the beautiful water. We tried to make our first rest
at Sutherland Island; but we found it so barricaded by
the precipitous ice-belt that it was impossible to land.
I clambered myself from the boat's mast upon the platform and filled our kettles with snow, and then, after

cooking our supper in the boats, we stood away for Hakluyt. It was an ugly crossing: we had a short chopping sea from the southeast; and, after awhile, the *Red* swamped. Riley and Godfrey managed to struggle to the *Faith,* and Bonsall to the *Hope;* but it was impossible to remove the cargo of our little comrade: it was as much as we could do to keep her afloat and let her tow behind us. Just at this time, too, the *Hope* made a signal of distress; and Brooks hailed us to say that she was making water faster than he could free her.

The wind was hauling round to the westward, and we could not take the sea abeam. But, as I made a rapid survey of the area around me, studded already with floating shreds of floe ice, I saw ahead to the low gray blink of the pack. I remember well the experience of our Beechey Island trip, and knew that the margin of these large fields is almost always broken by inlets of open water, which give much the same sort of protection as the creeks and rivers of an adverse coast. We were fortunate in finding one of these and fastening ourselves to an old floe, alongside of which our weary men turned in to sleep without hauling up the boats.

When Petersen and myself returned from an unsuccessful hunt upon the ice, we found them still asleep, in spite of a cold rain that might have awakened them. I did not disturb them till eight o'clock. We then retreated from our breakwater of refuge, generally pulling along by the boat hooks, but sometimes dragging our boats over the ice; and at last, bending to our oars as the water opened, finally reached the shore of

Hakluyt Island. It was hardly less repulsive than the ice-cliffs of the day before; but a spit to the southward gave us the opportunity of hauling up as the tide rose, and we finally succeeded in transferring ourselves and all our fortunes to the land-ice, and thence to the rocks beyond.

It snowed hard in the night, and the work of caulking went on badly, though we expended on it a prodigal share of our remaining white lead. We laboriously rigged up a tent for the sick and reinforced our bread dust and tallow supper by a few birds. We had shot a seal that day, but we lost him by his sinking.

In the morning of the twenty-second we pushed forward through the snowstorm for Northumberland Island, and succeeded in reaching it a little to the eastward of my former landing place. Myriads of auks greeted us, and we returned their greeting by the appropriate invitation to our table. A fox also saluted us with an admirable imitation of the "Huk-huk huk," which among the Esquimaux is the never unheeded call of distress; but the rascal, after seducing us a mile and a half out of our way, escaped our guns.

Our boats entered a little patch of open water that conducted us to the beach, directly below one of the hanging glaciers. The interest with which these impressed me when I was turning back from my Beechey Island effort was justified very fully by what I saw of them now. It seemed as if a caldron of ice inside the coast-ridge was boiling over, and throwing its crust in huge fragments from the overhanging lip into the sea below. The glacier must have been eleven hundred feet high; but even at its summit we could see the lines of viscous movement.

We crossed Murchison Channel on the twenty-third, and encamped for the night on the land floe at the base of Cape Parry—a hard day's travel, partly by tracking over ice, partly through tortuous and zigzag leads. The next day brought us to the neighborhood of Fitz-Clarence Rock, one of the most interesting monuments that rear themselves along this dreary coast: in a region more familiar to men, it would be a landmark to the navigator. It rises from a field of ice like an Egyptian pyramid surmounted by an obelisk.

The next day gave us admirable progress. The ice opened in leads before us, somewhat tortuous, but, on the whole, favoring, and for sixteen hours I never left the helm. We were all of us exhausted when the day's work came to a close. Our allowance had been small from the first; but the delays we seemed fated to encounter had made me reduce them to what I then thought the minimum quantity, six ounces of bread dust and a lump of tallow the size of a walnut: a paste or broth, made of these before setting out in the morning and distributed occasionally through the day in scanty rations, was our only fare. We were all of us glad when, running the boats under the lee of a berg, we were able to fill our kettles with snow and boil up for our great restorative tea. I may remark that, under the circumstances of most privation, I found no comforter so welcome to the party as this. We drank immoderately of the tea, and always with a good advantage.

While the men slept after their weary labor, McGary and myself climbed the berg for a view ahead. It was a saddening one. We had lost sight of Cary Island; but shoreward, up Wostenholm Channel, the ice seemed as if it had not yet begun to yield to the influences of summer. Everything showed how intense the last winter had been. We were close upon the first of July, and had a right to look for the North Water of the whalers where we now had solid ice or close pack, both of them almost equally unfavorable to our progress. Far off in the distance—how far I could not measure—rose the Dalrymple Rock, projecting from the lofty precipice of the island ahead; but between us and it the land-ice spread itself from the base of Saunders's Island unbroken to the far south.

The next day's progress was of course slow and wearisome, pushing through alternate ice and water for the land-belt. We fastened at last to the great floe near the shore, making our harbor in a crack, which opened with the changes of the tide.

The imperfect diet of the party was showing itself more and more in the decline of their strength. They seemed scarcely aware of it themselves, and referred the difficulty they found in dragging and pushing to something uncommon about the ice or sludge rather than to their own weakness. But now, as we endeavored to renew labors through the morning fog, belted in on all sides by ice-fields so distorted and rugged as to defy our efforts to cross them, the truth seemed to burst upon everyone. We had lost the feeling of hunger, and were almost satisfied with our pasty broth and the large draughts of tea which accompanied it. I was anxious to send our small boat, the *Eric*, across to the lumme-hill of Appah, where I knew from the Esquimaux we should find plenty of birds; but the strength of the party was insufficient to drag her.

We were sorely disheartened, and could only wait for the fog to rise in the hope of some smoother platform than that which was about us, for some lead that might save us the painful labor of tracking. I had climbed the iceberg; and there was nothing in view except Dalrymple Rock, with its red brassy face towering in the unknown distance. But I hardly got back to my boat before a gale struck us from the northwest, and a floe, taking upon a tongue of ice about a mile to the north of us, began to swing upon it like a pivot and close slowly in upon our narrow resting place.

At first our own floe also was driven before the wind; but in a little while it encountered the stationary ice at the foot of the very rock itself. On the instant the wildest imaginable ruin rose around us. The men sprang mechanically each one to his station, bearing back the boats and stores; but I gave up for the moment all hope of our escape. It was not a nip, such as is familiar to Arctic navigators, but the whole platform, where we stood and for hundreds of yards on every side of us, crumbled and crushed and piled and tossed itself madly under the pressure. I do not believe that of our little body of men, all of them disciplined

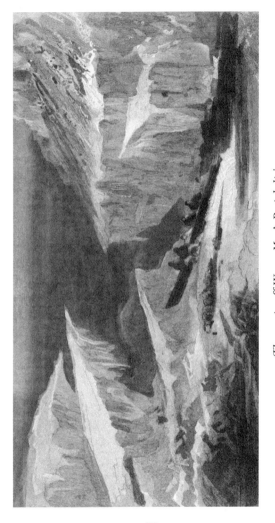

The escape off Weary Men's Rest, belt-ice

James Hamilton, from a sketch by Dr. Kane

403

in trials, able to measure danger while combating it—
I do not believe there is one who this day can explain
how or why—hardly when, in fact—we found ourselves afloat. We only know that in the midst of a
clamor utterly indescribable, through which the bray-
ing of a thousand trumpets could no more have been
heard than the voice of a man, we were shaken and
raised and whirled and let down again in a swelling
waste of broken hummocks, and, as the men grasped
their boat hooks in the stillness that followed, the boats
eddied away in a tumultuous skreed of ice and snow
and water.

We were borne along in this manner as long as the
unbroken remnant of the inshore floe continued revolving—utterly powerless and catching a glimpse
every now and then of the brazen headland that looked
down on us through the snowy sky. At last the floe
brought up against the rocks, the looser fragments that
hung round it began to separate, and we were able by
oars and boat hooks to force our battered little flotilla
clear of them. To our joyful surprise, we soon found
ourselves in a stretch of the land-water wide enough
to give us rowing room, and with the assured promise
of land close ahead.

As we neared it, we saw the same forbidding wall
of belt-ice as at Sutherland and Hakluyt. We pulled
along its margin, seeking in vain either an opening of
access or a nook of shelter. The gale rose, and the ice
began to drive again; but there was nothing to be done
but get a grapnel out to the belt and hold on for the

rising tide. The *Hope* stove her bottom and lost part of her weather boarding, and all the boats were badly chafed. It was an awful storm; and it was not without constant exertion that we kept afloat, baling out the scud that broke over us, and warding off the ice with boat hooks.

At three o'clock the tide was high enough for us to scale the ice-cliff. One by one we pulled up the boats upon a narrow shelf, the whole sixteen of us uniting at each pull. We were too much worn down to unload; but a deep and narrow gorge opened in the cliffs almost at the spot where we clambered up; and, as we pushed the boats into it on an even keel, the rocks seemed to close above our heads, until an abrupt turn in the course of the ravine placed a protecting cliff between us and the gale. We were completely encaved.

Just as we had brought in the last boat, the *Red Eric,* and were shoring her up with blocks of ice, a long unused but familiar and unmistakable sound startled and gladdened every ear, and a flock of eiders flecking the sky for a moment passed swiftly in front of us. We knew that we must be at their breeding grounds; and, as we turned in wet and hungry to our long coveted sleep, it was only to dream of eggs and abundance.

We remained almost three days in our crystal retreat, gathering eggs at the rate of twelve hundred a day. Outside, the storm raged without intermission, and our egg hunters found it difficult to keep their feet; but a merrier set of gourmands than were gathered within never surfeited in genial diet.

On the third of July the wind began to moderate, though the snow still fell heavily; and the next morning, after a patriotic eggnog, the liquor borrowed grudgingly from our alcohol flask, and diluted till it was worthy of temperance praise—we lowered our boats and bade a grateful farewell to "Weary Man's Rest." We rowed to the southeast end of Wostenholme Island; but the tide left us there, and we moved to the ice-foot.

For some days after this we kept moving slowly to the south, along the lanes that opened between the belt-ice and the floe. The weather continued dull and unfavorable for observations of any sort, and we were off a large glacier before we were aware that further progress near the shore was impracticable. Great chains of bergs presented themselves as barriers in our way, the spaces between choked by barricades of hummocks. It was hopeless to bore. We tried for sixteen hours together without finding a possibility of egress. The whole sea was rugged and broken in the extreme.

I climbed one of the bergs to the height of about two hundred feet, and, looking well to the west, was satisfied that a lead which I saw there could be followed in the direction of Conical Rocks, and beyond toward Cape Dudley Digges. But, on conferring with Brooks and McGary, I was startled to find how much the boats had suffered in the rude encounters of the last few days. The *Hope* was in fact altogether unseaworthy: the ice had strained her bottommost timbers, and it required nearly all our wood for repairs; bit by bit we had already cut up and burned the runners and cross-bars of two sledges; the third we had to reserve as essential to our ice-crossings.

In the meantime, the birds, which had been so abundant when we left Dalrymple's Island, and which we had counted on for a continuous store, seemed to have been driven off by the storm. We were again reduced to short daily rations of bread dust, and I was aware that the change of diet could not fail to tell upon the strength and energies of the party. I determined to keep inshore, in spite of the barricades of ice, in the hope of renewing, to some extent at least, our supplies of game. We were fifty-two hours in forcing this rugged passage: a most painful labor, which but for the disciplined endurance of the men might well have been deemed impracticable.

* * * *

Once through the barrier, the leads began to open again, and on the eleventh we found ourselves approaching Cape Dudley Digges, with a light breeze from the northwest. It looked for some hours as if our troubles were over, when a glacier came in sight not laid down on the charts, whose tongue of floe extended still farther out to sea than the one we had just passed with so much labor. Our first resolve was to double it at all hazards, for our crews were too much weakened to justify another tracking through the hummocks, and the soft snow which covered the land floes was an obstacle quite insuperable. Nevertheless, we forced our way into a lead of sludge, mingled with the comminuted ice of the glacier; but the only result was a lesson of gratitude for our escape from it. Our frail and weather-worn boats were unequal to the duty.

I again climbed the nearest berg—for these ice-mountains were to us like the lookout hills of men at home—and surveyed the ice to the south far on toward Cape York. My eyes never looked on a spectacle more painful. We were ahead of the season: the floes had not broken up. There was no "western water." Here in a cul-de-sac, between two barriers, both impassable to men in our condition, with stores miserably inadequate and strength broken down, we were to wait till the tardy summer should open to us a way.

I headed for the cliffs. Desolate and frowning as they were, it was better to reach them and halt upon the inhospitable shore than await the fruitless ventures of the sea. A narrow lead, a mere fissure at the edge of the land-ice, ended opposite a low platform: we had traced its whole extent, and it landed us close under the shadow of the precipitous shore.

Where the cape lies directly open to the swell of the northwest winds, at the base of a lofty precipice there was left still clinging to the rock a fragment of the winter ice-belt not more than five feet wide. The tides rose over it and the waves washed against it continually, but it gave a perfectly safe perch to our little boats. Above, cliff seemed to pile over cliff, until in the high distance the rocks looked like the overlapping scales of ancient armor. They were at least eleven hundred feet high, their summits generally lost in fog and mist; and all the way up we seemed to see the birds whose home is among their clefts. The nests were thickest on the shelves some fifty yards above the water; but both lumme and tridactyl gulls filled the entire air with glimmering specks, cawing and screeching with an incessant clamor.

To soften the scene, a natural bridge opened on our right into a little valley cove, green with mosses, and beyond and above it, cold and white, the glacier.

This glacier was about seven miles across at its "debouche"; it sloped gradually upward for some five miles back, and then, following the irregularities of its rocky substructure, it suddenly became a steep crevassed hill, ascending in abrupt terraces. Then came two intervals of less rugged ice, from which the glacier passed into the great *mer de glace.*

On ascending a high craggy hill to the north, I had a sublime prospect of this great frozen ocean, which seems to form the continental axis of Greenland—a vast undulating plain of purple-tinted ice, studded with islands, and absolutely gemming the horizon with the varied glitter of sun-tipped crystal.

The discharge of water from the lower surface of the glacier exceeded that of any of the northern glaciers except that of Humboldt and the one near Etah. One torrent on the side nearest me overran the ice-foot from two to five feet in depth, and spread itself upon the floes for several hundred yards; and another, finding its outlet near the summit of the glacier, broke over the rocks and poured in cataracts upon the beach below.

The ranunculus, saxifrages, chickweeds, abundant mosses, and Arctic grasses flourished near the level of the first talus of the glacier: the stone crops I found some two hundred feet higher. The thermometer was at ninety degrees in the sun; in the shade at thirty-eight degrees.

I have tried to describe the natural features of the scene, but I have omitted its most valued characteristic. It abounded in life. The lumme, nearly as large as canvas backs, and, as we thought, altogether sweeter and more juicy; their eggs, well known as delicacies on the Labrador coast; the cochlearia, growing superbly on the guano-coated surface—all of them in endless abundance: imagine such a combination of charms for scurvy-broken, hunger-stricken men.

I could not allow the fuel for a fire; our slush and tallow were reduced to very little more than a hundred pounds. The more curious in that art which has dignified the memory of Lucullus[1], and may do as much for Soyer[2], made experiments upon the organic matters within their reach—the dried nests of the kittiwake, the sods of poa, the heavy mosses, and the fatty skins of the birds around us. But they would none of them burn; and the most fastidious consoled himself at last with the doubt whether heat, though concentrating flavor, might not impair some other excellence.

[1]Lucius Lucullus: a Roman general who lived and ate lavishly.
[2]Alexis Soyer: a famous nineteenth-century French cook.

We limited ourselves to an average of a bird a piece per meal—of choice, not of necessity—and renewed the zest of the table with the best salad in the world—raw eggs and cochlearia.

It was one glorious holiday, our week at Providence Halt, so full of refreshment and all-happy thoughts that I never allowed myself to detract from it by acknowledging that it was other than premeditated. There were only two of the party who had looked out with me on the bleak ice-field ahead, and them I had pledged to silence.

Providence cliffs

XXXI

Deliverance

IT WAS the eighteenth of July before the aspects of the ice about us gave me the hope of progress. We had prepared ourselves for the new encounter with the sea and its trials by laying in a store of lumme; two hundred and fifty of which had been duly skinned, spread open, and dried on the rocks, as the *entremets* of our bread dust and tallow.

My journal tells of disaster in its record of our setting out. In launching the *Hope* from the frail and perishing ice-wharf on which we found our first refuge from the gale, she was precipitated into the sludge below, carrying away rail and bulwark, losing overboard our best shotgun, Bonsall's favorite, and, worst of all, that universal favorite, our kettle—soup kettle, paste kettle, teakettle, water kettle, in one. I may mention before I pass, that the kettle found its successor in the remains of a tin can which a good aunt of mine had filled with ginger nuts two years before, and which had long survived the condiments that once gave it dignity. "Such are the uses of adversity."[1]

Our descent to the coast followed the margin of the fast ice. After passing the Crimson Cliffs of Sir John Ross, it wore almost the dress of a holiday excursion—

[1] Adapted from Shakespeare's *As You Like It*, Act II, sc. i.

a rude one perhaps, yet truly one in feeling. Our course, except where a protruding glacier interfered with it, was nearly parallel to the shore. The birds along it were rejoicing in the young summer, and when we halted it was upon some green clothed cape near a stream of water from the ice-fields above. Our sportsmen would clamber up the cliffs and come back laden with little auks; great generous fires of turf, that cost nothing but the toil of gathering, blazed merrily; and our happy oarsmen, after a long day's work, made easy by the promise ahead, would stretch themselves in the sunshine and dream happily away till called to the morning wash and prayers. We enjoyed it the more, for we all of us knew that it could not last.

This coast must have been a favorite region at one time with the natives—a sort of Esquimaux Eden. We seldom encamped without finding the ruins of their habitations, for the most part overgrown with lichens and exhibiting every mark of antiquity. One of these, in latitude 76°20′, was once an extensive village. Our cairns for the safe deposit of meat stood in long lines, six or eight in a group; and the huts, built of large rocks faced each other as if disposed on a street or avenue.

Some of these huts were washed by the sea or torn away by the ice that had descended with the tides. The turf, too, a representative of very ancient growth, was cut off even with the water's edge, giving sections two feet thick. I had not noticed before such unmistakable evidence of the depression of this coast: its converse elevation I had observed to the north of

Wostenholme Sound. The axis of oscillation must be somewhere in the neighborhood of latitude 77°.

We reached Cape York on the twenty-first, after a tortuous but romantic travel through a misty atmosphere. Here the land-leads ceased, with the exception of some small and scarcely practicable openings near the shore, which were evidently owing to the wind that prevailed for the time. Everything bore proof of the late development of the season. The red snow was a fortnight behind its time. A fast floe extended with numerous tongues far out to the south and east. The only question was between a new rest, for the shore-ices to open, or a desertion of the coast and a trial of the open water to the west.

We sent off a detachment to see whether the Esquimaux might not be passing the summer at Episok behind the glacier of Cape Imalik, and began an inventory of our stock on hand.

I give the result:

Dried lumme	195 birds
Pork slush	112 pounds
Flour	50 pounds
Indian meal	50 pounds
Meat biscuit	80 pounds
Bread	348 pounds

Six hundred and forty pounds of provision, all told, exclusive of our dried birds, or some thirty-six pounds a man. Tom Hickey found a turf, something like his native peat, which we thought might help to boil our kettle; and with the aid of this our fuel account stood thus:

Turf, for two boilings a day	. . . .	7 days
Two sledge runners.	. . . . . .	6 days
Spare oars, sledges, and an empty cask	.	4 days

Seventeen days in all; not counting, however, the *Red Eric*, which would add something, and our emptied provision bags, which might carry on the estimate to about three weeks.

The party's return from Imalik gave us no reason to hesitate. The Esquimaux had not been there for several years. There were no birds in the neighborhood.

I climbed the rocks a second time with Mr. Mc-Gary and took a careful survey of the ice with my glass. The "fast," as the whalers call the immovable shore-ice, was seen in a nearly unbroken sweep, passing by Bushnell's Island and joining the coastline not far from where I stood. The outside floes were large and had evidently been not long broken; but it cheered my heart to see that there was one well-defined lead that followed the main floe until it lost itself to seaward.

I called my officers together, explained to them the motives that governed me and prepared to reembark. The boats were hauled up, examined carefully, and, as far as our means permitted, repaired. The *Red Eric* was stripped of her outfit and cargo, to be broken up for fuel when the occasion should come. A large beacon cairn was built on an eminence, open to view from the south and west; and a red flannel shirt, spared with some reluctance, was hoisted as a pennant to draw attention to the spot. Here I deposited a succinct record of our condition and purposes, and then directed our course south by west into the ice-fields.

By degrees the ice through which we were moving became more and more impacted; and it sometimes required all our ice-knowledge to determine whether a particular lead was practicable or not. The irregularities of the surface, broken by hummocks and occasionally by larger masses, made it difficult to see far ahead; besides which, we were often embarrassed by the fogs. I was awakened one evening from a weary sleep in my fox skins, to discover that we had fairly lost our way. The officer at the helm of the leading boat, misled by the irregular shape of a large iceberg that crossed his track, had lost the main lead some time before and was steering shoreward far out of the true course. The little canal in which he had locked us was hardly two boat-lengths across, and lost itself not far off in a feeble zigzag both behind and before us: it was evidently closing, and we could not retreat.

Without apprising the men of our misadventure, I ordered the boats hauled up and, under pretence of drying the clothing and stores, made a camp on the ice. A few hours after, the weather cleared enough for the first time to allow a view of the distance, and McGary and myself climbed a berg some three hundred feet high for the purpose. It was truly fearful: we were deep in the recesses of the bay, surrounded on all sides by stupendous icebergs and tangled floe pieces. My sturdy second officer, not naturally impressible and long accustomed to the vicissitudes of whaling life, shed tears at the prospect.

There was but one thing to be done: cost what it might, we must harness our sledges again and retrace our way to the westward. One sledge had been already used for firewood; the *Red Eric,* to which it had belonged, was now cut up, and her light cedar planking laid upon the floor of the other boats; and we went to work with the rue-raddies as in the olden time. It was not till the third toilsome day was well spent that we reached the berg which had bewildered our helmsman. We hauled over its tongue and joyously embarked again upon a free lead with a fine breeze from the north.

Our little squadron was now reduced to two boats. The land to the northward was no longer visible; and whenever I left the margin of the fast to avoid its deep sinuosities, I was obliged to trust entirely to the compass. We had at least eight days' allowance of fuel on board; but our provisions were running very low, and we met few birds and failed to secure any larger game. We saw several large seals upon the ice, but they were too watchful for us; and on two occasions we came upon the walrus sleeping—once within actual lance thrust; but the animal charged in the teeth of his assailant and made good his retreat.

On the twenty-eighth I instituted a quiet review of the state of things before us. Our draft on the stores we had laid in at Providence Halt had been limited for some days to three raw eggs and two breasts of birds a day; but we had a small ration of bread dust besides; and when we halted, as we did regularly for meals, our fuel allowed us to indulge lavishly in the great panacea of Arctic travel, tea. The men's strength was waning under this restricted diet; but a careful reckoning up of our remaining supplies proved to me now that even this was more than we could afford ourselves without an undue reliance on the fortunes of the hunt. Our next land was to be Cape Shackleton, one of the most prolific bird colonies of the coast, which we are all looking to, much as sailors nearing home in their boats after disaster and short allowance at sea. But, meting out our stores through the number of days that must elapse before we could expect to share its hospitable welcome, I found that five ounces of bread dust, four of tallow, and three of bird meat must from this time form our daily ration.

So far we had generally coasted the fast ice: it had given us an occasional resting place and refuge, and we were able sometimes to reinforce our stores of provisions by our guns. But it made our progress tediously slow, and our stock of small shot was so nearly exhausted that I was convinced our safety depended on an increase of speed. I determined to try the more open sea.

For the first two days the experiment was a failure. We were surrounded by heavy fogs; a southwest wind brought the outside pack upon us and obliged us to haul up on the drifting ice. We were thus carried to the northward, and lost about twenty miles. My party, much overworked, felt despondingly the want of the protection of the land-floes.

Nevertheless, I held to my purpose, steering SSW as nearly as the leads would admit and looking constantly for the thinning out of the pack that hangs around the western water.

Although the low diet and exposure to wet had again reduced our party, there was no apparent relaxation of energy; and it was not until some days later that I found their strength seriously giving way.

It is a little curious that the effect of a short allowance of food does not show itself in hunger. The first symptom is a loss of power, often so imperceptibly brought on that it becomes evident only by an accident. I well remember our look of blank amazement as, one day, the order being given to haul the *Hope* over a tongue of ice, we found that she would not budge. At first I thought it was owing to the wetness of the snow-covered surface in which her runners were; but, as there was a heavy gale blowing outside, and I was extremely anxious to get her on to a larger floe to prevent being drifted off, I lightened her cargo and set both crews upon her. In the land of promise, off Crimson Cliffs, such a force would have trundled her like a wheelbarrow: we could almost have borne her upon our backs. Now, with incessant labor and standing hauls, she moved at a snail's pace.

The *Faith* was left behind and barely escaped destruction. The outside pressure cleft the floe asunder, and we saw our best boat, with all our stores, drifting rapidly away from us. The sight produced an almost hysterical impression upon our party. Two days of want of bread, I am sure, would have destroyed us; and we had now left us but eight pounds of shot in all. To launch the *Hope* again, and rescue her comrade or share her fortunes, would have been the instinct of other circumstances; but it was out of the question now. Happily, before we had time to ponder our loss, a flat cake of ice eddied round near the floe we were upon; McGary and myself sprang to it at the moment and succeeded in floating it across the chasm in time to secure her. The rest of the crew rejoined her by only scrambling over the crushed ice as we brought her in at the hummock lines.

* * * *

Things grew worse and worse with us: the old difficulty of breathing came back again, and our feet swelled to such an extent that we were obliged to cut open our canvas boots. But the symptom which gave me most uneasiness was our inability to sleep. A form of low fever which hung by us when at work had been kept down by the thoroughness of our daily rest: all hopes of escape were in the refreshment of the halt.

It must be remembered that we were now in the open bay, in the full line of the great ice-drift to the Atlantic, and in boats so frail and unseaworthy as to require constant baling to keep them afloat.

It was at this crisis of our fortunes that we saw a

large seal floating—as is the custom of these animals— on a small patch of ice and seemingly asleep. It was an ussuk, and so large that I at first mistook it for a walrus. Signal was made for the *Hope* to follow astern, and, trembling with anxiety, we prepared to crawl down upon him.

Petersen, with the large English rifle, was stationed in the bow, and stockings were drawn over the oars as mufflers. As we neared the animal, our excitement became so intense that the men could hardly keep stroke. I had a set of signals for such occasions, which spared us the noise of the voice; and when about three hundred yards off, the oars were taken in, and we moved on in deep silence with a single scull astern.

He was not asleep, for he reared his head when we were within rifle shot; and to this day I can remember the hard, careworn, almost despairing expression of the men's thin faces as they saw him move: their lives depended on his capture.

I depressed my hand nervously, as a signal for Petersen to fire. McGary hung upon his oar, and the boat, slowly but noiselessly sagging ahead, seemed within certain range. Looking at Petersen, I saw that the poor fellow was paralyzed by his anxiety, trying vainly to obtain a rest for his gun against the cutwater of the boat. The seal rose on his fore-flippers, gazed at us for a moment with frightened curiosity and coiled himself for a plunge. At that instant, simultaneously with the crack of our rifle, he relaxed his long length on the ice, and at the very brink of the water, his head fell helpless to one side, very close within our reach.

I would have ordered another shot, but no discipline could have controlled the men. With a wild yell, each vociferating according to his own impulse, they urged both boats upon the floes. A crowd of hands seized the seal and bore him up to safer ice. The men seemed half crazy: I had not realized how much we were reduced by absolute famine. They ran over the floe, crying and laughing and brandishing their knives. It was not five minutes before every man was sucking his bloody fingers or eating long strips of raw blubber.

Not an ounce of this seal was lost. The intestines found their way into soup kettles without any observance of the preliminary home processes. The cartilaginous parts of the fore-flippers were cut off in the melee and passed round to be chewed upon; and even the liver, warm and raw as it was, bade fair to be eaten before it had seen the pot. That night, on the large halting floe, to which in contempt of the dangers of drifting we happy men had hauled our boats, two entire planks of the *Red Eric* were devoted to a grand cooking fire, and we enjoyed a rare and savage feast.

This was our last experience of the disagreeable effects of hunger. In the words of George Stephenson, "The charm was broken, and the dogs were safe." The dogs I have said little about, for none of us liked to think of them. The poor creatures Toodla and Whitey had been taken with us as last resources against starvation. They were, as McGary worded it, "meat on the hoof," and "able to carry their own fat over the floes."

Once, near Weary Man's Rest, I had been on the point of killing them; but they had been the leaders of our winter's team, and we could not bear the sacrifice.

I need not detail our journey any farther. Within a day or two we shot another seal, and from that time forward had a full supply of food.

On the first of August we sighted the Devil's Thumb, and were again among the familiar localities of the whalers' battling ground. The bay was quite open, and we had been headed due east for two days before. We were soon among the Duck Islands and, passing south of Cape Shackleton, prepared to land.

"Terra firma! Terra firma!" How very pleasant it was to look upon, and with what a tingle of excited thankfulness we drew near it! A little time to seek a cove among the wrinkled hills, a little time to exchange congratulations, and then our battered boats were hauled high and dry upon the rocks, and our party, with hearts full of our deliverance, lay down to rest.

And now, with the apparent certainty of reaching our homes, came that nervous apprehension which follows upon hope long deferred. I could not trust myself to take the outside passage, but timidly sought the quiet water channels running deep into the archipelago that forms a sort of labyrinth along the coast.

Thus it was that at one of our sleeping halts upon the rocks—for we still adhered to the old routine—Petersen awoke me with a story. He had just seen and recognized a native, who, in his frail kayak, was evidently seeking eider-down among the islands. The man had once been an inmate of his family. "Paul Zacharias, don't you know me? I'm Carl Petersen!" "No," said the man; "his wife says he's dead"; and, with a stolid expression of wonder, he stared for a moment at the long beard that loomed at him through the fog, and paddled away with all the energy of fright.

Two days after this, a mist had settled down upon the islands which embayed us, and when it lifted we found ourselves rowing, in lazy time, under the shadow of Karkamoot. Just then a familiar sound came to us over the water. We had often listened to the screeching of the gulls or the bark of the fox, and mistaken it for the "huk" of the Esquimaux; but this had about it an inflection not to be mistaken, for it died away in the familiar cadence of a "halloo."

"Listen, Petersen! oars, men!" "What is it?"—and he listened quietly at first, and then, trembling, said, in a half whisper, "Dannemarkers!"

I remember this, the first tone of Christian voice which had greeted our return to the world. How we all stood up and peered into the distant nooks; and how the cry came to us again, just as, having seen nothing, we were doubting whether the whole was not a dream; and then how, with long sweeps, the white ash cracking under the spring of the rowers, we stood for the cape that the sound proceeded from, and how nervously we scanned the green spots which our experience, grown now into instinct, told us would be the likely camping ground of wayfarers.

By-and-by—for we must have been pulling a good

half hour—the single mast of a small shallop showed itself; and Petersen, who had been very quiet and grave, burst out into an incoherent fit of crying, only relieved by the broken exclamations of Danish mingled with English. "Tis the Upernavik oilboat! The *Fraulein Flaischer!* Carlie Mossyn, the assistant cooper, must be on his road to Kingatok for blubber. The *Mariane* (the one annual ship) has come, and Carlie Mossyn—" and here he did it all over again, gulping down his words and wringing his hands.

It was Carlie Mossyn, sure enough. The quiet routine of a Danish settlement is the same every year, and Petersen had hit upon the exact state of things. The *Mariane* was at Proven, and Carlie Mossyn had come up in the *Fraulein Flaischer* to get the year's supply of blubber from Kingatok.

Here we first got our cloudy vague idea of what had passed in the big world during our absence. The friction of its fierce rotation had not much disturbed this little outpost of civilization, and we thought it a sort of blunder as he told us that France and England were in league with the Mussulman [Muslim] against the Greek Church. He was a good Lutheran, this assistant cooper, and all news with him had a theological complexion.

"What of America? eh Petersen?"—and we all looked, waiting for him to interpret the answer.

"America?" said Carlie; "we don't know much of that country here, for they have no whalers on the coast; but a steamer and a barque passed up a fortnight

Kasarsoak, Sanderson's Hope, Upernavik

James Hamilton, from a sketch by Dr. Kane

ago, and have gone out into the ice to seek your party."

How gently all the lore of this man oozed out of him! he seemed an oracle, as, with hot tingling fingers pressed against the gunwale of the boat, we listened to his words. "Sebastopol ain't taken." Where and what was Sebastopol?

But "Sir John Franklin?" There we were at home again—our own delusive little speciality rose uppermost. Franklin's party, or traces of the dead which represented it, had been found nearly a thousand miles to the south of where we had been searching for them.

Another sleeping halt has passed, and we have all washed clean at the freshwater basins and furbished up our ragged furs and woolens. Petersen had been foreman of the settlement, and he calls my attention, with a sort of pride, to the tolling of the workmen's bell. It is six o'clock. We are nearing the end of our trials. Can it be a dream?

We hugged the land by the big harbor, turned the corner by the old brewhouse, and, in the midst of a crowd of children, hauled our boats for the last time up on the rocks.

For eighty-four days we had lived in the open air. Our habits were hard and weather worn. We could not remain within the four walls of a house without a distressing sense of suffocation. But we drank coffee that night before many a hospitable threshold and listened again and again to the hymn of welcome, which, sung by many voices, greeted our deliverance.

CONCLUSION

WE RECEIVED all manner of kindness from the Danes of Upernavik. The residents of this distant settlement are dependent for their supplies on the annual trading ship of the colonies, and they, of course, could not minister to our many necessities without much personal inconvenience. But they fitted up a loft for our reception, and shared their stores with us in liberal Christian charity.

They gave us many details of the expeditions in search of Sir John Franklin, and added the painful news that my gallant friend and comrade, Bellot[1], had perished in a second crusade to save him. We knew each other by many common sympathies: I had divided with him the hazards of mutual rescue among the ice-fields; and his last letter to me, just before I left New York, promised me the hope that we were to meet again in Baffin's Bay, and that he would unite himself with our party as a volunteer. The French service never lost a more chivalrous spirit.

[1]Joseph-René Bellot was a gallant young officer who several times obtained leave from the French navy to participate in the search for Franklin. He endeared himself with all who met him, including the Inuit. He drowned while on the Inglefield expedition when he went through a sudden fissure in the ice. He was twenty-seven when he died.

The Danish vessel was not ready for her homeward journey till the fourth of September; but the interval was well spent in regaining health and gradually accustoming ourselves to indoor life and habits. It is a fact, which the physiologist will not find it difficult to reconcile with established theories, that we were all more prostrated by the repose and comfort of our new condition than we had been by nearly three months of constant exposure and effort.

On the sixth I left Upernavik with all our party, in the *Mariane*, a stanch but antiquated little barque, under the command of Captain Ammondson, a fine representative of the true hearted and skillful seamen of this nation, who promised to drop us at the Shetland Islands. Our little boat, the *Faith*, which was regarded by all of us as a precious relic, took passage along with us. Except the furs on our backs, and the documents that recorded our labors and trials, it was all we brought back of the *Advance* and her fortunes.

On the eleventh we arrived at Godhavn, the inspectorate of North Greenland, and had a characteristic welcome from my excellent friend, Mr. Olrik. The *Mariane* had stopped only to discharge a few stores and receive her papers of clearance; but her departure was held back to the latest moment in hopes of receiving news of Captain Hartstene's squadron, which had not been heard of since the twenty-first of July.

We were upon the eve of setting out, however, when the lookout man at the hilltop announced a steamer in the distance. It drew near, with a barque in tow, and we soon recognized the stars and stripes of our own country. The *Faith* was lowered for the last time into the water, and the little flag that had floated so near the poles of both hemispheres opened once more to the breeze. With Brooks at the tiller and Mr. Olrik at my side, followed by all the boats of the settlement, we went out to meet them.

Not even after the death of the usuk did our men lay to their oars more heartily. We neared the squadron and the gallant men who had come out to seek us; we could see the scars that their own ice-battles had impressed on the vessels; we knew the gold lace of the officers' cap-bands, and discerned the groups who, glass in hand, were evidently regarding us.

Presently we were alongside. An officer, whom I shall ever remember as a cherished friend, Captain Hartstene, hailed a little man in a ragged flannel shirt, "Is that Dr. Kane?" and with the "Yes!" that followed, the rigging was manned by our countrymen, and cheers welcomed us back to the social world of love they represented.

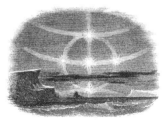

Parhelia, drawn by Mr. Sontag

Index

INDEX

437

List of The Lakeside Classics

The Lakeside Classics

Designed, typeset, printed, and bound by
R.R. Donnelley & Sons Company.
Text was set and pages output by ComCom,
the R.R. Donnelley composition facility
located in Allentown, Pennsylvania.
The body typeface is 11/12 pt. Bulmer.
Images were scanned and proofed
on state-of-the-art equipment in the
Crawfordsville, Indiana,
Book Manufacturing Division
electronic prepress center.
Maps were created by GeoSystems of
Lancaster, Pennsylvania.
Electronic information was converted into
press-ready plates using computer-to-plate technology.
The book was printed and bound
in the Crawfordsville Book Manufacturing Division.
Paper stock is 50-pound
White Lakeside Classics Opaque,
a 50-percent recycled sheet manufactured by Glatfelter.
Cloth for the one-piece case binding is
Roxite C Vellum Chocolate Brown,
manufactured by Holliston Mills, Inc.